SEXUAL CULTURES IN EUROPE

Themes in sexuality

edited by
Franz X. Eder, Lesley A. Hall & Gert Hekma

Manchester University Press
Manchester & New York

distributed exclusively in the USA by St. Martin's Press

Copyright © Manchester University Press 1999

While copyright in the volume as a whole is vested in Manchester University Press, copyright in individual chapters belongs to their respective authors, and no chapter may be reproduced wholly or in part without the express permission in writing of both author and publisher

Published by Manchester University Press
Oxford Road, Manchester M13 9NR, UK
and Room 400, 175 Fifth Avenue, New York, NY 10010, USA
http://www.man.ac.uk/mup

Distributed exclusively in the USA by
St. Martin's Press, Inc., 175 Fifth Avenue, New York,
NY 10010, USA

Distributed exclusively in Canada by
UBC Press, University of British Columbia, 6344 Memorial Road,
Vancouver, BC, Canada V6T 1Z2

British Library Cataloguing-in-Publication Data
A catalogue record for this book is available from the British Library

Library of Congress Cataloging-in-Publication Data applied for

ISBN   0 7190 5320 x *hardback*
       0 7190 5321 8 *paperback*

First published 1999

05   04   03   02   01   00   99   10   9   8   7   6   5   4   3   2   1

Typeset in Monotype Bell
by Koinonia, Manchester
Printed in Great Britain
by Bell & Bain Ltd, Glasgow

UNIVERSITY OF
WOLVERHAMPTON
KNOWLEDGE • INNOVATION • ENTERPRISE

Harrison Learning Centre
City Campus
University of Wolverhampton
St Peter's Square
Wolverhampton WV1 1RH
Telephone: 0845 408 1631
Online Renewals:
www.wlv.ac.uk/lib/myaccount

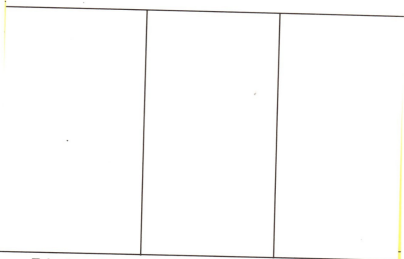

Telephone Renewals: 01902 321333 or 0845 408 1631
Online Renewals: www.wlv.ac.uk/lib/myaccount
Please return this item on or before the last date shown above.
Fines will be charged if items are returned late.
See tariff of fines displayed at the Counter.

MANCHESTER
UNIVERSITY PRESS

Contents

Contributors

Franz X. Eder is a historian at the Institute for Economic and Social History, University of Vienna. He has carried out research on quantitative methods and on the history of the family and labour organisation. Current projects on the history of sexuality include sexual discourses in the German speaking countries, eighteenth to twentieth centuries. He is co-editor of *Geschichte der homosexualitäten* (Österreichische Zeitschrift für Geschichtswissenschaften 1998, no. 3); forthcoming is a book on *Sexual Cultures in Germany and Austria, 1700–2000*.

Roger Davidson is Reader in Economic and Social History at the University of Edinburgh. He has published widely on the social history of VD and its role in the regulation of sexuality. He is currently completing a book on *Dangerous Liaisons: The Social History of VD in Twentieth-century Scotland*, and is preparing a co-edited volume (with Lesley Hall) on VD and European Society since 1870.

Willem de Blécourt is an Honorary Research Fellow at the Huizinga Institute, Amsterdam, and an Associate Fellow in the Department of History, University of Warwick. His publications include *Het Amazonenleger. Irreguliere genezeressen in Nederland, ca. 1850–1930* (Amsterdam, 1998). His current research interests are lay healers and the twentieth-century cultural history of abortion and contraception.

Kate Fisher recently completed her Oxford D.Phil, 'An Oral History of Birth Control Practice *c.*1925–50: A Study of Oxford and South Wales' and is currently working at the Cambridge Group for the History of Population and Social Structure on a project entitled *Marriage, Fertility and Sexuality: An Oral History Study*.

Lesley A. Hall is Senior Assistant Archivist, Contemporary Medical Archives Centre, Wellcome Institute for the History of Medicine,

London, and Honorary Lecturer in History of Medicine, University College London. She has published *Hidden Anxieties: Male Sexuality 1900–1950* (Oxford, 1991); (with Professor Roy Porter) *The Facts of Life: The Creation of Sexual Knowledge in Britain, 1650–1950* (New Haven CT, 1995) and numerous articles, chapters and reviews on questions of sex, gender, birth control, eugenics, etc. She is currently working on a biography of British feminist sex radical Stella Browne (1880–1955), a textbook on sex, gender and social change in Britain since 1880, and (with Roger Davidson) an edited volume on the social history of venereal diseases in Europe 1870–2000.

Emily Hamer is an independent scholar and the author of *Britannia's Glory: A History of Twentieth-century Lesbians* (London, 1996).

Gert Hekma is a lecturer in gay and lesbian studies at the University of Amsterdam where he co-chairs the gender, sexuality and culture stream of courses. He has published widely in the field of the history and sociology of (homo)sexuality, is an editor of *Thamyris* and a regular contributor to *Sexualities*.

Dorelies Kraakmann is a historian specialising in the history and cultural study of sexualities. She teaches gay and lesbian studies at the University of Amsterdam.

Angus McLaren, professor of history at the University of Victoria, British Colombia, is the author of numerous works on the history of birth control, eugenics and sexuality. His most recent books include *Trials of Masculinity: Policing Sexual Boundaries 1870–1930* (Chicago: Chicago University Press, 1997) and *Twentieth-century Sexuality: A History* (Oxford, forthcoming).

Lutz Sauerteig is Research Fellow and Lecturer at the Institute for the History of Medicine, University of Freiburg. His latest publications include *Krankheit, Sexualität, Gesellschaft: Geschlechtskrankheiten under Gesundsheitpolitik in Deutschland im 19. und frühen 20. Jahrhundert* (Stuttgart, 1999); 'Sex, Medicine and Morality during the First World War' in R. Cooter and M. Harrison (eds), *War, Medicine and Modernity, 1860–1945* (Stroud, Gloucs., 1999) and (with Roger Davidson) 'Law, Medicine and Morality: A Comparative View of Twentieth-century Sexually Transmitted Diseases' in J. Woodward and R. Jütte (eds), *Coping with Sickness: Medicine, Law and Human Rights* (Manchester, forthcoming). He is currently researching the medical market place in twentieth-century Germany.

Dr Anne-Marie Sohn is Professor of Contemporary History at the University of Rouen (France). She is a specialist in Women's history and the social history of France. Her publications include *Chrysalides. Femmes dans la vie privée. XIXème-XXème siècles* (Paris, 1996) and *Du premier baiser à l'alcôve. La sexualité des Français au quotidien. 1850–1950* (Paris, 1996). On-going research project: 'Teenagers and the young generation in the French 1960's'.

Simon Szreter is a University Lecturer in the Faculty of History, University of Cambridge, a Fellow and Director of Studies in History, St John's College Cambridge, and an Honorary Research Associate of the Cambridge Group for the History of Population and Social Structure. He has published *Fertility, Class and Gender in Britain, 1860–1940* (Cambridge, 1996) and articles on related topics, as well as being Guest Editor for the Special Issue of *Social History of Medicine* on the General Register Office (1991).

Bertrand Taithe read history at the Sorbonne and Manchester University where he completed a thesis on the Contagious Diseases Acts. He has published a number of articles on gender and the history of sexuality. He has published *The Essential Mayhew: Representing and Communicating the Poor* (Rivers Oram, 1996); edited *Prophecy: The Power of Inspired Language in History* (Sutton, 1997); *War: Identities in Conflict* (Sutton, 1998) and *Propaganda: Political Rhetoric and Systems of Belief* (Sutton, 1999). His next monograph, *Defeated Flesh: Welfare, Warfare and the Making of Modern France* will be published by Manchester University Press in 1999. He is an editor of *European Review of History/revue europeenne d'histoire*.

Acknowledgements

The editors would like to thank the Forum on Sexuality, at The Netherlands' Universities Institute for Co-ordination of Research in Social Sciences (SISWO), Amsterdam, for its support for the workshop conference 'Sexual Cultures of Europe 1700–1995', 21–3 June 1996, at which early versions of the chapters in this volume were discussed by all contributors, and the Wellcome Trust for providing travel funding for several participants. They extend further gratitude to the participants at the conference for the lively and useful discussion of the papers which took place. Particular thanks are extended to Andrew Blaikie, Sam Pryke, Hugo Röling and Cornelie Usborne, who, although their papers are absent from this volume, made invaluable contributions during discussion to the outcome of this project.

Angus McLaren's chapter in this volume draws on material which appeared in a different form in Angus McLaren, *The Trials of Masculinity* ©1997 by the University of Chicago: the kind permission of the University of Chicago Press is acknowledged.

Introduction

There has been a debate on the nature of the object and perspective of women's studies. These are nowadays generally accepted as gender, being understood as the cultural organisation of sexed roles. Sexed roles include not only feminine and masculine, but also androgynous, unfeminine and unmasculine, third-gender roles and so forth. Women's studies rejects the bipolar model of sexes current in biology, in traditional humanities and social sciences, and in society, in favour of the broader question of gender. As historians of sexuality have made a similar move from nature to culture, so sex, sexuality or sexology are no longer adequate descriptions of the object, or of the terrain, of historical research. We suggest a change from sex and sexuality to sexual culture, comparable to the change from sex to gender in women's studies, while an adequate name for the discipline could well be, instead of sexology, sexual studies, in line with the new concepts of cultural studies and gender studies. The term 'sexual cultures' covers both individual experience and collective interpretations and does not favour one or the other side.[1]

This volume and its companion, *Sexual Cultures in Europe: National Histories*, are based on an acceptance that society has a strong influence on the shapes and definitions of sexuality, which has been underlined during the 1980s and 1990s by research into the social and historical forms of sexuality. But if the social forms of sexuality vary from culture to culture and epoch to epoch, what does this mean for sexuality and sexual emancipation in contemporary Europe?

The chapters in this volume aim to advance our understanding of European sexual cultures by looking at specific aspects of sexual culture as they are or have been manifested in particular countries at particular times. We initially made a much longer list of possible

themes, but constraints of time, space and the available histori-
ography have led us to restrict these themes to three: 'dangerous
sexualities,' perceived to be imperilling the well-being of both state
and individuals and the means taken to combat them; 'stigmatised
sexualities', forms of sexual orientation and behaviour which have
been condemned, marginalised and penalised; and sex and reproduction, another area in which the interests of the individual and of
the state are involved and may be in conflict.

The volume includes some transnational overviews, for example
Hekma's chapter on male homosexuality in a European context, Kraakman's analysis of pornography, McLaren's comparative analysis of
differing national responses to the often ill-understood phenomenon
of transvestism, and Szreter's aerial map of the differential demography of modern European nations. Other chapters, such as Taithe's
unravelling of the 'syphilisation' debate of the mid nineteenth century,
Sohn's presentation of French Catholics oscillating between 'abstinence and "appeasement of lust"', Hamer's portrayal of an interlinked
network of lesbian doctors, and de Blécourt's and Fisher's studies of
specific local cultures of abortion, provide rather more snapshot
views. Others, such as Sauerteig's narrative of the extended history
of sex education in Germany and Davidson's depiction of Scotland's
'culture of compulsion', take a longer look at the interaction of
national traditions with particular aspects of sexual culture. The
differing historical methodologies deployed by the contributors point
to the various ways in which it is possible to uncover this often
occluded subject and the diverse sources to which the historian can turn.

Although the essays have been classified under particular
headings, their interest is not necessarily restricted to these themes.
A number of the chapters shed interesting lights on the relationships
between sexuality and religious belief and practice. For example,
Davidson's analysis of the control of sexually transmitted diseases
invaluably demonstrates the influence on sexual culture of Calvinist
Protestantism as well as providing a useful study of regional differences (a topic we should have liked to include) within the United
Kingdom and the tension between Scottish tradition and laws and
those of England. Fisher's analysis of oral testimony about the practice
of abortion in South Wales, however, indicates that, on the level of
private conduct in the area of reproductive control, the pervasive
'chapel' culture had remarkably little influence. Sohn's study of the
marital and contraceptive anguish of devout Catholics in the 1930s

reveals that, even while apparently rejecting it, these couples could not ignore the pervasively secularist Malthusian tendencies with which they were surrounded. This chapter also provides an insight into changing patterns of expectations of marriage, another area which we were not able to deal with as extensively as we should have liked.

Sex has frequently been regarded as a source of danger, both *per se* and because of venereal disease. Sauerteig's overview of the German tradition of sex education reminds us that much early sex education consisted of awful warnings about the dangers of excess in general and in particular of self-abuse. It was not until the early twentieth century that sex education became one public health response to the perceived threat to national well-being presented by sexually transmitted diseases. Even then, as Sauerteig demonstrates, there were powerful forces ranged against any explicit education of the young in the avoidance of venereal disease or indeed provision of any degree of sexual enlightenment.

The problem of venereal diseases had not been ignored during the nineteenth century, but medico-moral policing of prostitutes was usually the main measure of prevention. Taithe, in his unravelling of the contest for claims over the scientific 'truths' of syphilis and its prevention or cure, reveals the extent to which factors of medical status and access to power groups influenced the acceptance of particular theories about the nature of the disease and the implications for policy. Auzias-Turenne's inoculation theory threatened too many vested interests in mid-nineteenth-century France for it to be a potential contender against Ricord's hegemony in the field.

The British tradition in venereal-disease control has often been described as hostile to medico-moral policing, given the political debacle of the Contagious Diseases Acts of the 1860s. The 'British system' initiated in 1917 was based in a rhetoric of voluntarism. Davidson, in an illuminating study of the situation in Scotland, argues that, although the system was largely similar to that in other parts of Britain, local forces of Calvinistic probity and an authoritarian tradition of civic interventionism continued to locate venereal disease in stigmatised disorderly bodies, with powerful implications for the actual implementation of centrally formulated policies.

When considering stigmatised sexualities, the one that perhaps most often springs to mind and has most often been the cause of legal prosecution is male homosexuality. In his consideration of same-sex relations between men since 1700, Hekma examines the lively debate about the emergence of the 'molly' or 'queen' identity (as opposed to the sodomite) during the eighteenth century and suggests that ideas about same-sex sexual manifestations do not exist in a vacuum but have to be related to the context of discourses about gender and sexuality and wider cultural factors. He also suggests that there are different stories to be told of the 'guilt' cultures of northern Europe and the 'shame' cultures of the Mediterranean. In an account which cannot be regarded as one of uncomplicated progression from darkness to light, he indicates the paradoxical, or at least syncopated, relationship between moves towards emancipation and the more intensive legal regulation of unacceptable desires. He notes that (perhaps provided that persecution is not so rigorous as to enforce silence) it is countries such as the United Kingdom which are less than wholly liberal towards the gay community that have a wider and more politicised activist movement.

In her study of the rise and fall of pornographic literature Kraakman examines the way that explicit writing about sex became split off from other kinds of writing into a genre which was simply about predictably aroused transient pleasure, not merely through acts of censorship but through changes in literary form and concepts of appropriateness. She argues that the idea of a 'Golden Age' of politically radical subversive pornography is not entirely tenable although pornography has from time to time served this function, and suggests that this apparently vitiated and formulaic genre may yet find new life in providing a way for sexual minorities or silenced groups to voice their desires.

Although the late nineteenth century saw an efflorescence of definitions of sexual deviants,[2] there was often an endeavour to conflate the various paraphilias into variant manifestations of 'sexual inversion'. McLaren demonstrates the persistent tendency to assume cross-dressing, at least in the male, to be almost an aggressive act of homosexual solicitation. While in women travesty might have a transgressive sexual allure, or be perceived as an understandable attempt to mimic the more privileged sex, male cross-dressing aroused much deeper horror. Concern about the practice, and attempts to elucidate its mysteries, he shows as varying widely in different European countries, and tending to be stimulated rather than silenced by the legal oppression of sexual minorities (compare Hekma's chapter).

While lesbianism has rarely been the subject of legal regulation in European nations during the modern era, it has been argued that the sexological definition of the 'female invert' increasingly precluded the kind of same-sex affectionate (and possibly sexual) relationships which had been available to women during the nineteenth century and earlier. Hamer, in her chapter on an interconnected network of British professional women, suggests that there were other models available to women to identify their bonds to other women besides that presented by Radclyffe Hall in *The Well of Loneliness*, and other languages besides that of the discourse of 'inversion'. While demonstrating that such definitions are never all-encompassing, her essay also points to the importance of the availability of certain social and economic freedoms for women in enabling them to define their own sexual lifestyles.

Reproductive sex has often been seen as the only licit form of sexual activity, but even this has not been without its problems and difficulties. From the later nineteenth century the hitherto apparently inevitable connection between heterosexual intercourse and reproduction was visibly being eroded. In his overview of 'the fertility decline', Szreter points out that this is no longer seen as a unitary and monolithic occurrence following one set of rules. He analyses the demographic data available for a range of European nations to demonstrate not only that the decline in the birth rate took place at different periods in different areas but that the mechanisms by which it occurred would appear to have been very various and that specific national patterns were engendered by local cultural traditions. Similarly, he suggests, we may be perceiving apparent homogenisation and modernisation of European cultures which are in fact responding in very different ways to the phenomena of the late twentieth century. Furthermore, caution is appropriate about making too broad generalisations even on the national level: as Szreter has established,[3] national population decline is made up of diverse micro-declines taking place in specific groups of the population.

Much of the debate around the exact mechanisms by which the population fell and sex was detached from reproduction must remain hypothetical and speculative. Yet it is possible to reconstruct some of the means by which individuals attempted to control their own fertility. De Blécourt examines the culture of illegal (operative) abortion in The Hague. As with so much data about sex in history, the evidence is somewhat skewed by resulting from occasions when things went wrong, in this case when abortionists fell foul of the law (in the Netherlands it was not necessary for a patient to die for prosecution to take place). None the less, there was a flourishing culture or cultures of abortion in The Hague, not the exclusively female network sometimes posited but also involving men as both seekers and providers of abortion.

A rather different subculture is described in Fisher's study of abortion in South Wales, based on oral history interviews. It is not clear whether the differences between these subcultures are absolute or national, or due to a distinction between unwanted pregnancy in illicit relationships and in marriage, or whether these two chapters deal with different stages of the attempt to terminate a pregnancy. Fisher's interviewees did mention instrumental abortion (though never in relation to themselves) but spoke much more of attempts using drugs and other self-administered remedies. They also, in spite of belonging to a community with strongly religious (Protestant) moral norms, made very little allusion to any religious or moral qualms about inducing miscarriage.

Robert Nye has described elsewhere the importance of fulfilled conjugal sexuality to French self-definitions.[4] Anne-Marie Sohn provides a study of the trials concerning marital sexuality experienced by a group of unusually devout followers of Roman Catholicism in a society increasingly composed of purely formal adherents to the church, or even non-believers. Their scrupulous agonies over the right place of sexuality within marriage recall Foucault's concept of 'the confessional', and demonstrate the tradition within French Catholicism on which he was drawing. Sohn's analysis of the letters received by the Abbé Viollet reveals the tightening-up of religious policing of private moral behaviour within the Catholic church during the interwar period within a context of changing ideals of the conjugal relationship and an increasing acceptance in society as a whole of the 'Malthusian' limited family as desirable, and the problems this caused for those who wished to be good Catholics and also to enjoy good marriages.

These chapters, it is hoped, will provide stimulus, and suggest agendas, for further investigations into the very rich subject of the sexual cultures of Europe.

Notes

1 This paragraph is shared with the companion volume: Franz X. Eder, Lesley A. Hall and Gert Hekma (eds), *Sexual Cultures in Europe: National Histories* (Manchester, Manchester University Press, 1999).
2 See Oosterhuis in *Sexual Cultures: National Histories*.
3 S. Szreter, *Fertility, Class and Gender in Britain, 1860–1940* (Cambridge, Cambridge University Press, 1996).
4 Nye in *Sexual Culture: National Histories*.

Dangerous sexualities and their control

1

Sex education in Germany from the eighteenth to the twentieth century

Lutz D. H. Sauerteig

The history of sex education in Germany from the eighteenth to the twentieth century is fascinating and revealing. By showing who took the initiative in bringing the topic of sex education of children and young people into the political agenda (the medical profession, pedagogues, clerics, the women's movement or other political groups), and what their motivations were, this chapter raises several key questions. Who should educate (doctors, clerics, teachers or parents) and where? How far should one go into anatomical and biological details of reproduction? What kind of sexual ethics should be taught? The dichotomy between the rights of parents to educate their children themselves and the public task of the state to preserve and control the health of its citizenry was, however, a problem which has stood in the foreground of the discourse only since the nineteenth century. In the eighteenth century such a 'private' as opposed to a 'public' sphere did not exist.[1]

The eighteenth century was perceived by many contemporary writers as a period of increased sexual desire. A strong sexual urge was recognised as physically implanted in men and women from puberty and accepted as being 'natural' and God-given. Whereas the Catholic church kept on insisting that complete continence was absolutely possible, eighteenth-century writers assumed it to be harmful and unhealthy. The sexual drive was, as Isabel Hull shows, 'celebrated as the motor of society and the mark of the independent, adult, productive citizen'. The cultural and social changes in the Age of Enlightenment were interpreted not only as increasing sexual desire through wealth, exotic food and drink, luxurious clothing, excessive reading and other amusements, and thereby causing moral confusion and enslaving habits such as masturbation, but also as curing them. The 'normal' way to control and moderate sexual urges and thus to avoid masturbation was marriage. Here, sexual urge converted into love. Hence, as Hull convincingly argues, the aim of eighteenth-century doctors, pedagogues, state theorists and philosophers was not sexual repression but moderation through self-control and advocating a generally 'reasonable lifestyle'. This was the route from being a slave of one's desires to freedom and to a healthy and happy life. To achieve this aim, young people had to be educated.[2]

Already prior to the eighteenth century there had been a widespread store of literature expounding advice on sexual matters, some of it being repeatedly revised and reissued with success over a two-hundred-year period. These endeavours to impart knowledge about the anatomy and function of the sexual organs, about love as well as reproduction and the emergence of life, were intensified in the Age of Enlightenment. Through systematic investigation of the sexual drive, laws of human sexual behaviour and principles of 'normality' were to be established. A controversial issue in this expanding discourse on sexual matters that created much worry was – and still is – whether transmitting knowledge to readers makes them aware of practices against which they should actually be warned for moral reasons. Only guides that were supposed to introduce couples to the world of marriage were spared this worry, for intercourse in marriage was considered 'natural' and was socially desirable, though only for reproductive purposes. The situation was different with the works that warned against masturbation. While those doctors, pedagogues and Protestant theologians who felt themselves committed to the Enlightenment assumed that a lack of knowledge does not protect against the hazards of temptation, Catholic theologians especially tried to decree silence on this subject. However, a huge range of sexual advice literature emerged in the last decades of the eighteenth century through which readers may have discovered exactly what 'unnatural' practices of intercourse existed and how to masturbate. Or, by reading recommendations of which positions during intercourse and which sexual acts to avoid so as not to endanger the success of marital coitus, namely conception, they may have learned exactly the techniques of contraception.[3]

One of the threatening symptoms of increasing sexual desire was seen in childhood masturbation, a phenomenon assumed to occur more frequently than before. As sexual enjoyment was strictly reserved for adults, masturbation appeared as dangerous sexual behaviour. This became a key subject in eighteenth-century sexual advice literature. Whereas before masturbation was constructed in a religious context as 'sin', it now shifted into a medical context and became a dangerous disease which finally might lead to death.[4] The turning point is marked by *De l'onanisme* by the Swiss physician Samuel Auguste David Tissot, first published in Latin in 1758 and quickly translated several times into French, German, Italian and English. Tissot's views were popularised in Germany especially by Jean-Jacques Rousseau's *Émile ou de l'éducation* (1762), which became the central pedagogical text for German intellectuals. Influenced by Tissot and Rousseau, the Philanthropists, a group of pedagogues such as Christian Gotthilf Salzmann, Joachim Heinrich Campe and Johann Bernhard Basedow, started an educational campaign against the dangerous disease of masturbation.[5]

The anti-masturbation campaign moved children and young people and their sexual behaviour into the centre of interest. For the educators sexual behaviour was not a naturally given fact but could be influenced through education. As ignorance and unsatisfied curiosity were considered to be much more dangerous than appropriate knowledge, the Philanthropists saw the necessity of enlightening young people about sexuality. They saw the task of education as being to stifle the senses and passions of young people by rational means, subject them to rational self-control, and thus to prevent them from masturbating. Sensitivity was considered to be an epidemic caused by an illness that Salzmann felt had befallen all of Germany, namely masturbation. As antidotes against unleashed sensitivity and its consequences, they recommended chastity, self-control and moderation. This was best achieved, on the one hand, by physical toughening and work, ideally gardening, as well as by a dietetic life style and, on the other hand, by constantly watching over children to ensure that these measures were adhered to. To answer children's questions about reproduction, parents should refer to the world of plants and animals. The main emphasis was to be placed on reproduction as the social function of marriage, on pregnancy and on pain in delivery, not so much on procreation, and not at all on lust or eroticism. Hence, deterrence through fear and horror, by describing the dreadful effects of masturbation and the insufferable pain of childbirth, was the main educational method of the Philanthropists.[6]

However, at the end of the eighteenth century these first attempts at sexual education came to a halt. The Philanthropists became resigned because they perceived their concept of rational education to have failed in controlling the sexual drive.[7] During the nineteenth century the educational aim was to preserve innocence in the young. This principle was especially propagated by the Protestant and Catholic churches. Sexual education would only direct the interest of young people to sexuality and arouse their curiosity. Under the influence of the Benedictine Aegidius Jais and the Jesuit Joseph Deharbe, Catholic religious education successfully imposed a far-reaching and long-lasting taboo on anything sexual. Their catechisms were both reprinted several times during the nineteenth century.[8] If sexuality was to be mentioned at all, it was only in the confessional. The position of the nineteenth-century alliance of clergy, pedagogues and physicians, the 'medico-moral alliance', was therefore described by Peter Gay as 'learned ignorance'.[9] This, however, resulted in the dilemma of how to preserve innocence without giving any explanation what this meant and thereby hinting at the world of sexuality. Whether the young were successfully kept in innocent ignorance is questionable.[10]

From the second half of the nineteenth century the discourse on sexuality became more medicalised, and the focus of research moved from the 'normal' to the pathological. Sexual drive outside marriage or without reproduction as its aim was now considered as 'perversion' and the concept of masturbation changed from a disease causing mainly physical harm to a nervous disease finally leading to madness.[11] Upholding the dogma of sexual innocence for the young became more and more difficult or even impossible. Industrialisation and urbanisation had changed living circumstances too drastically. Cramped living conditions among urban labourers, prolonged schooling for the middle class and, hence, the ensuing extended phase of 'youth', as well as the raising of the marriage age, are just a few points to be mentioned. The turn of the century marked the beginning of a rapidly spreading discussion about sex instruction. For many contemporaries around 1900 the 'social question' seemed to be pushed aside in favour of the 'sexual question'. The Berlin sexologist Iwan Bloch spoke of sex education as a 'burning contemporary issue'.[12]

The discussion on sex education was stimulated by several other discourses, one being the debate about the effects of 'smutty and trashy literature' on the young.[13] Pedagogues began to think about how to educate the young about sexual behaviour on the basis of middle-class values. Additional impetus for dealing with sex education and the sexual problems of youths came from the life and sex reform movements and the youth movements. The topics discussed ranged from homosexuality and masturbation, the relationship between nature and the body, the declining birth rate and population politics, to birth control and abortion.[14] And last but not least, the emergence of practitioners of sexology and psychoanalysis (particularly Wilhelm Fliess and Sigmund Freud) directed attention again towards child sexuality, thus triggering off controversial debates around the turn of the century.[15]

Since a comprehensive analysis of the history of sex education in Germany is still lacking, not all aspects can be analysed here.[16] Thus I shall concentrate mainly on those aspects that played a significant role in the discussion about venereal disease (VD), which was an essential thread of the twentieth-century controversy about sex education.[17] Around 1900, VD, like tuberculosis and alcoholism, was considered a social disease yet to be conquered. One of the public health strategies pursued to combat VD was to educate people about the imminent hazards that VD posed to themselves, their families, the state and ultimately the 'race'. VD education was, however, not possible without a certain measure of sex education.

Among the first groups to support sexual and moral education of the young around the turn of the century were the German abolitionists.[18] These women from the radical wing of the German women's movement were not only demanding the abolition of state-regulated prostitution but were also fighting against the middle-class double moral standard. Instead they propagated a sexual morality equally valid for men and women, a standard that viewed marriage, sexuality and reproduction as a unit. In their campaigns they sought to appeal to juveniles at as early an age as possible. For example, in Hamburg they organised educational talks for leavers of primary schools in 1899. In these talks male and female doctors instructed boys and girls, respectively, about the consequences of 'immorality' to health and pointed out the responsibility that each individual had with regard to sexual behaviour towards herself or himself and the coming generation. Lida Gustava Heymann championed an educational concept that, although beginning in the plant and animal world, ultimately did go into human sexuality. She did not want to stay at the birds-and-bees level. With regard to girls she considered it particularly important to emphasise the role of the woman as a mother.[19]

At the same time as the abolitionists, the naturopathy movement began to commit itself to sex education, since the causes of health problems both physical and mental were seen to lie in sexual behaviour. Journals, brochures and guides of the naturopathy movement were repeatedly devoted to sexual issues. Many of its health manuals contained detailed figures of the sexual organs, dealt with the physiological processes of reproduction and informed readers about birth control. Naturopaths saw lack of knowledge on the subject as a great danger to the development of the mental and physical health of young people. After the turn of the century naturopathy organisations began to sponsor educational talks for their male and female members, and they had special educational evenings for young people which attracted great interest. The naturopathy doctrine preached moderation as its ideal: moderate conservation of sexual energy and the prevention of every kind of unhealthy exaggeration. Those involved in naturopathy, therefore, struggled not only against masturbation but also against premarital and extramarital sexual intercourse. Instead they expected sexual restraint from young people.[20]

Following the turn of the century, radical women found a new forum for their sexual ethics demands in the Union for the Protection of Mothers (Bund für Mutterschutz, BfM), an organisation established in 1905 along the lines of the 'New Ethics' drafted by German feminist Helene Stöcker.[21] Stöcker and her sympathisers declared 'regular sexual intercourse between sexually mature' males and females 'who are attracted to each other' to be something 'natural' as long as both assumed an appropriate measure of responsibility for each other, an aspect lacking, for example, in prostitution.[22] In the BfM's journal Maria Lischnewska argued in favour of answering eight-year-olds who asked where children came from, not with the fable about the stork but rather with an explanation about pregnancy and birth suitable for their age.[23] The 'New Ethics' encountered adamant resistance because it advocated living together without the legitimisation of marriage; it was vehemently fought by social purity organisations and the middle-class women's movement as being a modernistic attack on traditional social order.

Other advocates of sex education for the young at an early stage included various socialists, such as the Berlin physician and sexologist Max Hodann and the Munich physician Julian Marcuse, as well as women like Clara Zetkin and Henriette Fürth. Although the

Social Democrats did not officially demand early sex education, they published relevant articles in their journals and brochures.[24] The German Society for Combating Venereal Disease (Deutsche Gesellschaft zur Bekämpfung der Geschlechtskrankheiten, DGBG), founded in 1902 by leading German venereologists, entered the discourse on sex education shortly after the turn of the century.[25] Since the DGBG insistently warned that the spread of VD was a threat to the state and the nation, it succeeded in interesting even conservative circles in issues of sex education. In the years to follow, the DGBG became a driving force in the discussion on sex education.

Altogether, sex education had become a topic of public debate by the turn of the century. One of the first highlights was the third congress of the DGBG held in May of 1907, devoted solely to the topic of sex education.[26] In the same year Sigmund Freud published a short article in which he pointed out the necessity of providing children and young people with adequate sex education.[27] Because the DGBG combined fear of the spread of VD with demands for more detailed sex education for the young, it succeeded in gradually persuading the Ministries of Culture of the German states and the municipal school authorities to collaborate. Hence, in 1908 the Imperial Health Council (Reichsgesundheitsrat), the most important committee of medical and public health experts consulted by the Imperial Office of the Interior (Reichsamt des Innern), emphasised the importance of sex education. The great majority of the experts demanded more intensive instruction of the young: however, they found they were not in a position to set up uniform and universal principles.[28]

The Chairman of the DGBG, the eminent Breslau venereologist Professor Albert Neisser, called sexual and moral education one of the most prominent goals and tasks for the DGBG.[29] Stressing ethical and biological education as a dual aim, Neisser differentiated the DGBG from the moralistic objectives of the social purity movements. The goal of the DGBG was to enlighten the young sexually, on the one hand, and to discipline them towards self-control and self-restraint, on the other. Although many doctors in the DGBG could agree on this dual strategy, they stressed it differently. The physician Martin Chotzen, who was one of the DGBG's experts on sex education, stressed 'that sexual awareness of man needs careful, early, and continuously nurtured education just as any other aspect of emotional life'.[30] Up until then, he admitted, this notion had not penetrated the consciousness of the public. Hence, in view of the neglect in general sex education, the goal of sexual ethics, at least at first, would have to be postponed in favour of the 'more urgent task of bringing sex education ... to the masses of the people'.[31] The Berlin venereologist and Secretary General of the DGBG, Alfred Blaschko also stressed that the emphasis had to be placed on sexual enlightenment first: 'Hence, we had to admit that for our educational work we had to create a totally new and healthy substrate and that the absolute prerequisite of any effective education had to be rational sexual instruction.'[32]

The DGBG's programme for sexual ethics was a dietetic educational regimen with the motto 'a sound soul can live only in a sound body'.[33] Since sexual drive in most humans was 'so tremendous', according to Blaschko, it 'could not always be led to that which is right by means of rational instruction and insight'. For this reason, he declared the 'strengthening of will-power' to be the foremost goal of sex education.[34] Therefore, the entire organism would have to be strengthened and become accustomed to exhausting physical activity.[35] Being pampered, leading a dissolute way of life, drinking alcohol and being mentally strained, on the other hand, were to be avoided.

The novel entitled *Helmut Harringa* (1910) by the teetotaller Hermann Popert, a bestseller in the youth movement, contributed to the glorification of this chastity cult. Popert furnished the prewar generation with the ideal of a Germanic youth looking into the future with purity, asceticism and strength. In his novel Popert made alcohol the culprit involved in all evil. Alcohol obfuscates the mind of the hero's brother, Friedrich Harringa, a member of a *Burschenschaft* (students' society), and leads him to a brothel. Afflicted with syphilis, Friedrich finally drowns himself in the Baltic Sea. His brother, Helmut, who is a judge in Hamburg, thereupon becomes an ardent supporter of the temperance movement.[36]

At the aforementioned session of the Imperial Health Council in 1908 the leading Prussian medical officer, Martin Kirchner, took up the idea of strengthening will-power by means of dietetics. The young must be rendered capable of sexual chastity by educating them in self-restraint and self-control. They should be raised to respect women and should view the founding of a 'happy family' and the 'production of healthy offspring' as a 'marvellous and worthwhile task for every citizen'. On the other hand they should loathe prostitutes. According to Kirchner, a youth must learn 'to look at naked people without becoming physically aroused'. For this reason, Kirchner wished that schools would place more value on physical education and sports, so that young people could become 'physically toughened'.[37]

Very detailed explanation of human sexuality, the sexual organs and sexual intercourse was, however, not planned for the schools.[38] Alfred Blaschko insisted that the biological principles of sexuality should be explained in terms of gradually progressing educational instruction. False impressions about sexuality (which occurred particularly among urban youth) and ensuing systematic ignorance were to be eliminated as early as the primary school level. For Blaschko it was 'a grievous error to believe that young people, because these things had been passed over in total silence, would grow in purity and chastity, untouched by all things sensual'.[39] A more detailed sex education could then be integrated into the lessons on general hygiene in the vocational schools (*Fortbildungsschulen*) and at the upper levels of higher education.[40]

But there was still strong opposition to any form of biological sex education. In particular the Protestant and Catholic churches, as well as social purity organisations, propagated a strictly moral ethical education without touching on biological questions of sexuality. Instead, will-power training was at the core of the Catholic church's educational concept. Around the turn of the century, however, the taboo placed on sexual issues was cautiously criticised from within the Catholic church. Various Catholic pedagogues were in favour of sex education for children and teenagers which, however, should be done very cautiously and in keeping with their age while maintaining the maxims of modesty and purity. The official church line still rejected, however, any sex education that went into the physical aspects of reproduction, calling it highly dangerous, especially since thereby Darwinistic teachings would be introduced into school instruction. Therefore the Catholic church continued to warn about the negative consequences of general sex education. And in the pastoral letter of the Fulda Bishops' Conference of 1908 the German bishops called for having children strictly educated towards decency and chastity.[41]

One of the leading pedagogues, Friedrich Wilhelm Foerster, read and esteemed by both Protestant and especially Catholic clergy and teachers, was chiefly concerned with getting moral and religious values across to young people.[42] Foerster, coming from a liberal background, kept himself entirely separate from the 'Moderns', the advocates of the sex reform movement, such as Helene Stöcker and her 'New Ethics'. He strictly rejected general sex education by schools and propagated a pedagogy against 'mounting sexual degeneration and negligence',[43] to transmit moral and religious values to the young and bring them closer to the ideals of monogamy. According to him, young people did not primarily have to be warned against the risks of extramarital sexual intercourse but rather had to be educated towards self-control. Only then could young people be in a position to subdue the 'nature' of their sexual drive to their 'spirit'.[44] Foerster recommended 'will-power gymnastics', which he expanded to make an all-encompassing system of 'will-power training'. Any sex education would 'primarily' have to become 'will-power training'.[45] One aspect of this training was, for example, fasting or bearing pain, subjecting oneself to oaths of silence and, naturally, praying.[46] As he saw it, the solution to the sexual issue was to be achieved not 'from below, in terms of matter', in other words by sex education, but rather 'from above', by religion.[47]

The Protestant churches did not reject sex education in principle, but only in the form of pure communication of biological facts. Hence sex education was mainly supposed to be education towards morality, extinguishing all sensuality even within marriage. The Protestant churches, therefore, were against sex education in school and referred this task to the parents as well as to ecclesiastical charity associations and social purity organisations.[48]

To equip parents (primarily mothers) for educating their children about sexuality, or to motivate them at least to support sex education in schools, the DGBG produced in 1907 a manual about sex education. In collaboration with the school authorities, popular education organisations (*Volksbildungsvereine*) and the churches, the local branches of the DGBG conducted evening meetings for parents at which doctors spoke on the most significant issues in sex education.[49] Social Democrats, such as the doctors Julian Marcuse and Max Hodann, the feminist Henriette Fürth and the teacher Otto Rühle, published brochures on sex education for the working class.[50] Those who advocated sex education within the school argued that most fathers and mothers were far too deficient in sexual knowledge, and thus fell short in or completely refrained from educating their children on sexual matters.[51] Sigmund Freud, therefore, advocated leaving sex education up to the school if the parents could not or did not want to educate their children on this subject. To him it was the task of the school 'to discuss the major facts of life' in biology class and to point out the 'social significance' of these facts, doing so as early as the last year of primary school.[52] Whereas sex education at school was advocated by the sexologist Iwan Bloch, his opponent, Albert Moll, felt that the mother must assume this task or, in cases where this was impossible, the family doctor.[53] Along with moral objections the strongest argument voiced by the critics of sex education in schools was that teachers lacked the necessary training. The churches stood firm on their standpoint that sex education was a task to be entrusted primarily to parents, especially mothers, as only they were endowed with the capacity to deal with children individually. In particular, the Catholic organisations for mothers were asked to commit themselves to this.

In the years prior to the First World War, despite all the objections in the Ministries of Culture of the German states and although the prerequisites had not been met in the training of teachers, some school authorities had permitted lectures on sex education for those leaving school. These lectures were usually given by doctors, some of them in the presence of teachers and parents. A survey conducted by the DGBG's Berlin branch among the directors of several secondary schools in Greater Berlin showed that, of the sixty-two participating schools, twenty-three were in favour of and thirty against sex education lectures. Such lectures had already been given at ten of the schools, at eight of them by a doctor.[54]

After the war and the political changes of the November revolution in 1918, attitudes towards sex education changed considerably. For example, the Hamburg Supervisory School Authority (Oberschulbehörde), which had prohibited any form of sex education in primary schools in 1901, lifted the ban in July 1919; it now recommended not only going into issues of sexual ethics in class but also speaking about the biological aspects of reproduction.[55] In December 1919 the Supervisory School Authority presented a draft for a syllabus on sex education. According to this syllabus teachers were supposed to talk about procreation to twelve- to thirteen-year-olds and, to fourteen to sixteen-year-olds, more precisely about the sexual organs and the consequences of masturbation. At the same time the pupils were also to be given dietetic guidance on relieving sexual tension (sports, nutrition, etc.). The subject of VD would not be touched upon until the upper forms; however, those leaving school at the age of sixteen would have to obtain such instruction earlier. Even the female pupils of high schools for girls were supposed to have sex education according to these syllabus drafts and be instructed about VD. This syllabus, however, was never put into practice and the decision as to how sex education could be carried out best was left again to the individual teacher.[56] Just how far these guidelines were followed by Hamburg teachers in practice is unknown. Most likely, only a few particularly open-minded teachers attempted to apply these guidelines in their classroom instruction. In vocational schools (*Berufsschulen*), however, sex education was compulsory. But of those Hamburg women interviewed by the historian Karen Hagemann none could recall having had sex education in school between 1922 and 1933.[57]

In the 1920s the Hamburg system of sex education was held to be very 'modern' and met with criticism in other mainly rural German states (such as Mecklenburg-Schwerin and Oldenburg) without big cities.[58] Nationalistic and Christian conservative circles continued to reject strictly any form of more liberalised sex education. The managing director of the DGBG, the venereologist Hermann Röschmann, also did not wish to go as far as the Hamburg sex education system. Röschmann advocated early sex education in the lower forms where children should be made aware of 'origins and development in nature'. Sexual reproduction, however, should be explained only on the basis of examples from the plant and lower animal worlds. Röschmann believed it was not necessary to go into human sexual reproduction; one could rely on children to transfer the concept.[59] This was basically the attitude of the majority to non-ecclesiastical sex education in the Weimar Republic. Only a few were willing to go beyond any analogous education in terms of birds and bees. At best they were willing to go into human sexuality in the lectures on VD for school-leavers.[60]

Even the Social Democrats were in favour of sex education in terms of disciplining children to observe premarital abstinence and moral purity. Children should be warned about the risks of premarital sexual intercourse and be instilled with the need to control their sexual drive and to exercise self-control. Prior to the First World War, Social Democratic views on sex education held that reproduction should be discussed with children only on the basis of examples from the plant and animal world. It was only during the Weimar Republic that working-class parents were exhorted to educate their children on sexuality. They were to begin with examples from nature with younger children and then educate the older ones explicitly about human reproduction as well. Although the notions of the Social Democrats about sex education were held to be 'progressive' in the Weimar Republic, their goals hardly differed from those of liberal middle-class pedagogues and doctors.[61]

It was the sex reform movement of the 1920s which became the spearhead of sex education. The sex reform movement created an infrastructure for sex education not only with its magazines, brochures and lecture evenings, which were sometimes attended by as many as two thousand listeners, but above all with its counselling centres. Through these centres they probably reached more people than their members, whom they claimed numbered over 150,000. The advocates of sex reform came from the radical wing of the women's movement, the political left, from science and the medical profession, and from the homosexual movement. They all were convinced that it was better to regulate the sexual conduct of humans than to suppress it. While non-medical sex reformers kept on defending the principle of self-help, the influence of female and male doctors on the sex reform movement increased from the mid-1920s. Atina Grossmann speaks of a medicalisation and politicisation of the sex reform movement.[62] Although the principal aims of the sex reform movement were to provide its adherents with instruction about birth control, to supply contraceptive devices and to fight against the ban on abortion, it did discuss important aspects of sex education as well: education towards a fulfilling sex life for both partners, but especially for the woman. From the mid-1920s, a number of marriage guides promoted eroticism in marriage. With its activities and publications the sex reform movement transmitted the necessary anatomical and physiological knowledge about sexuality and reproduction. Thus the sex reform movement, with its various branches and directions, was concerned with both eroticism in marriage and rationalisation of sexuality. It believed that a more fulfilled sex life in marriage would produce a better marriage and healthier children.[63]

The most liberal and certainly most progressive position in the debate on sex education in the Weimar Republic was taken by the socialist and director of the Berlin-Reinickendorf public health office, Max Hodann.[64] He became the best-known and most controversial medical sex educationalist in the Weimar Republic. Some of his books on sex were even banned. His first major work, *Bub und Mädel* (*Guy and Gal*), addressed working-class young people; his book *Woher die Kinder kommen* (*Where Children Come From*), published in 1926, was written especially for children.[65] Hodann attempted to answer young people's most burning questions about sexuality in a simple, understandable language and with clear-cut, self-explanatory drawings. Going far beyond the majority of sex educationalists in the Weimar Republic, Hodann spoke openly about the basic biological facts of human sex life. He not only addressed young people but considered sex education for adults to be urgently needed as well.[66] Another channel for sex education of adults, especially working-class adults, was the advice columns in various journals of the sex reform movement in which Max Hodann and other sexologists answered questions.[67]

Although Hodann and his colleagues had a great number of readers, especially among the working class and the proletarian youth movement, and although many attended their numerous lectures, it remains uncertain how much of what was read or heard could actually be applied by parents, for example in educating their children, and to what extent parents really could overcome their fears as well as their reticence in speaking about sexuality.[68] On the other hand, influenced by Hodann's books, the socialist working-class youth movement practised a far more direct form of sex education. This was confirmed in particular by girls and women who had been taught in detail not only about sexuality and reproduction but also about birth-control methods.[69]

In a sense the Catholic church marked the extreme opposite pole in the discourse on sex education. For the most part it did not change its attitude to the sex education of young people during the Weimar Republic. On the contrary, the changes in the way women perceived themselves in the Weimar Republic and were termed 'New Women' – such as their more self-confident attitude, changes in their outer appearance (page-boy hairdo, short skirt, silk stockings, make-up, smoking cigarettes) and the image they imparted of leading a sexually emancipated life – were interpreted as a threat to purity and morality and, hence, as a hazard for the nation.[70] The Catholic church and its youth groups wanted children and young people to grow up as 'innocently' and as 'chastely' as possible in an atmosphere free from all sexual stimuli.[71] VD was still seen by the church as a punishment by God for violating the chastity commandment. The *Leitsätze und Weisungen zu verschiedenen modernen Sittlichkeitsfragen* (*Guiding*

Principles and Instructions on Various Modern Questions of Morality) promulgated by the Fulda Bishops' Conference in 1925 clearly stressed the principles of 'shamefulness and morality' as 'protective barriers' set up by God around chastity. The German bishops rejected all modernising efforts (including gymnastics and swimming instruction on a co-educational basis, modern dance classes, nudism etc.) as these entailed 'violating chasteness and modesty'. People were exhorted to act against the 'tendency towards evil lust' that lay dormant in them 'in a life-long moral battle … with the aid of divine mercy'.[72] However, in the public debate on this subject these guidelines scarcely had any meaning.[73] In 1929 Breslau's Prince-Bishop Bertram published his *Erwägungen zu Fragen der Sexual-Pädagogik* (*Considerations on Questions of Sexual Instructions*) in which he referred to Foerster's theory of sex education: instead of sex education *per se* he advocated educating the mind towards modesty and chastity.[74] And finally, in 1929 and again in 1931, Pope Pius XI warned German Catholics against sex education in one of his encyclicals and in a special circular.[75]

Thus the churches attempted to defend the traditional ideals of chastity and purity as a bulwark against what they perceived as being the moral decay of society. They struggled against any form of sex education which threatened to lift the protective coat of innocence, a coat that was, in their opinion, necessary. Thus, they demanded education for young people in terms of a form of sexual ethics that would lead them along the path of a life centred on Christian values. Education in terms of sexual ethics, according to the churches, was the task of the home, primarily the mother, and not a public task to be fulfilled by the schools. If the parents were not in a position to do so or did not want to, the churches and their welfare organisations were obligated to provide moral instructions.

So far we have looked at the discourse on sex education and its implementation. One question remains to be tackled: what and how much did children really know about sexuality? To find a clear answer is, however, difficult. In the middle class, as in the working class, sexuality remained a taboo far into the twentieth century. In most families sex education did not take place. At most, working-class parents gave their older children a book to read about sex or the children discovered it either by chance or put intentionally by their parents on the table. Most working-class children obtained their knowledge about sexuality from friends, often by way of smutty talk and dirty jokes, from their older brothers or sisters, in some cases from their grandmothers – and later in the Weimar Republic, in part, from classroom instruction or through youth organisations. Even when their daughters began menstruating, many mothers did not find it necessary to have a talk with them about sexuality except, at most, to caution them urgently about pregnancy.[76] Even at the beginning of the 1990s the vast majority of children and young people in Germany, especially the males, learned the most important sexual facts not at school or at home but from their mates on the street or from magazines for young people (like *Bravo*).[77]

Although in rural areas 'natural' sex education was quite common,[78] it is debatable what working-class children saw of their parents' sex life in cramped living conditions and to what extent they were confronted by the corporeality of their brothers, sisters or parents.[79] Recent case studies based on oral history came to the conclusion that in working-class families, despite sleeping together, there were strict barriers of shame which prevented children from seeing the sex life of their parents – except perhaps in some unintentional and rare cases.[80] But even if children did see or hear anything, they most likely neither really understood it nor found it a substitute for sex education. Most working-class daughters were totally innocent and inexperienced right up to adulthood. Some not only had their first sexual experiences at work in the factory but also obtained a good deal of their knowledge about sexuality there.[81]

The innocence of middle-class girls in the nineteenth century has already become a legend, especially if one calls to mind Wedekind's Wendla Bergmann in his play *Frühlings Erwachen* (*Spring Awakening*) from 1891.[82] On the other hand, Alain Corbin speculates whether middle-class girls had not in part only assumed the role of a 'silly goose' and were actually better informed than they would admit or be permitted to show.[83] For them a likely source of sexual knowledge could have been the maid who was employed in many middle-class households. The vast social barrier between them may have facilitated the daughter overcoming her shame to speak about sexuality to the maid.[84]

Conclusion

Whereas in the second half of the eighteenth century the initiative for sex education came from the Philanthropist pedagogues and some physicians, the decisive moves towards educating young people about biological and moral-ethical matters of sexuality came at the beginning of the twentieth century from the women's movement and increasingly from the medical profession. They all questioned the churches' monopoly of interpretation over questions of sexual ethics. While eighteenth- and twentieth-century pedagogues wanted to enlighten young people sexually out of the fear of the dangerous consequences of ignorance, the motivation to a more explicit type of sex education in the late nineteenth- and early twentieth-century women's movement stemmed from their struggle against the middle-class double moral standard, especially against state regulation of prostitution. The motivation in the medical profession came in the eighteenth century from the devastating supposed consequences of masturbation and in the nineteenth and early twentieth century from the worry about the spread of VD. In 'the name of decency' they all wanted to take a stand against the stranglehold that ignorance had on this subject.[85] Although they were aware of the necessity of sex education, they usually never went beyond making references to the birds and bees.

In the Weimar Republic the topic of sex education remained highly controversial. It generated a dispute about different notions of sexual morals, concerning the function of marriage and the family in society and the role of women in the relations between the sexes. German Nationalist and Christian conservative groups, fearing both a progressive undermining of prevailing sexual moral standards and disintegration of the family, viewed sex education as a means of conveying and strengthening their moral and religious notions. Liberals and Socialists, out of fear of the consequences that VD and prostitution might have for the health of the nation, advocated more explicit sex education and propagated a 'rationalisation' of reproduction. But they did not reject marriage as an institution.[86]

Since sex education in schools could barely gain acceptance in the 1920s because of the objections and reservations of school authorities, churches and parents, the DGBG made the strategic decision to seek a broader alliance consisting of the medical profession, churches and charity organisations in order to push its efforts through. In view of this medico-moral alliance, the balance was inevitably shifted more towards the ethical aspects of sex education. With this basis, and in collaboration with school administrations of some cities, seminars on sex education could be held for teachers. In this context it was then possible to draw up curricula for sex education; however, special classes on sex education *per se* did not exist at school. Sex education was mainly integrated into religion or biology classes. How this worked in practice, however, cannot be assessed using the currently available sources.

The majority of the Weimar Republic's literature for sex education was aimed at working-class young people. Both adequate physiological knowledge about sexuality and reproduction, and middle-class moral standards, were to be conveyed. The purpose of such literature was to control the sexual conduct of the working class, which appeared considerably depraved from the perspective of the middle class, and hence appeared a threat to the morals and health of the nation. Middle-class conservative sex education was not so much concerned with conveying knowledge but saw its foremost role rather as the protection of children against harmful influences from the outside and in safeguarding childhood innocence. The goals of sexual ethics were to curb and suppress sexual drive as well as to divert attention from it. The sex reform movement with its strong affiliations with the political left, on the other hand, aimed both at an eroticisation of marriage, particularly in the working class, and at a rationalising of sexuality with the help of medicine.

It was only in the late 1960s that the Ministries of Culture of the German states agreed that sex education should form a part of general school education.[87] Since then the discourse on sex education has changed again more into a pedagogical discourse and centred on the old question of where the private sphere of the family ends and where the duty of the state to interfere begins.[88] It seems that each society has to draw this line again and again. In Germany this has been done for the present by a forty-page decision of the Federal Constitutional Court in 1977. The Constitutional Court decided that sex education is primarily the educational right of the family. The state, however, has the right to implement sex education at school, but has to take different value systems into consideration and abstain from any form of indoctrination of children and young people.[89] In practice the conflict between those who consider the presentation of biological facts of sexuality enough and those who insist on sex education and thus on ethical values is still unsolved.

Notes

I would like to thank Franz X. Eder (Vienna), Lesley Hall (London), Thomas Schlich (Freiburg) and Cornelie Usborne (London) for their useful comments, and Margret Andergassen (Freiburg) for her help with the translation. The Wellcome Trust London generously provided me with a travel grant.

1 On this question see I. V. Hull, *Sexuality, State, and Civil Society in Germany, 1700–1815* (Ithaca and London, Cornell University Press, 1996), especially pp. 95–7, 190–5 and chapter 10.

2 Hull, *Sexuality*, pp. 229–44, quotation p. 238. On moderation as a medical principle see M. Lindemann, *Health and Healing in Eighteenth-century Germany* (Baltimore and London, Johns Hopkins University Press, 1996), pp. 262–71; E. Seidler, *Lebensplanung und Gesundheitsführung: Franz Anton Mai und die medizinische Aufklärung in Mannheim* (Mannheim, Boehringer, 1975).

3 Hull, *Sexuality*, pp. 258–80; K. Braun, *Die Krankheit Onania: Körperangst und die Anfänge moderner Sexualität im 18. Jahrhundert* (Frankfurt and New York, Campus, 1995), pp. 118–39; R. Porter, 'The Literature of Sexual Advice before 1800', in R. Porter and M. Teich (eds), *Sexual Knowledge, Sexual Science: The History of Attitudes to Sexuality* (Cambridge, Cambridge University Press, 1994); P. Crawford, 'Sexual Knowledge in England, 1500–1750', in Porter and Teich (eds), *Sexual Knowledge.*

4 Braun, *Krankheit Onania*. Another topic, closely related to the anti-masturbation campaign of the Philanthropists, was their fight against wet-nursing: see Simon Richter, 'Wet-nursing, Onanism, and the Breast in Eighteenth-century Germany', *Journal of the History of Sexuality*, 7 (1996).

5 Braun, *Krankheit Onania*, pp. 95–9; J. Stengers and A. van Neck, *Histoire d'une grande peur: la masturbation* (Brussels, Editions de l'Université de Bruxelles, 1984), chapters 5 and 6; Hull, *Sexuality*, pp. 252 and 260; Isabel Hull, '"Sexualität" und bürgerliche Gesellschaft', in U. Frevert (ed.), *Bürgerinnen und Bürger: Geschlechterverhältnisse im 19. Jahrhundert* (Göttingen, Vandenhoeck & Ruprecht, 1988), pp. 57–9.

6 Hull, *Sexuality*, p. 276; H. Hentze, *Sexualität und Pädagogik des späten 18. Jahrhunderts* (Frankfurt am Main, Peter Lang, 1979).

7 Braun, *Krankheit Onania*, p. 252.

8 A. Jais, *Das Wichtigste für Eltern, Erzieher und Aufseher der Jugend* (Munich, Lentner, 1787); J. Deharbe, *Katholischer Katechismus, oder Lehrbegriff* (Lucerne, 1847).

9 F. Mort, *Dangerous Sexualities: Medico-moral Politics in England since 1830* (London and New York, Routledge & Kegan Paul, 1987), p. 86; P. Gay, *The Bourgeois Experience: Victoria to Freud*, vol. 1 (Oxford, Oxford University Press, 1984), p. 278.

10 See Gay, *Bourgeois Experience*, vol. 1, pp. 281–94.

11 L. A. Hall, 'Forbidden by God, Despised by Men: Masturbation, Medical Warnings, Moral Panic, and Manhood in Great Britain, 1850–1950', *Journal of the History of Sexuality*, 2 (1991/92); R. P. Neuman, 'Masturbation, Madness, and the Modern Concepts of Childhood', *Journal of Social History*, 7 (1974/75); H. T. Engelhardt, 'The Disease of Masturbation:

Values and the Concept of Disease', *Bulletin of the History of Medicine*, 48 (1974).

12   I. Bloch, *Das Sexualleben unserer Zeit in seinen Beziehungen zur modernen Kultur* (Berlin, Louis Marcus, 1907), p. 741.

13   M. F. Stieg, 'The 1926 German Law to Protect Youth against Trash and Dirt: Moral Protectionism in a Democracy', *Central European History*, 23 (1990); G. Jäger, 'Der Kampf gegen Schmutz und Schund: Die Reaktion der Gebildeten auf die Unterhaltungsindustrie', *Archiv für Geschichte des Buchwesens*, 31 (1988).

14   A. Grossmann, *Reforming Sex: The German Movement for Birth Control and Abortion Reform, 1920–1950* (Oxford, Oxford University Press, 1995), pp. 3–20; C. Regin, *Selbsthilfe und Gesundheitspolitik: Die Naturheilbewegung im Kaiserreich (1889 bis 1914)* (Stuttgart, Franz Steiner, 1995), pp. 100–251; U. Geuter, *Homosexualität in der deutschen Jugendbewegung: Jungenfreundschaft und Sexualität im Diskurs von Jugendbewegung, Psychoanalyse und Jugendpsychologie am Beginn des 20. Jahrhunderts* (Frankfurt am Main, Suhrkamp, 1994); C. Usborne, *The Politics of the Body in Weimar Germany: Women's Reproductive Rights and Duties* (Ann Arbor, University of Michigan Press, 1992), pp. 1–30; U. Linse, '"Geschlechternot der Jugend": Über Jugendbewegung und Sexualität', in T. Koebner, R.-P. Janz and F. Trommler (eds), *'Mit uns zieht die neue Zeit': Der Mythos Jugend* (Frankfurt am Main, Suhrkamp, 1985); W. R. Krabbe, *Gesellschaftsveränderung durch Lebensreform: Strukturmerkmale einer sozialreformerischen Bewegung im Deutschland der Industrialisierungsperiode* (Göttingen, Vandenhoeck & Ruprecht, 1974).

15   See P. Gay, *Freud: A Life for our Time* (London, J. M. Dent & Sons, 1989), pp. 142–9; F. J. Sulloway, *Freud, Biologist of the Mind: Beyond the Psychoanalytic Legend* (London, Burnett Books, 1982), pp. 171–88, 210–13, 277–9, 468–71; H. F. Ellenberger, *The Discovery of the Unconscious: The History and Evolution of Dynamic Psychiatry* (London, Allen Lane/The Penguin Press, 1973), pp. 500–10.

16   H. Röling, 'Sexual Knowledge as the Boundary between Youth and Adulthood and the Ideal of Innocence in the Dutch Debate on Sexual Instruction 1890–1960', *Paedagogica Historica*, 29 (1993), p. 231; Gay, *Bourgeois Experience*, vol. 1, pp. 278–327. See M. Waweerzonnek, *Implizite Sexualpädagogik in der Sexualwissenschaft 1886 bis 1939* (Cologne, Pahl-Rugenstein, 1984); for Imperial Germany, see M. Schuster, 'Sexualaufklärung im Kaiserreich', in A. Bagel-Bohlau and M. Salewski (eds), *Sexualmoral und Zeitgeist im 19. und 20. Jahrhundert* (Opladen, Leske & Budrich, 1990); for Weimar and Nazi Germany, see R. Barkow, *Die Sexualpädagogik von 1918–1945* (dissertation, Münster, 1980).

17   See for more details L. Sauerteig, *Krankheit, Sexualität, Gesellschaft: Geschlechtskrankheiten und Gesundheitspolitik in Deutschland im 19. und frühen 20. Jahrhundert* (Stuttgart, Franz Steiner, 1999); L. Sauerteig, 'Moralismus versus Pragmatismus: Die Kontroverse um Schutzmittel gegen Geschlechtskrankheiten zu Beginn des 20. Jahrhunderts im deutsch-englischen Vergleich', in M. Dinges and T. Schlich (eds), *Neue Wege in der Seuchengeschichte* (Stuttgart, Franz Steiner, 1995).

18 See L. Sauerteig, 'Frauenemanzipation und Sittlichkeit: Die Rezeption des englischen Abolitionismus in Deutschland', in R. Muhs, J. Paulmann and W. Steinmetz (eds), *Aneignung und Abwehr: Interkultureller Transfer zwischen Deutschland und Grossbritannien im 19. Jahrhundert* (Bodenheim, Philo-Verlagsgesellschaft, 1998).

19 K. Hagemann, *Frauenalltag und Männerpolitik: Alltagsleben und gesellschaftliches Handeln von Arbeiterfrauen in der Weimarer Republik* (Bonn, Dietz, 1990), pp. 238–9; K. Ahrens, 'Entwicklung einer Konzeption für sexuelle Aufklärung an Hamburger Schulen (1901–1929)', in H.-P. de Lorent and V. Ullrich (eds), *Der Traum von der freien Schule: Schule und Schulpolitik in Hamburg während der Weimarer Republik* (Hamburg, Ergebnisse, 1988), pp. 306–7.

20 Regin, *Selbsthilfe*, pp. 212–20.

21 See A. T. Allen, *Feminism and Motherhood in Germany, 1800–1914* (New Brunswick, N.J., Rutgers University Press, 1991), pp. 173–205; C. Wickert, *Helene Stöcker, 1869–1943: Frauenrechtlerin, Sexualreformerin und Pazifistin. Eine Biographie* (Bonn, Dietz, 1991); T. Wobbe, *Gleichheit und Differenz: Politische Strategien von Frauenrechtlerinnen um die Jahrhundertwende* (Frankfurt am Main and New York, Campus, 1989), pp. 99–130; B. Nowacki, *Der Bund für Mutterschutz (1905–1933)* (Husum, Matthiesen, 1983); R. J. Evans, *The Feminist Movement in Germany 1894–1933* (London and Beverly Hills, Sage, 1976), pp. 115–39.

22 Helene Stöcker, 'Prostitution und Enthaltsamkeit', *Mitteilungen der Deutschen Gesellschaft zur Bekämpfung der Geschlechtskrankheiten* (henceforth *MDGBG*), 2 (1904), pp. 125–7.

23 M. Lischnewska, 'Die geschlechtliche Belehrung der Kinder', *Mutterschutz*, 1 (1905).

24 See Hagemann, *Frauenalltag*, pp. 227–9; R. P. Neuman, *Socialism, the Family and Sexuality: The Marxist Tradition and German Social Democracy before 1914* (Evanston, Ill., dissertation, Northwestern University, 1972, Microfilm Ann Arbor); E. Fromm, *Arbeiter und Angestellte am Vorabend des Dritten Reiches: Eine sozialpsychologische Untersuchung*, ed. Wolfgang Bonss (Stuttgart, Deutsche Verlags-Anstalt, 1980), p. 194.

25 See Sauerteig, *Krankheit*, chapter 3.

26 See Lida Gustava Heymann's comment on the DGBG Congress on Sexual Education, *Zeitschrift für Bekämpfung der Geschlechtskrankheiten* (henceforth *ZBG*), 7 (1907), p. 168; M. Chotzen, 'Die sexualpädagogische Tätigkeit der Deutschen Gesellschaft zur Bekämpfung der Geschlechtskrankheiten: Ein Bericht, erstattet der XI. Jahresversammlung der DGBG 1913', *ZBG*, 14 (1912–14), pp. 364–5; H. Haustein, 'Statistik der Geschlechtskrankheiten', in J. Jadassohn (ed.), *Handbuch der Haut- und Geschlechtskrankheiten*, vol. 22 (Berlin, Julius Springer, 1927), p. 706.

27 S. Freud, 'Zur sexuellen Aufklärung der Kinder: Offener Brief an Dr. M. Fürst', in S. Freud, *Gesammelte Werke*, vol. 7 (Frankfurt am Main, S. Fischer, fourth ed. 1966).

28 Bundesarchiv Berlin (henceforth BAB), 15.01/11866, pp. 232–54: Imperial Health Office (Reichsgesundheitsamt), report on measures to control VD, December 1908, p. 11.

29 A. Neisser, 'Die Aufgaben der Deutschen Gesellschaft zur Bekämpfung der Geschlechtskrankheiten', *MDGBG*, 1 (1902/03), p. 32.

30 M. Chotzen, 'Praktische Vorschläge für die Durchführung einer sexuellen Erziehung', *ZBG*, 12 (1911/12), p. 368.

31 Chotzen, 'Sexualpädagogische Tätigkeit', p. 353.

32 A. Blaschko, *Die Deutsche Gesellschaft zur Bekämpfung der Geschlechtskrankheiten* (Leipzig, J. A. Barth, 1920), p. 7.

33 Blaschko, *Gesellschaft*, p. 7. See A. Eulenburg, 'Sexuelle Diätetik', *ZBG*, 7 (1907).

34 Blaschko, *Gesellschaft*, p. 7.

35 A. Blaschko, 'Hygiene der Geschlechtskrankheiten', in A. Gärtner (ed.), *Weyls Handbuch der Hygiene*, vol. 8 (Leipzig, J. A. Barth, second ed. 1918–22), p. 429.

36 H. Popert, *Helmut Harringa: Eine Geschichte aus unsrer Zeit* (Dresden, A. Köhler, 1905). See Linse, 'Geschlechternot', pp. 263–4; W. Laqueur, *Die deutsche Jugendbewegung: Eine historische Studie* (Cologne, Wissenschaft und Politik, 1962, second ed. 1978), pp. 56–8.

37 BAB, 15.01/11866, pp. 103–8: Martin Kirchner, 'Massnahmen zur Bekämpfung der Geschlechtskrankheiten im Deutschen Reiche', paper given at a meeting of the Imperial Health Council, March 1908, pp. 3–4.

38 See the papers given at the 1907 DGBG Congress on Sexual Education: K. Höller, 'Die Aufgabe der Volksschule', *ZBG*, 7 (1907), pp. 86–7; M. Enderlin, 'Die sexuelle Frage und die Volksschule', *ZBG*, 7 (1907), p. 66; Kemsies, 'Die sexuelle Aufklärung in den höheren Lehranstalten', *ZBG*, 7 (1907); W. Fürstenheim, 'Die sexuelle Belehrung der Abiturienten', *ZBG*, 7 (1907), pp. 150 and 153. See M. Doell, 'Die sexuelle Frage im Erziehungsplan des Gymnasiums: Vortrag, gehalten in der Gymnasiallehrer-Vereinigung zu München', *ZBG*, 12 (1911/12); Chotzen, 'Praktische Vorschläge', pp. 372–3; Blaschko, 'Hygiene', p. 430.

39 Blaschko, 'Hygiene', p. 430.

40 A. Blaschko, 'Geschlechtskrankheiten', in A. Grotjahn and I. Kaup (eds), *Handwörterbuch der sozialen Hygiene*, 2 vols, vol. 1 (Leipzig, F. C. W. Vogel, 1912), p. 405.

41 Pastoral letter, Fulda Bishops' Conference, 12 August 1908, in *Akten der Fuldaer Bischofskonferenz*, vol. 3 (Mainz, Matthias-Grunewald, 1985), no 134, p. 121. See M. Langer, *Katholische Sexualpädagogik im 20. Jahrhundert: Zur Geschichte eines religionspädagogischen Problems* (Munich, Kösel, 1986), pp. 15–27 and 47–55; Barkow, *Sexualpädagogik*, pp. 25–134; W. Braun, *Geschlechtliche Erziehung im katholischen Religionsunterricht: Ein Beitrag zur katholischen Religionspädagogik von der Reformation bis zur Gegenwart* (Trier, Spee, 1970), pp. 143–54 and 167–82.

42 See H.-G. Ziebertz, *Sexualpädagogik im gesellschaftlichen Kontext: Studien zur Konzeptentwicklung katholischer Sexualerziehung* (Kampen, J. H. Kok and Weinheim, Deutscher Studien Verlag, 1993), pp. 75–86.

43 F. W. Foerster, *Sexualethik und Sexualpädagogik: Eine Auseinandersetzung mit den Modernen* (Kempten and Munich, Kösel, 1907), p. 20.

44 Foerster, *Sexualethik*, pp. 44–52.

45 Foerster, *Sexualethik*, p. 58.

46 Foerster, *Sexualethik*, pp. 63–5 and 86–93.

47 Foerster, *Sexualethik*, p. 93.

48 See Steinweg, 'Leitsätze für die "gemeinschaftliche Aufklärungsarbeit mit den Verbänden der Wohlfahrtspflege"', *MDGBG*, 22 (1924); Barkow, *Sexualpädagogik*, pp. 49–50.

49 See Blaschko's comment at DGBG Congress on Sexual Education in *ZBG*, 7 (1907), p. 184; Chotzen, 'Praktische Vorschläge', pp. 369–70; Chotzen, 'Sexualpädagogische Tätigkeit', pp. 355 and 358–9; Chotzen, 'Unsere sexualpädagogische Aktion', *MDGBG*, 11 (1913), p. 2.

50 J. Marcuse, *Geschlechtliche Erziehung in der Arbeiterfamilie* (Berlin, Buchandlung Vorwärts, 1907) (Arbeiter-Gesundheits-Bibliothek, ed. I. Zadek, vol. 15); H. Fürth, *Die Geschlechtliche Aufklärung in Haus und Schule* (Leipzig, Frauen-Rundschau, 1903); O. Rühle, *Die Aufklärung der Kinder über geschlechtliche Dinge* (Bremen, Sozialdemokratische Verein Bremen, 1908).

51 See E. Meirowsky, 'Leitsätze für ein von der D.G.B.G. herauszugebendes Elternmerkblatt', *ZBG*, 7 (1907), pp. 182–3; Barkow, *Sexualpädagogik*, pp. 174–9.

52 Freud, 'Aufklärung', p. 26.

53 Bloch, *Sexualleben*, pp. 746–7. See Wawerzonnek, *Sexualpädagogik*, pp. 57–8.

54 O. Rosenthal, 'Über die sexuelle Belehrung von Abiturienten: Eine Enquete', *ZBG*, 12 (1911/12), pp. 274–5.

55 See BAB, 15.01/11875, pp. 312–13: Minutes of a meeting of the Hamburg Supervisory School Authority, 29 July 1919, extract.

56 Hagemann, *Frauenalltag*, pp. 239–40; see Ahrens, 'Entwicklung', pp. 309–10.

57 Hagemann, *Frauenalltag*, pp. 240–1; Ahrens, 'Entwicklung', p. 312.

58 See BAB 15.01/11876, pp. 89–92: Report of the Imperial Health Office, 11 April 1920.

59 BAB, 15.01/11876, 99. 100–2: Report of conference on combating VD, prostitution and crime through social measures, in Bielefeld, 6 October 1920, pp. 2–3; see *MDGBG*, 19 (1921), pp. 32–5.

60 See Barkow, *Sexualpädagogik*, pp. 206–16.

61 See H. Rosenbaum, *Proletarische Familien: Arbeiterfamilien und Arbeiterväter im frühen 20. Jahrhundert zwischen traditioneller, sozialdemokratischer und kleinbürgerlicher Orientierung* (Frankfurt am Main, Suhrkamp, 1992), pp. 199 and 372; Hagemann, *Frauenalltag*, pp. 228–9; Linse, 'Geschlechternot', pp. 279–82; Neuman, *Socialism*.

62 Grossmann, *Reforming Sex*, chapter 2.

63 Grossmann, *Reforming Sex*, pp. 14–135; Usborne, *Politics*, pp. 95 and 102–33; K. v Soden, *Die Sexualberatungsstellen der Weimarer Republik 1919–1933* (Berlin, Edition Hentrich, 1988), pp. 9–12 and 44–144.

64 See W. Wolff, *Max Hodann (1894–1946): Sozialist und Sexualreformer* (Hamburg, von Bockel, 1993); my critical review of Wolff's book in *Paedagogica Historica*, 30 (1994), pp. 996–9; Grossmann, *Reforming Sex*; Hagemann, *Frauenalltag*, pp. 229–31.

65 M. Hodann, *Bub und Mädel: Gespräche unter Kameraden über die Geschlechterfrage* (Leipzig, Ernst Oldenburg, 1924; 5th edition Rudolstadt,

Greifen, 1926, 8th edition 1927); M. Hodann, *Woher die Kinder kommen: Ein Lehrbuch für Kinder lesbar* (Rudolstadt, Greifen, 1926), new edition with the title *Bringt uns wirklich der Klapperstorch? Ein Lehrbüchlein für Kinder lesbar* (Berlin, Universitas, 1928).

66 See M. Hodann, *Geschlecht und Liebe in biologischer und gesellschaftlicher Beziehung* (Rudolstadt, Greifen, 1927; further editions were published with Büchergilde Gutenberg, Berlin, 1932, and with Universitas, Berlin, 1932, an English translation appeared in 1932 and a French one in 1933); M. Hodann, *Sexualelend und Sexualberatung: Briefe aus der Praxis* (Rudolstadt, Greifen, 1928).

67 Grossmann, *Reforming Sex*, pp. 24 and 28–9.

68 Hagemann, *Frauenalltag*, p. 231.

69 See Hagemann, *Frauenalltag*, pp. 233–6.

70 See C. Usborne, 'The New Woman and Generational Conflicts: Perceptions of Young Women's Sexual Mores in the Weimar Republic', in M. Roseman (ed.), *Generations in Conflict: Youth Revolt and Generation Formation in Germany, 1770–1968* (Cambridge, Cambridge University Press, 1995); Usborne, *Politics*, pp. 85–101.

71 Archbishop Bertram, Breslau, at the Fulda Bishops' Conference, 22 and 23 August 1916, in *Akten der Fuldaer Bischofskonferenz*, vol. 3 (1985), no. 306, p. 274. See I. Götz von Olenhusen, 'Geschlechterrollen, Jugend und Religion: Deutschland 1900–1933', in M. Kraul and C. Lüth (eds), *Erziehung der Menschen-Geschlechter: Studien zur Religion, Sozialisation und Bildung in Europa seit der Aufklärung* (Weinheim, Deutscher Studien Verlag, 1996); Langer, *Sexualpädagogik*, pp. 56–71.

72 'Katholische Leitsätze und Weisungen zu verschiedenen modernen Sittlichkeitsfragen', *Amtsblatt für die Erzdiözese München und Freising* (1925), p. 28.

73 Langer, *Sexualpädagogik*, pp. 103–4.

74 A. Bertram, *Reverentia Puero! Katholische Erwägungen zu Fragen der Sexual-Pädagogik* (Freiburg, Herder, 1929). See Langer, *Sexualpädagogik*, pp. 104–6.

75 Encyclicals *De christiana iuventae educatione*, 31 December 1929 and *Decretum de 'educatione sexuali' et de 'eugenica'*, 21 March 1931, *Amtsblatt für die Erzdiözese München und Freising* (1931), pp. 104–5.

76 C. Lipp, 'Die Innenseite der Arbeiterkultur: Sexualität im Arbeitermilieu des 19. und frühen 20. Jahrhunderts', in R. van Dülmen (ed.), *Arbeit, Frömmigkeit und Eigensinn: Studien zur historischen Kulturforschung*, vol. 2 (Frankfurt am Main, Fischer, 1990), pp. 224–6; Hagemann, *Frauenalltag*, pp. 225–7 and 232–7; Rosenbaum, *Proletarische Familien*, pp. 188 and 196–9.

77 A. Hilgers, '25 Jahre Sexualerziehung in der Schule: Richtlinien und Unterrichtspraxis auf dem Prüfstand', *SOWI: Sozialwissenschaftliche Information*, 24 (1995), p. 80.

78 A. Corbin, 'Kulissen', in P. Ariès and G. Duby (eds), *Geschichte des privaten Lebens*, vol. 4 (Frankfurt am Main, S. Fischer, 1992), pp. 461–2 and 547.

79 Hagemann, *Frauenalltag*, p. 225; Lipp, 'Innenseite', pp. 223–4; Rosenbaum, *Proletarische Familien*, pp. 195–6; G. A. Ritter and K. Tenfelde, *Arbeiter im Deutschen Kaiserreich 1871 bis 1914* (Bonn, Dietz, 1992), pp. 627 and 642–3.

80 Rosenbaum, *Proletarische Familien*, pp. 195–6; Lipp, 'Innenseite', pp. 224 and 227–8; H. P. Duerr, *Der Mythos vom Zivilisationsprozess*, vol. 1 (Frankfurt am Main, Suhrkamp, 1988).

81 Rosenbaum, *Proletarische Familien*, p. 198; Lipp, 'Innenseite', pp. 223 and 230–7.

82 F. Wedekind, *Frühlings Erwachen: Eine Kindertragödie* (Stuttgart, Reclam, 1971), act 2, scene 2.

83 Corbin, 'Kulissen', pp. 461–2.

84 G.-F. Budde, *Auf dem Weg ins Bürgerleben: Kindheit und Erziehung in deutschen und englischen Bürgerfamilien 1840–1914* (Göttingen, Vandenhoeck & Ruprecht, 1994), pp. 213–14.

85 Gay, *Bourgeois Experience*, vol. 1, p. 319.

86 See Usborne, *Politics*, pp. 77–8; Hagemann, *Frauenalltag*, pp. 244–5.

87 'Empfehlung zur Sexualerziehung in den Schulen', *Sammlung der Beschlüsse der Ständigen Konferenz der Kultursminister der Länder der Bundesrepublik Deutschland* (Neuwied, Luchterhand, 1969), no. 659, 3 October 1968.

88 See Hilgers, 'Sexualerziehung'.

89 *Entscheidungen des Bundesverfassungsgerichts*, 47 (1978), decision no. 2, 21 December 1977. See Hilgers, 'Sexualerziehung'.

2

The rise and fall of European syphilisation: the debates on human experimentation and vaccination of syphilis, *c.* 1845–70

Bertrand Taithe

Michel Foucault's distinction between Western *scientia sexualis* and *ars erotica*[1] cannot be better exemplified than by the role of the history of venereology in the history of sexuality. The 'art' of venereology and the science of genitals were two *loci* of scientific power and definitions of sexuality. The debate on syphilisation illustrates how the mental universe of syphilology, a scientific obsession rather than a specialisation in our modern understanding, came to be constructed across Europe between 1845 and 1870. The debates considered in this chapter between Joseph-Alexandre Auzias-Turenne and Philippe Ricord were European while still very Parisian, and they marked both the decline of the French clinic and the crucial problems in the construction of a science of diseases of sexual organs. Pioneer philosopher and sociologist of science Ludwik Fleck did not choose by mistake to illustrate his concept of coercive 'thought collective' with examples taken from the history of syphilology.[2] Perhaps no other area of the social history of medicine offers examples of 'self-fulfilling scientific expectations'.[3] While Fleck's analysis of the Wassermann test remains debated,[4] his innovative concepts help in analysing the thirty-year dispute that shook French and European syphilology.[5]

Apart from his few friends and followers, historians of venereology often refer to Dr Auzias-Turenne's life-work as an exemplary failure of nineteenth-century medical research.[6] They condescendingly use his example as an anecdote from the age of heroic medicine. Syphilisation, his theory of the supposed immunisation against syphilis through repeated injections of syphilis, was a tragic mistake borne of a confusion between chancroid and syphilitic chancres, worth recalling only for the ethical implications of human experiments. Accounts of his struggle to have his theories accepted between 1845 and 1870 conclude on the philosophical necessity of his oblivion.

This chapter tackles this latter argument. It aims to expose how and why the French medical establishment rejected Auzias-Turenne and his theories almost *a priori* and how this national condemnation sealed their fate at an international level. It dwells on Auzias-Turenne's publications, private archive, diaries and notes,[7] on the extensive record kept at the Préfecture de Police Archives of Paris and on various medical journals and other contemporary narratives.[8] Syphilisation was a scientific debate which originated within the medical establishment and which was successfully marginalised. This containment of a medical theory which promised immunity from the most dangerous venereal disease demonstrated not only the social mechanism which defined and excluded quacks but also the limits of medical intervention and experimentation in the sexual field. This was an area which proved to have so many correlations and effects that experimenting with sexually transmitted diseases amounted to no less than meddling with human nature itself. Syphilisation might have put lives at risk but it also undermined fundamental religious and scientific assumptions on the role of sexuality in the making of the individual self.

The syphilisation debate, 1845–70

The syphilisation debate started in 1845 with Auzias-Turenne's experiments on animal syphilis and lasted until his death in 1870 and that of the Norwegian syphilisator Carl Wilhelm Boeck in 1875.[9] A full account of this debate is excessively repetitive and tends to be dominated by Auzias-Turenne's side of the story.[10] The narrative structure of Auzias-Turenne's version of the events resembles the never-ending combat between David and Goliath. The two characters of Ricord and Auzias-Turenne contrasted two types of intellectual and social developments in Second-Empire France. Ricord was a product of the French academic world of the 1830s who eventually dominated the Hôpital du Midi.[11] His sense of humour and congenial love of life made him the 'most popular physician' in Paris, and also the wealthiest.

Born in 1800 in Baltimore,[12] Philippe Ricord benefited from a series of useful patrons: Lesueur,[13] who took him to Paris, and Baron Cuvier.[14] Under the supreme patronage of Cuvier, Ricord managed to develop a complex and effective patronage-seeking career as a medical student, from Broussais[15] to Dupuytren,[16] to Dupuytren's enemy, Lisfranc.[17] Ricord knew better than most how the French institutions worked and how one could obtain desired senior hospital posts.[18] He passed the relevant competitive examination in 1828 and was put in charge of a surgical ward at the Midi venereal hospital. From this ill-reputed hospital Ricord erected a dogmatic fortress. In 1838 he published the classic nineteenth-century textbook on VD, *Traité pratique des maladies vénériennes*. This book was a landmark in the renewed interest in venereology, and Ricord discriminated between various venereal symptoms and established the biorhythm of syphilis. This study, based on Hunter[19] but dwelling on an historical tradition of clinical observations dating from Fernel d'Amiens,[20] also used many conclusions derived from experiments on self-inoculated chancres.[21] Ricord developed three fundamental paradigms of syphilology: the disease was specifically human, it progressed through three periods and it was contagious only in the first stage. The book was a fine specimen of empirical clinical work, and, if it was not revolutionary, it seemed much sharper and authoritative than previous observations of syphilis. More importantly, Ricord's organisation of venereal diseases in a clear nosology created the template of all subsequent medical discussions of sexually transmissible diseases. Indeed, contemporaries expressed the view that Ricord's writings and his art of arranging evidence had saved 'syphilology' from chaos.[22] His prose re-created an orthodox and coherent syphilology based on 'virus' transmission.[23]

While he reorganised the pathology of syphilis, his views were also reassuring: the propagation of syphilis seemed limited, the potential dangers greatly circumscribed by the curative uses of metallic treatments like mercury in its various forms.[24] Most of Ricord's influence derived from this book,[25] and in 1844 he became a prominent member of the Society of Surgery. Republican in 1848,[26] Bonapartist in 1851, his remarkable career of political versatility did not end with his retirement in 1860. He carried on his private practice from his grand house, rue de Tournon,[27] and obtained more money than he could spend from his aristocratic clients.[28] In 1868 he became the president of the then very conservative Académie de Médecine. A year later, he became the consulting surgeon of the Emperor, who was afflicted with kidney stones.[29] After the 1870 upheaval he converted to the new republic and even became a

Parisian hero through a careful management of his image as the head of war ambulances.[30] After the war the old man remained a prominent scientific figure of the new regime. He died a rich man in 1889, one of few medical Commandeurs de la Légion d'Honneur. His fortune amounted to several million francs and he became a model of medical and social success. His very close association with whatever regime could favour his career and ambition matched his technical mastering of the medical establishment. Ricord managed to keep his social and political prestige intact in spite of fundamental scientific objections to his work. Until the end Ricord viewed syphilis as a curable disease mostly confined to the genitalia.[31] Ricordian views of pox combined a lighthearted approach to the disease, the butt of his many jokes, and a heavy-handed use of mercury and cauterisation. This attitude was rather symbolic of a 'morally neutral' medicine in a regulationist country and explains his fortunes.

Joseph-Alexandre Auzias-Turenne always sought to reflect another reality of French medicine. Born in 1812, Auzias-Turenne went to Montpellier and then Paris to struggle his way through to the doctorate. He became acquainted with Etienne Geoffroy Saint-Hilaire, who treated him like a son.[32] The modalities of this prestigious patronage were strikingly different from that of Cuvier for Ricord, and Auzias-Turenne slowly had to make his way to the doctorate. In 1842 he eventually graduated but failed to become an intern and thus could never apply for a hospital job or faculty teaching position. On the other hand, he had, through the Geoffroy dynasty, constant access to the Museum d'Histoire Naturelle[33] and its collections.[34] In 1844, while following Ricord's clinical teaching at the Midi hospital, Auzias-Turenne heard him repeat his view that syphilis was specifically human. This position took up Cuvier's appraisal of the place of man in the animal estate.[35] Auzias-Turenne reacted as a disciple of Geoffroy Saint-Hilaire, and he saw the specificity of syphilis as an anomaly. To check this point he obtained from his patron the right to experiment with monkeys on the innocuousness of syphilis to animals. After a few inoculations following which monkeys appeared to develop chancres, Auzias-Turenne attempted to display the universality of syphilis in public in 1845. He selected monkeys with which he had obtained positive results previously, chose some more harmful pus but the experiment failed. Discredited for a time, Auzias-Turenne reflected on the possibility of acquired immunity from the repeated inoculation of syphilis.[36] He thought of this method as a 'vaccine' and he secretly practised upon himself the series of inoculations known as syphilisation. The method was quite simple: one had to choose a ripe bubo of fully developed primary syphilis, slice it open and puncture some clear pus. The experimenter later introduced 'the active principle' under the skin on the arm or the chest. Auzias-Turenne would then renew this process several times until symptomatic reactions lessened, thus 'showing' acquired immunity. This renewed series of inoculations was only comparable with mithridatisation (the acquired immunity to poison) and did not really fit with any recent medical practices, in spite of efforts to compare it with Jenner's work. Auzias-Turenne spent a few years establishing a small clinical sample validating his experimental model. One major obstacle to a breakthrough of syphilisation was the length of time it took him to find volunteers to experiment upon.[37] He still had no official appointment within any hospital ward. Without the *internat* he stood little chance of ever getting one.

His political choices also proved less than judicious: a friend of François-Vincent Raspail, a republican in 1848, an agnostic if not a militant atheist (his burial, in 1870, provided an opportunity for an anti-clerical demonstration), his political and ethical choices lacked Ricord's pragmatism. His experiment on monkeys tended to prove that venereal diseases had no moral or religious dimension.[38] Syphilis was merely one disease among many others. 'The advantages of syphilisation applied to prostitutes are very important', he wrote to the Emperor Napoléon III, '1. The main source of syphilis would dry up, 2. One could go to see a prostitute safely ... it would follow that one would not seek to satisfy natural needs elsewhere than in brothel houses.'[39] Auzias-Turenne integrated syphilis within the nosology and equated it with smallpox, neglecting major discrepancies in their means of propagation. He refused to deal with promiscuity; if anything, his argument in favour of syphilisation showed a total lack of concern for the moral implications of brothels. His argument in favour of brothels could easily be turned on its head against police regulation. With syphilisation the need for policed brothels would disappear since any form of sexual regulation would lose its hygienic legitimacy.

In the light of his overt opposition to everything Ricord stood for or even made a living from, it was not surprising that Auzias-Turenne faced serious antagonism when he applied to the French police to obtain authorisation to experiment with a 'process' of immunisation against syphilis at the prostitute hospital wing of Saint-Lazare prison on 9 February 1852.[40] He offered to serve in the lock-hospital at no cost to the police for a full clinical trial of syphilisation.[41] His original excuse was to continue the treatment undertaken by some inmates before their imprisonment. His application created a strong interest from the Police Second Bureau in charge of regulating Paris prostitution.[42] The regulation of prostitution in Paris followed two major lines: the institution of authorised and controlled brothels, and fortnightly medical visits. The first measure aimed at clearing the streets of prostitutes. It partially failed, and ever more prostitutes resorted to working freelance, subjected only to the police medical examination (*filles en cartes*). Unregistered prostitutes, rebellious and infected ones, were locked in the prison lock-hospital of Saint-Lazare. Once 'administratively' detained, prostitutes underwent the current mercurial treatment administered by third-rate and underpaid visiting physicians. As Alain Corbin pointed out, this medical supervision was a late addition to regulation that gradually justified all policing practices. Paris regulation sprang from a spy system of the *ancien régime*,[43] and originally regulation worked without much medical examination.[44] Prostitutes were often unpaid police informers.[45] Medical examination became a part of the police routine later, and the number of medical men paid for this task increased only gradually throughout the century. The sanitary part of the examination slowly took over as the shortcomings of police regulation became more obvious.[46]

Even when submitted to experimental treatment, prostitutes rarely had the opportunity to voice their consent or their objections.[47] While it was a routine task for the police, prostitutes dreaded the first stay in prison. Syphilis, even if 'cured', entailed a social climb-down from the brothel to the street and bar back-rooms. Many prostitutes, however, escaped police regulation, and middle-class *demi-mondaines* seldom ended up in Saint-Lazare. The human stock Auzias-Turenne applied to experiment upon was the poorest and the least respectable. While most prostitutes were at the margin of the criminal world, sick prostitutes had even fewer friends. Auzias-Turenne nevertheless wished to apply experimental therapeutics only to consenting human beings. Similar experiments took place in other Paris hospitals (such as Val-de-Grâce) on less-informed patients. Considering the class prejudices against prostitutes, Auzias-Turenne's choice reflected an existing double standard of morality but did not innovate in this respect. More surprising is the fact that he applied to the police to counteract the likely consequences of an Academy of Medicine inquiry on his techniques.[48] The real paradox was that his early claims to a vaccine for syphilis would eventually make police regulation redundant. It was, to say the least, naive to believe that the French police, during the most severe political repression of 1852, would let such a useful tool disappear.[49]

Yet there were other concerns which counterbalanced an *a priori* negative appraisal of Auzias-Turenne's system.[50] The savings resulting from the general vaccination of sailors, soldiers and prostitutes (the three main groups at risk identified for preventive syphilisation) were potentially very attractive. 'Syphilisation is bound to be useful to the administration under these three accounts: savings, health and public morality.'[51] Considering its technical difficulties, Auzias-Turenne improperly presented syphilisation as fitting among well-known cheap preventive measures like vaccination in spite of the long and painful series of inoculations his methods required.[52]

The three deaths of syphilisation

Syphilisation died three times between 1845 and 1870. The Academy of Medicine rejected it in July 1852. The Police Committee followed in December 1852. Public opinion reproved the 1859 inoculation of secondary syphilis to volunteers. Each instance of condemnation was different: each time a different element of the theory, ethics and practice of syphilisation was condemned.

Auzias-Turenne's application had been public. The police had to react publicly. This was a fundamental element of the syphilisation debate at its early stages. During the whole debate the police committee published most of its reports, evidence and proceedings. On 14 February 1852 the 2ième Bureau sent letters to Piedmont and Belgium to check the credentials of Auzias-Turenne's followers. In June, and in June only, the police administrators sought advice from Ricord.[53] On his advice they set up a committee of five medical men which included two non-specialist physicians (Mélier, a very senior *académicien* who presided, and Conneau, Louis-Napoléon's physician) and three specialists: a military medical officer from the Val-de-Grâce hospital, recently disciplined for experimenting with syphilisation, Marchal (de Calvi); Dr Denis, surgeon at the police dispensaries; and Ricord himself. Ricord and Denis were known opponents of syphilisation. This administrative sentencing of syphilisation took place largely in the absence of the main promoter himself. Charles-Jacob Marchal, who had practised syphilisation in his military hospital of Val-de-Grâce, was alone defending the theory and his own unethical practice.[54] Marchal had recently lost his hospital practice and was in a difficult position. His military hierarchical superiors condemned his radical political choices of 1848, his left-wing writings and his experiments.[55] He merely supported some aspects of Auzias-Turenne's theory, principally the curative power of syphilisation, but he vehemently denied that syphilisation should be used preventively. His argument was contradictory. While defending his own 'curative' treatments using syphilisation, Marchal denounced preventive syphilisation as immoral and dangerous. Auzias-Turenne argued that prevention was better than cure, but he claimed syphilisation was good at both.

Before the Police Committee had developed its inquiry Ricord had pre-empted its decision and in many ways made it redundant by bringing the matter to the Academy of Medicine.[56] The Academy of Medicine committee did not follow Marchal's or even Malgaigne's partial redemption of syphilisation. Their committee condemned it *ex cathedra*, mostly on moral grounds. After a short, severe and debatable examination of Auzias-Turenne's and Marchal's clinical cases and a handful of accidents linked to syphilisation, Bégin delivered the final blow:

> The fundamental practice of any treatment is to prevent or erase as far as possible the taint pox might leave behind, one would think indifferently to multiply them without any restriction and to *ostensibly mark the patient's body with permanent scars of a disease he would have some concern, later, to pretend he was never afflicted with. This hideous tattoo, proof of youth's foolish years, can impose too damaging consequences on the women or men who have reached maturity and wish to contract a legitimate union.* To prevent a disease that is possible to avoid and probably possible to cure in most cases; to start treating it with inoculations aggravating the dangers; or to cure it multiplying its accidents and scars, saturating one's body with a virus to better kill it, is something neither common sense nor science can admit.[57]

When Ricord organised a committee for the police to examine syphilisation, he decided that syphilisation should be technically retold once and for ever. The tools he planned to use were his own clinical knowledge of venereology. He gave weight to the committee by attending every one of its meetings himself. His choice of three other members of the Paris hospital elite gave the committee more institutional value and made it appear as a valid scientific panel. Choosing Marchal to represent Auzias-Turenne's supporters was particularly shrewd. The Police Committee therefore appeared more impartial, more balanced than the Academy of Medicine's own. To invite Marchal to be the secretary of a police committee was a devious way of neutralising him. All of Marchal's republican colleagues were either 're-located' in Algeria or in prison.[58] Considering the very serious consequences syphilisation would have, any validation of Auzias-Turenne's theory could be interpreted as an infringement on the repressive prerogatives of the police and a blow against the Academy. It would also be an attack on his hierarchical superiors who had disciplined him a few months earlier over this issue. Considering the rebuttal from the Academy of Medicine, the Police Committee became almost a redundant tribunal whose sole purpose was to silence syphilisation definitively.

Paradoxically the Academy had taken the moral and ethical path while Ricord set up the Police Committee to prove Auzias-Turenne scientifically wrong by the standard of contemporary venereology and medicine. There were a number of scientific problems attached to syphilisation: neither Marchal nor Auzias-Turenne could explain exactly how syphilisation worked. The comparison with pre-Jennerian inoculation of smallpox was of limited use. When the inoculation of smallpox began it was common clinical observation that the disease did not usually recur.[59] Nothing of that kind could be asserted confidently about syphilis. Marchal and Auzias-Turenne were left with dubious semantic assimilation between smallpox and pox (*petite et grande vérole*). The only clinical evidence Auzias-Turenne could put forward was the case of the monkeys and his own limited practice. This violated two rules of French medical proceedings in 1852: his experimentation on monkeys and other animals preceded clinical observation and it was based on a highly debatable and literal assimilation of human beings with animals.[60] It was a common judgement, then, that experimental medicine should be subordinated to prior clinical observation.[61]

Ricord opposed Auzias-Turenne on both grounds. He put forward his long experience of hospital work against Auzias-Turenne's own lack of practice. Having established his pre-eminence in the field, Ricord rejected dogmatically the non-specificity of human syphilis. This is a rare instance of a conscious translation into medicine of the Geoffroy–Cuvier debate.[62] Isidore Geoffroy Saint-Hilaire backed Auzias-Turenne as the spiritual heir of his father. The need for purely experimental research was not compelling in venereology. Yet, when the committee decided to reproduce the 1845 experiments, two monkeys were locked in Saint-Lazare. Auzias-Turenne practised the inoculation of syphilis to both monkeys to reproduce his own experiment and prove the existence of animal syphilis and how syphilisation worked. When a chancre grew on the inoculated ears of the monkeys, Ricord denied that it was syphilis; other members of the committee were hesitant while Marchal alone was convinced. The experiment of syphilisation on monkeys was aborted and the poor animals were forgotten in prison.[63] Renouncing any experimental re-enactment of syphilisation, the committee satisfied itself with discussing a few cases, including one fatal accident. Auzias-Turenne's reluctance to give names (which would have been printed later) made controls difficult: 'M. Ricord advanced that a doctor had informed him of a drummer of the Garde Nationale whom I had cured, and, as this man was not rich, I might show him to the commission, I simply answered that I wished to keep secret everybody's privacy, rich or poor, and I kept quiet.'[64] Auzias-Turenne's self-styled puritanical ethics entangled him in contradictory attitudes towards the moral consequences of syphilis. Although he refused to consider syphilis as immoral *per se* ('innocent victims' were common in the literature and Auzias-Turenne worked on the dangers of vaccine syphilis contracted through arm-to-arm vaccination), he acknowledged society's moral condemnation of the victims of syphilis. He therefore refused to give the names of his patients. In later years the fear of being prosecuted would make him even more secretive and led him to avoid treating 'common people' who might go to hospitals before the end of their syphilisation.[65] In the context of the 1852, 1859 and 1867 inquiries, he also refused to show his own scars. Ricord spent some time attacking Auzias-Turenne's apparent fear of self-experimentation and accused him of being a coward and therefore a quack.

Meanwhile international support for syphilisation proved little use to Auzias-Turenne. From June 1852 the Foreign Office itself dealt with the correspondence.[66] The French government queried Dr Sperino's practice of syphilisation in Turin.[67] The Piedmontese government replied on his behalf on 20 August. On 28 August, the Interior ministry of Piedmont replied to the queries of the committee. By 4 September the same services sent a report highlighting ambiguities in the Turin Academy of Medicine's vote on Sperino's data (vote dated 1 August). The Italian experiment with syphilisation was short-lived. Sperino's data were flawed but, in spite of the ambiguities of his results, the Turin Academy waited for the French decision to replicate its conclusions in a way which was to become familiar during this whole debate. The Parisian model of syphilology had been established by Ricord and the Ecole du Midi, and challenges to this system were to be tried in Paris. One cannot talk of scientific centralisation but perhaps of intellectual jurisdiction. Paris in this regard remained the centre of the science of sexual diseases in the same way that it was deemed to be the main experimental ground for the regulation of prostitution.

On 29 September the negative report from Brussels arrived.[68] Clinical trials at Saint-Pierre Hospital, Brussels, provided harrowing evidence of infected buboes and unbearable pains. The patient eventually obtained the end of the experimentation, which was a form of repeated self-inoculation but which clearly did not follow Auzias-Turenne's method. This Belgian clinical trial on two prostitutes was the only one the committee looked at in any detail. In December the Police Committee decided to reject Auzias-Turenne's application for a permanent post at the Saint-Lazare hospital. On 28 January, nevertheless, the police services sent a letter to Dr Sigmund in Vienna.[69] However, the police services published the committee's negative report in May, before Sigmund had even answered.[70] It seems that, by that stage, the administrative system kept running its course and attempted to fulfil its information-gathering mission regardless of its immediate relevance.

Ricord had put all his scientific and institutional influence into attacking the experiment of the monkeys. Rejecting the fundamental act of syphilisation, he had the power to prevent the full-scale experiment on human beings from taking place at Saint-Lazare. Eventually the committee produced a report that strangely stated all the phases of the proceedings and the constant debate between Marchal and Ricord within it. In the end Marchal defended the possible curative aspects of syphilisation on desperate cases and condemned Auzias-Turenne as a dangerous quack. Ricord had won. He kept Auzias-Turenne at bay, away from any institutional functions.

This was the first police rebuttal of Auzias-Turenne, but he refused to give up his life ambition. Relentlessly he lobbied the Imperial Government to have his case reopened every year between 1853 and 1860. To each enquiry the police answered negatively: 'The real aim of their [Auzias-Turenne's and his friends'] request is money and above all the Imperial patronage on the application of the process of syphilisation.'[71] His patrons, the Emperor's cousin, the Emperor's personal cabinet even, received invariably the same answer: the 1852 committee's reports denied any scientific validity to syphilisation. Although he did not hold any official position within any Parisian hospitals, Auzias-Turenne managed to have access to patients in some hospitals as a visiting guest physician. Hospital consultants valued his knowledge of the physiology and pathology of syphilis. In 1859 he persuaded some of Velpeau's disciples at the Saint-Louis hospital to attempt the inoculation of secondary syphilis to three volunteers. Gibert and Auzias-Turenne conducted the experiment. It breached Ricord's fundamental dogma of the three stages of syphilis. This experiment aggravated the dangers of syphilis and considerably reduced the prospects of a permanent 'cure' with the mercurial treatment. Diday successfully re-enacted the experiment in Lyons.[72] At Auzias-Turenne's request the state asked the Academy to judge the results. A long public sitting of the whole Academy vindicated Auzias-Turenne (31 May 1859). Meanwhile Ricord and his friends of the Union Médicale orchestrated a polemical debate on the ethics of human experiments on the three volunteers. Although vindicated, Auzias-Turenne lost the right to experiment in public hospitals. His friends were prosecuted and he rightly felt even more threatened.[73] The original ethical condemnation of syphilisation applied again to experimentation on human beings. This experiment extended the period of contamination beyond the period of primary symptoms. It also renewed the general interest in venereology. An apparently cured syphilitic could enter the family. As a consequence of this inoculation, a multitude of works on new *syphiligraphie* and on syphilis within marriage appeared.[74]

For Auzias-Turenne, however, this 'successful' experiment was disastrous. He lost access to all public hospitals and had to open his own dispensary, Dispensaire du Midi, in 1861 next to Ricord's own Midi hospital. Ricord subsequently tried to close it down in 1863.[75] Definitively excluded from any French institutions, syphilisation and to a large extent the inoculation of syphilis became marginal practices.

Auzias-Turenne carried on his private teaching and work but he failed to obtain much recognition in spite of Malgaigne's support at the Academy.[76] The alternative medical circles in which he was most involved were very marginal in France.

European syphilisation

Across Europe, however, Auzias-Turenne enlarged the number of his followers and supporters: Dr Boeck at Christiania (now Oslo) University, Dr Sperino in Turin, Gamberini in Bologna,[77] Sigmund in Vienna, and at home Dr Guérault (a navy medical officer) and the Imperial Prince (second in line to the throne).[78] Professor Boeck of Christiania University organised a congress on the subject of syphilisation and obtained the support of up to twenty-seven Norwegian doctors.[79] Guérault, after a stay in Norway with Prince Napoléon, returned convinced of Auzias-Turenne's genius and wrote a thesis in favour of the rehabilitation of syphilisation.[80] This court patronage was nearly the breakthrough to an institutional position. The anti-clerical views of Prince Napoléon, however, and his opposition to Empress Eugénie somewhat undermined the usefulness of such a patron. The police services, which were very close to the Emperor, had no difficulty rejecting Auzias-Turenne's claims. The European network played an important part in making the survival of Auzias-Turenne's ideas possible and, slowly, in grinding down the Ricordian epistemological certitude attached to the science of venereal diseases.

Boeck accumulated the clinical evidence so badly missing in Auzias-Turenne's work,[81] and through his patronage Auzias-Turenne was awarded the highly prestigious Polar Star medal of Sweden in 1859.[82] During the 1859 secondary syphilis experimentation Boeck even intended to come and visit Diday in Lyon to demonstrate the use of syphilisation. The disciple was in danger of becoming the master. In fact Auzias-Turenne wanted to keep his position as the head of the syphilisation movement and successfully discouraged both Diday and Boeck. This might have been his major error: Boeck experimenting in France would have been more helpful than simple translations of his books from abroad. Boeck's prestige was still considerable and his academic and hospital positions would have guaranteed a fairer hearing.

Ricord's parallel network worked on the same basis but benefited from his social and scientific status. On a few occasions the two networks collided and either the two men faced each other directly, or their friends and followers denounced each other. This inter-nationalisation had its deadlock in Paris. Auzias-Turenne still used his international contacts to obtain a platform for his experimental approach to venereal diseases.

Still demonstrating the use of international gatherings as an ideal platform for marginal theories, Auzias-Turenne reaped the short-lived benefits of his international connections at the 1867 international conference in Paris. In an over-excited regulationist conference, his proposal to answer question three, relating to the spread of venereal diseases, by the syphilisation of volunteering prostitutes was well received until he had to face Ricord once again.[83] Ricord vilified him and had him condemned again by the Academy of Medicine in 1869. Broken but not fully defeated, Auzias-Turenne died a year later. His obituaries portrayed him as he would have wished, as a scientific man of great talent who did not try to use his methods for profit (unlike Ricord) and who died in poverty.[84] Radical medical journals reported his anticlerical burial and paid tribute to his contribution to the non-official teaching of medicine in Paris. By that date syphilisation was hardly on the medical agenda. His last will was to have his complete works published by his friends. Published eight years later, the book went unnoticed in medical journals. Although die-hard followers of Auzias-Turenne carried on their work in Sweden, the University of Christiania did not bother to claim its share of Auzias-Turenne's legacy for its medical school: Auzias-Turenne's own skeleton (it ended up at Montparnasse cemetery).

The nature of medical dead ends

It would be easy to dismiss syphilisation as Christiania University did Auzias-Turenne's corpse. However, in the light of Carl Wilhelm Boeck's career there, syphilisation was defeated across Europe more because Auzias-Turenne had achieved so little institutional status while he monopolised it as sole inventor than because his technique could not be reproduced or did not give satisfactory results. His results were just as positive or negative as Ricord's own, and neither Ricord nor Auzias-Turenne could cure a disease so badly understood.[85]

Auzias-Turenne was defeated because he could not be inte-grated without damaging the French medical establishment and because there was no other possible site for a science of sexual diseases. Ricord's teaching had structured venereology in France and abroad around his own successful career. Followers like William Acton could only look with envy at Ricord's social prestige and clinical practice. The fact that much of this brilliant career was the result of political nepotism did not subvert the fundamental axiom of social visibility:[86] talent, even recognised by many, was not the key to an institutional role, rather the reverse was true. Ricord was not alone in seeking Imperial patronage, and the stability of his career was fundamentally important for a science searching for itself. Ricord had made sense of syphilis, he exemplified what syphilology could lead to, he was the symbol of the professionalisation of venereology in the same way that later Pasteur or Charcot became emblematic figures of modern science and psychiatry respectively.[87] There were limits in this knowledge, and Ricord's empire did not stretch further than venereal diseases. His message was mostly reassuring and did not affect sexual practices or intend to undermine sexual representations and forms of social regulation.

Auzias-Turenne, on the other hand, undermined much of the scientific basis of Ricord's career; he also undermined his methodology and endangered the scientific validity of police regulation. Socially Auzias-Turenne was as obscure as most of his syphilological counterparts. He had failed to exploit the nepotistic system, although his calls for Imperial patronage prove that he was not totally adverse to it, and he eventually made a virtue of necessity. Scientifically and socially Auzias-Turenne missed his targets and did not set an example worth emulating. Auzias-Turenne was proved wrong because he tried to go against the grain of a Fleckian thought collective. His ideas could not be integrated as 'facts' of syphilology: they went against the accumulation of too many accepted popular and scientific practices and social rules. He was defeated also because his views undermined not only Ricord (Ricord successfully negotiated and integrated into his theories many contradictory observations to his own) but also the social ontology of syphilis. His method did not appear socially appropriate in the 1850s context.[88] His plan for vaccination identified groups of people likely to be infected – sailors, prostitutes and soldiers – but it neglected the moral issues linked with syphilis. While his 1859 experiment amplified and worsened the pathological dangers of the disease, it only aggravated objections to syphilisation. His practice of inoculation, of mithridatisation against syphilis by syphilis, went against accepted practice. He was not, however, judged on his dubious results, which were not examined until 1859, not even really on his methods; rather he was judged on his inability to adapt his theories and practice to moral norms and recognised methods. The ontological definition of the disease in contemporary venereology – its limited contagiousness, the many successful mercurial treatments offered – did not justify the need to invest in a revolutionary treatment of syphilis. As the police summed up: 'The application of syphilisation presents numerous inconveniences and real dangers. In this situation the administration could not and cannot without seriously engaging its responsibility accept requests of experimentation.'[89]

This lack of intellectual curiosity or even the fear of tackling innovations, even if only to prove them wrong, is certainly symptomatic of the significant decline of Parisian empiricism in the age of experimental medicine.[90] In spite of all its limitations, the syphilisation debate came at a critical period for the redefinition of syphilology and the problematisation of the regulation of prostitution. Its implications largely undermined Ricord's optimistic empiricism and opened up the field for further research.[91] Auzias-Turenne's experimental claims contributed to a renewal of medical thinking in his area both in France and abroad,[92] while the ethical implications of human experimentation re-opened Pandora's box. This emphasis on ethics and the purpose of medical control in the area of sexually transmitted diseases led directly to the 1870s and 1880s debate led by Josephine Butler, Yves Guyot and Pasteur Borel on the *Habeas Corpus* in regulationist Europe and on the distribution of epidemiological responsibility to both genders.[93]

Notes

This research was undertaken while I was a Wellcome fellow at the University of Manchester and completed with a grant from Huddersfield University. I would like to thank my colleagues at both institutions for their help and comments. John V. Pickstone and Patrice Pinell have influenced this text in various conversations we have had over the years, and Mark Jenner has read and commented on earlier drafts of this text, while the lively debates that took place in the Amsterdam workshop where this paper was presented certainly induced me to re-consider many of my earlier assumptions. I am grateful to all.
 1 Michel Foucault, *The History of Sexuality* (Chicago, Chicago University Press, 1978), pp. 58–9.

2 Ludwik Fleck, *Genesis and Development of a Scientific Fact* (Chicago, Chicago University Press, 1979).

3 *Ibid.*, p. 33.

4 See Anne-Marie Moulin, 'Fleck's Style', in Robert S. Cohen and Thomas Schnelle (eds), *Cognition and Fact: Materials on Ludwik Fleck (1896–1961)* (Boston, Kullwer, 1986), pp. 172–90; also Jonathan Harwood, 'Ludwik Fleck and the Sociology of Knowledge', *Social Studies of Science*, 16 (1986), pp. 173–87.

5 For an unreconstructed account of this debate see Diane Beyer Perett, 'Ethics and Error: The Dispute Between Ricord and Auzias-Turenne Over Syphilisation, 1845–1870', unpublished Ph.D. thesis, Stanford University, 1977.

6 Claude Quêtel, *Le Mal de Naples, histoire de la syphilis* (Paris, Seghers, 1986), pp. 143–4; Jacques Léonard, *La Médecine entre les savoirs et les pouvoirs* (Paris, Aubier, 1981), p. 144.

7 Auzias-Turenne's archives were deposited by his friends at the Bibliothèque de l'Arsenal in Paris (henceforth BA), ms. 6715–6750.

8 The archives relating to the regulation of prostitution are kept at the Archives de la Préfecture de Police de Paris (henceforth APdP), and most of the material relating to the Auzias-Turenne controversy is kept in boxes 229 and 230 of the huge series DA.

9 Stian W. Erichsen, 'Auzias-Turenne's Syphilisation Method in Norway', *American Journal of Syphilis, Gonorrhea and Venereal Diseases*, 35, 1 (1951), pp. 42–52; also Linda W. Peterson and Olof S. Skinsnes, 'Carl Wilhelm Boeck, 1808–1875', *International Journal of Leprosy and other Mycobacterial Diseases*, 41 (1975), pp. 154–5. Boeck was a respected dermatologist before he embraced syphilisation theories and became their most successful proponent.

10 Perett, 'Ethics and Error', for instance p. 229.

11 See A. Pignot, 'L'Hôpital du Midi et ses origines, recherches sur l'histoire médicale et sociale de la syphilis', Thèse de médecine, Paris, 1885.

12 Exceedingly famous during his lifetime, Philippe Ricord did not enjoy long-term fame. Apart from laudatory comments published after his death, the only published biography of Ricord was written in 1939 by a member of the Ligue de la Préservation Sociale, a eugenic group: C. Eginer, *Philippe Ricord, 1800–1889 sa vie son oeuvre* (Paris, Le François, 1939). In the same hagiographic vein see M. Guignard, 'Philippe Ricord: sa vie son oeuvre 1800–1889', Thèse de doctorat, Faculté de Médecine, Paris, 1978.

13 Jean-Baptiste Lesueur (1778–1857) became a correspondent of the Museum d'Histoire Naturelle of Paris. He settled in 1815 in Philadelphia and returned to France in 1844.

14 Georges Cuvier (1769–1832) was a leading figure of the newly created Museum d'Histoire Naturelle. In 1809 he organised the Science Faculty of the university of Paris; he was made a Baron in 1820 and a member of the Académie Française. See D. Outram, *Georges Cuvier: Vocation, Science, and University in Post-Revolutionary France* (Manchester, Manchester University Press, 1984); also P. Ardouin, *Georges Cuvier, promoteur de l'idée évolutionniste et créateur de la biologie moderne* (Paris, Expansion Scientifique, 1970).

Cuvier in the 1820s was at the summit of his power and was a most important political figure. On patronage and science in early nineteenth-century France see R. Fox, *The Patronage of Science in the 19th Century* (Leiden, Noordhoff International, 1976); also R. Fox and G. Weisz (eds), *The Organisation of Science and Technology in France, 1800–1914* (Cambridge, Cambridge University Press, 1980); N. and J. Dhombres, *Naissance d'un nouveau pouvoir, science et savants en France 1793–1824* (Paris, Payot, 1989). T. A. Appel, *The Cuvier–Geoffroy Debate: French Biology in the Decades before Darwin* (Oxford, Oxford University Press, 1987), pp. 31–65.

15 François-Joseph Broussais, (1772–1838), a military surgeon during the Napoleonic wars, after the war he violently attacked the Pinel School of Medicine and focused opposition on the establishment at the Val-de-Grâce military hospital where he obtained a chair. In 1830 he obtained public recognition and a chair at the faculty, but his *'physiologisme'* was soon perceived as obsolete. See Frédéric Dubois d'Amiens, *Éloge de Broussais* (Paris, Ballière, 1838); and A. Costes, *Histoire critique de la doctrine physiologique de Broussais* (Paris, Ballière, n.d.).

16 Guillaume Dupuytren (1777–1835) was a skilled surgeon of no special theory who followed Broussais's physiologism. He dominated the Hôtel-Dieu from 1812 until his death. He was close to the throne and a consulting surgeon to King Louis XVIII and Charles X. Made a Baron in 1820, he left a fortune of several million francs at his death. See H. Mondor, *Dupuytren* (Paris, Gallimard, 1945).

17 J. Lisfranc (1790–1847) specialised in 'women's diseases' and problems of the uterus.

18 Olivier Faure, *Genèse de l'hôpital moderne, les hospices civils de Lyon 1802–1845* (Lyon, Presses Universitaires de Lyon, 1982), chapters 1 and 2.

19 For example L. V. Lagneau, *Traité pratique des maladies syphilitiques*, 2 vols (Paris, Gabon, 1828). Ricord also dwelled on classic texts like J. Astruc, *Traité des maladies vénériennes* (Paris, Cavalier, 1743); H. Boerhaave, *Système sur les maladies vénériennes* (Paris, La Méthie, 1735); J. Hunter, *A Treatise on the Venereal Diseases* (1786), trans. G. Richelot with notes by P. Ricord (Paris, Firmin Didot Frères, 1845).

20 Its use is best illustrated in J. Fernel d'Amiens, *Le Meilleur Traitement du mal vénérien*, 1579, re-ed. L. Le Pilar (Paris, Masson, 1879). Jay Cassel gives very vivid descriptions of the effects of the mercury treatment on patients in *The Secret Plague: Venereal Diseases in Canada 1838–1939* (Toronto, Toronto University Press, 1987), pp. 51–62.

21 See J. De Castelnau, *Recherches sur l'innoculation* (Paris, Méquignan, 1841).

22 'Twenty years ago, doctrines on syphilis were in an awful chaos: people denied the existence of syphilis and rejected the idea of a virus.' M. Malgaigne, in *De la Syphilisation et de la contagion des accidents secondaires de la syphilis* (Paris, n.p., 1853); Auzias-Turenne, *La Syphilisation*, p. 179.

23 The term 'virus' was still very vague and debated.

24 Fleck, *Genesis and Development*, p. 4.

25 See imitators: Berthelaud, *Précis des maladies vénériennes, de leur doctrine et de leur traitement* (Strasbourg, n.p., 1852); Davila, *De la Prophilaxie de la syphilis*, (Strasbourg, Berger Levrault, 1852).

26 See J. Léonard, *La Médecine*, pp. 222–5.

27 Ricord's social climbing can be followed best with his changes of address. Starting in a modest house, his last lodging was a magnificent building displaying all the visible signs of wealth. He received numerous patients but had a system of waiting parlours which enabled his servants to isolate the rich seeking a discreet treatment. Ricord used this power over his patients as a tool and there are many anecdotes of his indiscreet jokes. He became extremely rich from his private practice (hospital work did not pay very well but it enabled him to raise his fees) and from the commercial use of his mercury pills.

28 'He takes a lot of gold and his patients a lot of mercury', wrote Auzias-Turenne in his diary, 'Mémoires d'un syphilisateur', 1859, vol. 1, p. 122. BA, ms 6736.

29 Ricord was asked to diagnose the Emperor's disease not long before the 1870 war. He clearly identified a stone of the size of a 'pigeon egg'. Under pressure from partisans of the authoritarian Empire hoping for a victorious war, Ricord made a false diagnosis. See Eginer, *Ricord sa vie son oeuvre*, p. 63.

30 Ricord led a network of ambulances organised with the money raised by the conservative press (*les ambulances de la Presse*). A. Cousin, *Ambulance de la Presse Française, service de Monsieur Demarquay* (Paris, Malteste, 1872), pp. 1–15; Ricord, *Ambulances de la Presse, annexes du ministère de la guerre pendant le siège et sous la Commune* (Paris, Ballière, 1873), pp. 12–30.

31 We are very far from Fracastor's descriptions of horrible syphilis. Fracastor had been translated in 1847: *La Syphilis*, trans. P. Yvaren (Paris, Ballière, 1847). Other accounts of the first clinical descriptions were translated and began to be studied systematically in the period with which we are concerned: C. Renault, 'La Syphilis au XVe siècle', thèse de doctorat, Faculté de Médecine, Paris, 1868; P. Rengifo, 'Etude sur les premiers syphilographes espagnols', thèse, Paris, 1863; C. V. Daremberg, 'Nouveaux documents pouvant servir à l'histoire de la syphilis au Moyen-Age', *Union Médicale* (Paris, 1868), 3 ser., vol. 6, pp. 465–70; A. Fournier, new trans., *La Syphilis* (Paris, Delahaye, 1870).

32 Etienne Geoffroy Saint-Hilaire (1772–1844) arrived at the Museum in 1795. Originally the patron and friend of Cuvier, he did not achieve as much power as Cuvier in the scientific establishment but held a firm grip on the Museum d'Histoire Naturelle. He left his gold watch to Auzias-Turenne. This was a very symbolic present (often a gift from father to an heir), and Auzias-Turenne remained very close to Geoffroy's widow. Introduction to Auzias-Turenne, *Oeuvres Complètes* (Paris, Ballière, 1878), pp. vii–ix; I. Geoffroy Saint-Hilaire, *Vie, travaux et doctrines scientifiques d'Étienne Geoffroy Saint-Hilaire* (Paris, Bertrand, 1847), repr. Brussels, 1968.

33 The Museum had been created from the royal gardens: see Y. Laissus and J. Torlains, *Le Jardin du Roi et le Collège Royal* (Paris, Hermann, 1987); and for later periods a good discussion can be found in T. A. Appel, *The Cuvier–Geoffroy Debate: French Biology in the Decades before Darwin* (New York, Oxford University Press, 1987), chapters 2 and 3.

34 Isidore-Geoffroy Saint-Hilaire (1805–61) took his father's chair at the Museum and became an historian of science and a specialist in abnormal developments and monstrosity, coining the word *teratology*. Auzias-Turenne, *Oeuvres*, pp. vi–ix.

35 The debate was very complex and there is no space to dwell on it here, but the place of human beings amongst the animal estate was certainly a central issue. The debate sought to determine whether the animal structure was conditioned by function or morphology. Etienne Geoffroy defended a unity of composition, somehow close to Lamarckian views on evolution. One of the key issues later debated in Darwin's work, the place of humans in creation was therefore part of the controversy. The specificity of syphilis could be defended only in a static view of creation in which humans stood alone, separate from animals. See Appel, *The Cuvier–Geoffroy Debate*, chapters 1 and 7 on the various uses of the debate; P. Ardouin, *Georges Cuvier*.

36 Auzias-Turenne, *Oeuvres*, pp. viii and 87.

37 Auzias-Turenne became an important member of several alternative research groups such as the Société Médicale du Panthéon (1850); he also published in *Le Courier Médical*, then the *Revue Étrangère Médico-chirurgicale*. He did some private teaching at the École Pratique de la Faculté de Médecine de Paris. He taught syphilisation there from 1851 to 1870. See Auzias-Turenne, *Oeuvres*, pp. xvi–xviii and 88–9. He was also a member of the Commission de l'enseignement médical libre, and campaigned for the freedom of teaching before 1870. See obituary in *Le Mouvement Médical*, 29 May 1870.

38 Isidore-Geoffroy Saint-Hilaire himself pointed out publicly that Auzias-Turenne's work was the medical application of his father's ideas. See Auzias-Turenne, 'Mémoires', vol. 2, p. 8.

39 APdP, DA 229/6, Auzias-Turenne's letter to His Majesty Napoleon III, March 1860.

40 Saint-Lazare, a medieval leper hospital, was turned into a convent, then into a prison during the Revolution. Rebuilt in 1823, it received all female convicts sentenced for less than a year, and prostitutes rebelling against the police administration. See E. Labédolière, *Le Nouveau Paris* (Paris, Barba, 1860), pp. 153–5.

41 Only one patient was granted authorisation to pursue her treatment with Auzias-Turenne. Letter to Dr Auzias-Turenne, 9 October 1852, Archives de la Police, ms DA 229.

42 The Préfecture de Police in Paris was a powerful tool, engineered during the 1789 Revolution and first Empire, which controlled many of the functions normally attributed to mayors. C. J. Lecour, *La Compagne contre la Préfecture de Police, envisagée surtout du point de vue du service des moeurs* (Paris, Asselin, 1881), pp. 31–5.

43 See J. C. Sournia, 'L'Idée de Police Sanitaire pendant la Révolution', *Histoire des Sciences Médicales*, 22, 3–4 (1988), pp. 269–75.

44 E. M. Benabou, *La Prostitution et la police des moeurs au XVIIIe siècle* (Paris, Perrin, 1987), chapters 1 and 3.

45 APdP, DA 230.

46 P. Sabatier, *Histoire de la législation sur les femmes publiques et les lieux de débauches* (Paris, n.p., 1828); A. Parent-Duchâtelet, *De la prostitution dans la ville de Paris* (Paris, Ballière, 1836); C. Béraud, *Les Filles publiques de Paris et la police qui les régit* (Paris, n.p., 1839); J. Garin, *De la police sanitaire et de l'Assistance Publique dans leurs rapports avec l'extinction des maladies vénériennes* (Paris, Masson, 1866). Parent's work was the medical theorisation of the police practice which had existed for over thirty-four years. See A. Corbin, *Les Filles de noce, misère sexuelle et prostitution au XIXe et XXe siècles* (Paris, Aubier, 1978).

47 Corbin, *Les Filles de noce*, pp. 136–61.

48 On the Academy and innovations see J. E. Lesch, 'The Paris Academy of Medicine and Experimental Science, 1820–1848', in W. Coleman and F. L. Holmes (eds), *The Investigative Enterprise: Experimental Physiology in Nineteenth-century Medicine* (Berkeley, University of California Press, 1988); George Weisz, *The Medical Mandarins: The French Academy of Medicine in the Nineteenth and Early Twentieth Centuries* (Oxford, Oxford University Press, 1995).

49 On the advent of the Second Empire see M. Agulhon, *1848 ou l'apprentissage de la liberté* (Paris, Seuil, 1873); J. M. Thompson, *Louis-Napoleon and the Second-Empire* (Oxford, Blackwell, 1965); A. Dansette, *Du 2 Décembre au 4 septembre* (Paris, Le Seuil, 1970).

50 Philippe Ricord brought to the Academy's attention the case of Lindeman, a student Auzias-Turenne and himself had syphilised. Ricord pre-empted Auzias-Turenne and used his influence to shape the inquiry. Perett, 'Ethics and Error', pp. 105–77.

51 APdP, DA 229, Letter from Auzias-Turenne, 23 September 1853.

52 Malgaigne quoted forty-three inoculations. Dr Thiry of Saint-Pierre Hospital (Brussels) made a harrowing description of the sixty-three inoculations he inflicted on a patient in 1851 while loosely following Auzias's method. *Rapport à M. Le Préfet de Police*, Union Médicale, 1853, pp. 92–108.

53 *Syphiligraphie* or *Syphilographie* or *Syphilologie* were terms coined around 1842, as competing scientific words for a new medical specialty. The diversity of spelling reflected the uncertainty over what the medical specialisation on syphilis really was.

54 Charles-Jacob Marchal (de Calvi), *Deux lettres à messieurs les membres de l'Académie de Médecine* (Paris, n.p., 1852); also in *La Gazette des Hôpitaux Civils et Militaires*, 12 August 1852, p. 95.

55 Marchal (de Calvi), *Émancipation du prolétariat, réalisation du droit aux instruments du travail* (Paris, Renouard, 1848).

56 Académie Nationale de Médecine, *De la syphilisation et de la contagion des accidents secondaires de la syphilis* (Paris, n.p., 1853). The Academy rejected both syphilisation and the contagiousness of secondary syphilis on which syphilisation was based.

57 This extract, the final part of Bégin's speech, was copied by the police official in charge of the case, his italics. APdP, DA 229, 'Rapport à Monsieur le Préfet', April 1857.

58 J. L. Louis, *Histoire de l'école impériale du service de santé militaire à Strasbourg* (Paris, Berger Levrault, 1898), pp. 185–6.

59 G. Miller, *The Adoption of Inoculation of Small Pox in England and France in the Eighteenth Century* (Philadelphia, University of Pennsylvania Press, 1957).

60 'Auzias-Turenne, sa vie son oeuvre', in Auzias-Turenne, *La Syphilisation* (Paris, Ballière, 1878), p. xv.

61 The Auzias-Turenne debate ran in parallel with the development of experimental medicine and Auzias-Turenne's experiments only partially fit with a 'modern' definition of experimental science. See G. Canguilhem, *Le Normal et le pathologique*, 2nd edn (Paris, Presses Universitaires de France, 1966), pp. 5 and 32–51. On Claude Bernard see M. Grmek, *Claude Bernard et la méthode expérimentale*, 2nd edn (Paris, Payot, 1991). Claude Bernard advised Auzias-Turenne to be more cautious with his evidence and to improve the presentation of his results. Auzias-Turenne, 'Mémoires', June 1864, vol. 2, p. 319.

62 Auzias-Turenne, 'Enseignement de la Syphilisation', première leçon (31 November 1851), *La Syphilisation*, p. 80.

63 One died in prison, the other was released six months later. APdP, DA 229, letter on the monkeys of Saint Lazare.

64 Auzias-Turenne, *Lettre à monsieur le Préfet de Police sur la syphilisation* (Paris, n.p., 1853), p. 17.

65 Auzias-Turenne, 'Lettre à M. Sperino', 8 January 1854, *La Syphilisation*, p. 232.

66 APdP, DA 229/6, correspondence, 1852.

67 Dr Cullerier, *Rapport sur l'ouvrage de M Sperino* (Paris, Plon, 1853). Dr C. Spérino, *De la syphilisation comme méthode curative et comme moyen prophylactique des maladies vénériennes* (Paris, Chamerot, 1853) and *Mémoire sur le vote adopté par l'Académie de Médecine de Paris dans sa séance du 21 août 1852* (Turin, Pons, 1852).

68 Dr Thiny, 'Rapport sur la syphilisation à Bruxelles, expérience à l'hôpital Saint-Pierre de Bruxelles', pp. 92–106, *Rapport à M. le Préfet de Police sur la question de savoir si M. le Dr Auzias-Turenne peut-être autorisé à appliquer la syphilisation à l'infirmerie de la Prison Saint-Lazare* (Union Médicale, Paris, 1853).

69 Carl Ludwig Sigmund, *Syphilis und Venerische Geschwindsformen* (Stuttgart, Enke, 1869).

70 APdP, DA 229, chronology established in 1857 in reply to a query from the Imperial Secretary.

71 APdP, DA 229, letter to the Emperor in answer to Mr Kaupmann's query about the authorisation of a voluntary hospital of syphilisation, February, 1856.

72 Auzias-Turenne, 'Lettres à M. Diday, ex-chirugien en chef de l'hôpital de l'Antiquaille à Lyon', 7 and 17 April 1860, BA, ms, 6737. Dr Boucaud, *Responsabilité médicale: les inoculations d'accidents secondaires syphilitiques* (Lyon, Vingtrinier, 1860). Diday did not warn the patient before inoculating secondary syphilis to treat a skin disease.

73 See Auzias-Turenne, 'Mémoires', vol. 1, pp. 11–46; vol. 2, pp. 216–44.

74 M. Robert, *Nouveau traité des maladies vénériennes* (Paris, n. p., 1861); E. Lancereaux, *Traité historique et pratique de la syphilis* (Paris, Baillière, 1866); G. Lagneau fils, *Recherches comparatives sur les maladies vénériennes dans le différentes contrées* (Paris, Baillière, 1867); E. Langlebert, *Traité*

théorique et pratique des maladies vénériennes (Paris, Savy, 1864) and *La Syphilis dans ses rapports avec le marriage* (Paris, Delaye, 1873); D. Delzeune, 'Des doctrines et des connaissances nouvelles en syphilographie' (Thèse de doctorat, Paris, 1867); L. L. Belhomme and A. L. Martin, *Traité de pathologie syphilitique et vénérienne* (Paris, Cocez, 1864); A. Rollet, *Recherches cliniques et expérimentales sur la syphilis, le chancre simple et la blénnoragie* (Lyon, Sacy, 1861).

75 Ricord complained to the Assistance Publique, which organised relief in Paris, about this unpleasant neighbour, and the Assistance Publique asked the police to close it down. This was followed by a costly trial, but the dispensary remained until Auzias-Turenne became too weak to work in 1870.

76 Malgaigne (1806–65) was very concerned with ethical issues in medicine, after 1852 he perceived that Auzias-Turenne was not given a fair trial and undertook to defend him at the academy until his death. Auzias-Turenne, 'Mémoires', January 1865, vol. 2, p. 333.

77 Pietro Gamberini, *La Sifilizzazione praticata nello spedale di si orsola di Bologna, lettra nella sessione del 2 ottobre 1851 della societa medico-chirurgica di Bologna* (Milan, Anuali Universali delle Scienze e dell'Industria, 1852).

78 Auzias-Turenne, *La Syphilisation*, pp. 503–10.

79 Wilhelm Boeck, *Recherches sur la syphilis, appuyées de tableaux statistiques tirés des archives des hôpitaux de Christiania* (Christiania, Tensen, 1862); *De la syphilisation appliquée aux enfants* (Paris, Bailly, Divry, 1863).

80 See papers and manuscripts of Guérault, kept with Auzias-Turenne's papers (BA, ms 6750).

81 Wilhelm Boeck, *Recherches cliniques sur la syphilisation* (Paris, Dupont, 1854).

82 Auzias-Turenne succeeded Baron Alexander von Humboldt (1769–1859).

83 The opposition between Auzias-Turenne, Ricord and their partisans spoilt the chance of any proper discussion. See APdP, DA 229, report, 1867. Auzias-Turenne, *La Syphilisation*, pp. 270–1.

84 *La France Médicale*, 8 June 1870, p. 12.

85 There was still a difficulty in finding the right chancre, and then in finding the right kind of pus. Once the source was identified, inoculation was easy to perform, yet the lack of a uniform source for syphilisation was a problem.

86 It was in fact a return to the situation of 1823. See Delaunay, 'Les Médecins, la Restauration et la Révolution de 1830', p. 50.

87 Charcot was very close to republicans and secularists. G. Guillain, *J. M. Charcot 1825–1893, sa vie son oeuvre* (Paris, Masson, 1955); V. Leroux-Hugon, *Des Saintes laïques: les infirmières à l'aube de la troisième république* (Paris, Sciences en Situation, 1992); Y. Knibiehler *et al.*, *Cornettes et blouses blanches: les infirmiers dans la société française 1880–1980* (Paris, Hadiette, 1984). Charcot himself wrote a conciliatory essay on the unity of all medical practices in science: J. M. Charcot, *La Médecine empirique et la médecine scientifique* (Paris, Delahaye, 1867).

88 See G. Weisz, 'Academic Debate and Therapeutic Reasoning in Mid-nineteenth Century France', in L. Löwy (ed.), *Medicine and Change,*

Colloque Inserm, no. 220 (Paris, INSERM, 1993), pp. 289–91.

89 APdP, ms. DA 229, letter to the Emperor's private office following a request by His Majesty the Imperial Prince, 7 April 1857.

90 John Harley Warner, 'Remembering Paris: Memory and the American Disciples of French Medicine in the Nineteenth Century', *Bulletin of the History of Medicine*, 65 (1991), pp. 301–25.

91 Alfred Fournier played a major part in a major re-evaluation of syphilis. Concerns about hereditary syphilis, innocent victims of contamination and, later, tabes were developed from the 1860s onwards. Only a few very isolated medical men before the 1860s felt that syphilis could be the cause of less obvious symptoms than those usually accepted and talked about as possible metamorphosis of syphilis. A. Fournier, *De la contagion syphilitique* (Paris, Delahaye, 1860); Auzias-Turenne, *De la contagion syphilitique à propos de la thèse de M. A. Fournier* (Paris, De Maquet, 1860) and *Correspondance syphilographique* (Paris, Leclerc, 1860), p. 13; H. Mireur, 'Essai sur l'hérédité de la syphilis', thèse de Médecine (Paris, 1867); A. Fournier, *L'Hérédité syphilitique* (Paris, Masson, 1891); P. Yvaren, *Des métamorphoses de la syphilis* (Paris, Ballière, 1854).

92 Boeck's message had been especially well received in the USA even if this breakthrough proved to be short-lived and relegated to history in the 1870s. See Freeman J. Bumstead, *The Pathology and Treatment of Venereal Diseases* (Philadelphia, Lea, 1879 fourth ed.), pp. 820–1.

93 See Bertrand Taithe, 'Consuming Desires: Prostitutes and Customers in France and England, 1850–1886', in M. Arnott and C. Osborne (eds), *Gender and Crime* (London, University College London Press, 1998).

3

The culture of compulsion:
venereal disease, sexuality and the state
in twentieth-century Scotland

Roger Davidson

Society's response to venereal disease has been shown to be a central strand in that 'whole web of discourses' that has constructed and regulated sexuality in modern society. During the late nineteenth and early twentieth centuries, VD became in many European countries a metaphor for physical and moral decay; for the forces of pollution and contamination that appeared to threaten the institutions of social order and racial progress. Alarm over the issue of VD offered an opportunity to express concern about the moral direction of society and changing standards of conduct. Given the supposedly wilful nature of its diffusion and its threat to 'social hygiene', it also provided a powerful justification for the social construction and proscription of dangerous sexualities.[1] An examination of VD policy therefore provides the historian of sexual culture with invaluable insights. By analysing the social and institutional factors shaping VD policy in modern Scotland, and the cluster of anxieties and assumptions which fuelled and circumscribed public health debate over sexually transmitted diseases, this chapter seeks to tease out some of the distinctive features of twentieth-century Scottish sexual culture and the forces defining it.

The campaign for controls

Social historians of sexuality in twentieth-century Britain have focused largely on the voluntarist strategies of treatment and moral propaganda implemented by central government in its attempts to reduce the incidence of sexually transmitted diseases.[2] However, within Scotland a more interventionist ideology was reflected in a succession of campaigns for VD controls involving compulsion. During the

1920s Scottish local health authorities, backed by a wide range of professional groups within Scottish society, repeatedly pressed for more stringent local authority powers to combat the spread of venereal disease.[3] In the course of the decade three separate bills were advanced – the most notable being the Edinburgh Corporation (Venereal Diseases) Bill of 1928 – seeking to notify, detain and penalise infected persons (as well as the parents of infected children) who refused to seek medical advice or to sustain a course of treatment until certified as non-infective. Despite the defeat of this campaign, many clinicians and local health authorities continued to lobby for additional VD controls throughout the 1930s. During the Second World War Scottish local authorities and social hygiene agencies renewed their efforts to secure more rigorous controls. They viewed wartime regulations, such as Defence Regulation 33B, which provided for the notification and possible prosecution of named sexual contacts, as insufficiently robust to deal with the dramatic rise in the incidence of VD, and, in 1944, persuaded the Scottish Office to fight the issue in the War Cabinet.[4] In the event the voluntarist ideology of the English Ministry of Health prevailed, but a further campaign for compulsion was launched in Scotland in the late 1940s. Although it had effectively run its course by 1950, as late as 1968 some Scottish politicians were still pressing for the compulsory examination and treatment of persons suspected of harbouring VD as a means of combating the moral panic surrounding the rising incidence of gonorrhoea.

The roots of compulsion

A range of explanations may be advanced for this distinctively compulsionist stance of Scottish public health administration towards sexually transmitted diseases. It was not primarily a function of the incidence of the diseases. In so far as data were available, there was, up to the 1950s, no marked divergence in trend between Scotland and England and Wales.

A more probable explanation may lie in longstanding social and institutional attitudes to sexuality and venereal infection and a strong tradition of civic authoritarianism and interventionism in Scotland. The overriding concern of early edicts relating to VD was to contain rather than to cure infection, with a consequential erosion of civil liberties. As early as 1497 repressive controls had been introduced by Aberdeen Town Council and the Privy Council of Scotland to contain the spread of 'glengore' or 'grandgore', as syphilis was commonly named in Scotland. As in most subsequent regulations, the Aberdeen edict especially targeted sexually active women, demanding that 'all light [loose] women ... dicist from thair vices and syn of venerie' and work for 'thair support on pain of being branded' or being banished from the town. The Edinburgh Statute of the same year, known as the Glengore Act and drawn up by James IV himself, ordered the immediate transportation of all infected individuals to the Island of Inchkeith in the Firth of Forth and the branding of the 'uncured' on the cheek as an additional stigma.[5]

Civic leaders, co-ordinated by the Convention of Scottish Royal Burghs, subsequently maintained this proactive commitment to the regulation and containment of venereal and other 'pestilential infections'. Scottish medical and legal ideology was heavily influenced by the European Enlightenment, and by the German tradition of 'medical police', involving wide-ranging powers of surveillance and intervention in personal and civic life in the cause of public health. Thus the Scottish cities were in the van of nineteenth-century initiatives to impose compulsory notification for infectious diseases, even where, as in the cases of TB and congenital gonorrhoea, social stigma surrounded them. Similarly Scottish health authorities proved notably aggressive in developing the powers conveyed by the 1897 Public Health (Scotland) Act to examine, to isolate and to prosecute infected persons endangering public health through immoral and unhygienic habits. Moreover, as in Sweden,[6] the relative autonomy of the Scottish 'city states' even after 1900 enabled this culture of interventionism to feed through into twentieth-century bylaws and local bills in which VD as a health issue was regularly mobilised as an adjunct to the policing of public morality.

Underlying the campaign for VD controls in twentieth-century Scotland was also a powerful moral agenda, drawing in part upon a vigorous tradition of church and community disciplining of sexual behaviour. Former patterns of church discipline administered by the kirk sessions and most vividly enshrined in the stool of penitence had been largely undermined by 1900.[7] None the less, as in many other European countries, the churches continued to play a critical role in defining the moral climate of Scottish civil society well into the twentieth century.[8] In the interwar period, both the Church of Scotland and the United Free Church issued a series of influential pronouncements on the laws relating to the age of consent, solicitation and censorship, and on the impact on sexual morality of social deprivation and poor housing. Indeed, as late as the early 1960s, local magistrates and church elders maintained 'the remarkable influence of puritanical religion' on Scottish popular life and 'criticism of illiberal presbyterian theocracy in local government was rife'.[9] Certain areas of church opinion did voice reservations about compulsory VD controls. Some ministers within the Episcopal Church and the Committee on Temperance and Morals of the United Free Church feared that it might lead to the concealment of disease and greater recourse to quack remedies, and were anxious that legal process in the pursuit of public health should not obscure fundamental issues of personal morality. The Roman Catholic Church in Scotland had no objection on doctrinal grounds but considered that the first priority was for the 'state purification' of entertainment and the media. However, in contrast to the Church of England's resolute opposition to compulsion, the Church of Scotland strongly endorsed the campaign for controls. In the view of its Church and Nation Committee, while the 'clear, reverent teaching of the true function of sex in human life, and the intimate and sacred relationship between body and spirit was vital', there was also an urgent need to 'secure compulsory notification and complete treatment of VD in the interests of the individual, the future family, and the community'.[10]

Local authority and church responses to VD drew additionally on a long tradition of penalising the transmission of VD under Scottish Common Law. In Scottish Civil Law the communication of VD by a husband to a wife justified separation on the grounds of cruelty.[11] In addition, under Scottish Criminal Law the communication of VD was treated as an aggravation of sexual offences such as rape and libidinous practices involving young girls.[12] The belief in ridding oneself of disease by means of transference was embedded in Scottish folk medicine and none more so than the widespread and lasting conviction that VD could be cured by intercourse with a virgin.[13] In this respect the legal system in early twentieth-century Scotland continued to view VD as much as a facet of criminal assault as an issue of public health.

The campaign for VD controls in Scotland was fuelled by an overriding preoccupation with the need to discipline those defaulting from treatment. In terms of the medico-moral ideology of twentieth-century health administrators and clinicians, this group of patients was doubly guilty. Not only had they contracted VD wilfully and 'venereally' by means of 'illicit' and 'promiscuous' sexual intercourse, but they also remained major vectors of disease both within their own families and within the community at large, by virtue of their failure to sustain treatment until cured and to modify their sexual behaviour. It was upon the defaulters that the burden of guilt for the continuing incidence of VD, despite the introduction of new medical therapies and facilities, was placed, and their categorisation and condemnation by state agencies were a potent example of the process of stereotyping in the social construction of 'dangerous sexuality'. Defaulters were regularly depicted by health officials and practitioners as promiscuous 'libertines', as 'hardened', 'incorrigible', 'intemperate' and 'habitual offenders' whose penchant for atavistic 'sexual indulgence' in the 'cult of phallic worship' rendered them unresponsive to the necessary discipline of medical therapy and undeserving of normal civil liberties.[14] Such behaviour not only offended public and professional opinion because of its implications for the spread of disease and its threat to 'social hygiene'. It also undermined the powerful moral agenda of welfare provisions within Scotland inherited from the nineteenth-century Board of Supervision which had rendered levels of poor relief (specifically, for women) conditional upon appropriate sexual behaviour.[15] The alleged propensity of defaulters to accept repeated but incomplete courses of free treatment at the VD clinics without modifying their sexual habits ran directly counter to this agenda. Indeed, in the opinion of many Scottish medical officials, it posed as serious a risk of reducing the VD services to 'a convenient aid to promiscuity' as the proposed issue of prophylactic packets or the establishment of post-coital ablution centres.

The moral agenda of those campaigning in Scotland for the compulsory notification and treatment of sexually transmitted diseases was strongly reinforced and legitimated by the apparent impact of default upon the cost-efficiency of the VD clinics; and especially so in a period of recurring public expenditure cuts and increased awareness of the health costs associated with sexual promiscuity. At all levels of Scottish health administration, the issue of 'wasted expenditure' and 'the interest of the taxpayer and rate-payer' were repeatedly cited in support of greater controls, and the free provision of treatment without associated powers to regulate sexual behaviour widely condemned as a subsidy to vice. In particular it offended against the principles of 'less eligibility' that those venereally infected through wilful promiscuity should be permitted to enjoy 'a free and unfettered regime' in the use of state-subsidised facilities, and especially so in the eyes of the petit-bourgeois, propertied, rate-paying local councillors who came to dominate the social politics of Scottish cities during the late nineteenth and twentieth centuries.

Although some limited research into the problem of default was undertaken, its prominence reflected very much the orchestration of social fears by experts and officials informed by ill-disguised Social Darwinism. It rested upon displaced anxieties about social disorder and moral decline, as well as bureaucratic self-interest. Certainly the ideology of professional expertise shaping the Social Hygiene Movement in Scotland was, as in other countries with compulsionist leanings, such as Germany and France,[16] heavily influenced by eugenics and its more coercive prescriptions for the 'degenerate'. Scottish VD administrators and clinicians closely identified national health and efficiency with sexual discipline. 'Promiscuity', broadly defined as non-marital intercourse, was viewed as a form of 'sexual atavism' that undermined racial fitness and evolution. Their operational philosophy therefore envisaged a proactive role based upon the registers and case notes of the clinics that would deploy nurse almoners and social work agencies, often in liaison with the magistrates and police, to identify and reform dangerous sexualities, and, where necessary, they anticipated the loss of civil liberties for those 'libertines' whose behaviour endangered the sexual health and efficiency of the nation. As a result, the Scottish Social Hygiene Movement adopted a distinctively interventionist view on VD policy. Whereas the efforts of the British Social Hygiene Council in England focused on educational issues and moral propaganda, the Scottish branch gave priority to co-ordinating the local authority campaigns for VD controls.

It may also be that the pattern of municipal health politics within Scotland, as in Germany, provided a stronger platform for the views of a generation of social hygienists whose outlook towards VD had been shaped by service in the medical corps in wartime, and who were concerned, by means of new controls, to establish the professional status of their expertise as venereologists. Possibly Scottish compulsionists within the Social Hygiene Movement, and especially the more prominent Medical Officers of Health such as Dr A. K. Chalmers, were able to exploit the more authoritarian culture of decision-making in Scotland and the greater willingness for medical expertise to shape civic agendas on issues of sexual behaviour and morality supposedly affecting public health.[17]

Also distinctive was the response of Scottish women's organisations to proposals for compulsory VD controls. While Scottish legislation encountered fierce opposition from a range of London-based feminist pressure groups, local branches of the Women's Citizens Association, Cooperative Women's Guild and the National Council of Women *were* prepared to give their conditional support. They shared the view of Scottish public health officials that additional powers were necessary to reduce the wilful or negligent spread of VD and to protect the welfare of women and children. Rather than undermining 'equal citizenship', they optimistically viewed compulsory measures as reinforcing it, by denying the right of infected men to 'pollute the springs of life' through marital intercourse. Female proponents of controls in Scotland dismissed the metropolitan agitation of other feminist groups such as the Women's Freedom League and the Association for Moral and Social Hygiene as unrepresentative of informed opinion in Scotland and as reflecting only the dogmatic and outdated anti-regulationist views of upper-middle-class suffragists from London and Plymouth.

In part, such divergence has to be seen within the context of the continuing struggle by public health administrators and practitioners to maintain a Scottish identity in health affairs, and their growing frustration with the apparent deference of the Scottish Board of Health to the 'libertarian fears' and moral laxity of 'the cathedral cities south of the border'. During the 1920s, opposition in Whitehall and Westminster to Scottish proposals became rapidly subsumed within the broader constitutional debate over Scottish legislative autonomy, fuelled by the cultural renaissance and resurgence of Scottish nationalism. In particular Cabinet opposition to the Edinburgh Venereal Diseases Bill of 1928 was viewed as an unwarranted interference with the moral agenda of Scottish civil society. After 1942 the issue of VD controls became once again an acid test of the autonomy of Scottish health administration. A prime consideration in the establishment of a separate Scottish Council for Health Education was to signify the distinctive Scottish commitment to a compulsionist strategy in matters affecting social hygiene, and, as late as the mid-1950s, the issue was to figure in evidence before the Royal Commission on Scottish Affairs as an illustration of the frustration of Scottish 'aims and aspirations' under a constitutional structure that denied adequate legislative devolution to Scottish affairs. Interestingly, this association between interventionism in the spheres of morality and sexuality and the quest for regional or national identity was paralleled elsewhere, as in Weimar Germany.[18]

VD and the regulation of sexual behaviour

As in many other European countries, the discourse surrounding VD in twentieth-century Scotland was shaped by more general community concerns to regulate sexual behaviour. Frequently moral panic surrounding VD provided a convenient peg upon which the local state could hang bylaws and procedures proscribing patterns of social intercourse. Conversely the desire of Scottish local authorities to maintain civic order and probity sustained an 'authoritarian' tradition of public health administration in the handling of infectious diseases, including VD. In the Scottish cities public order, public morality and public health remained inextricably linked both administratively and ideologically. While it is argued that, in England, government adopted a 'wider laissez-faire policy' towards sexual issues,[19] in Scotland the VD service and its clinicians remained heavily involved in strategies of moral reform, and the local state, as in Germany and Denmark,[20] remained highly interventionist on socio-sexual issues.

Various dimensions of stigmatisation and control characterised this quest for moral order. In the social construction of VD and the formulation of medico-moral strategies to contain it, female prostitution remained the defining link between public order and public health, and nineteenth-century discourses surrounding the 'Social Evil' continued to shape attitudinal and institutional responses to VD long after 1900. As issues of sexual immorality and sexual disease had become increasingly medicalised in Victorian Scotland, legal and medical agencies had collaborated to institutionalise and reform the promiscuous and venereally infected woman and isolate her from respectable society. VD had become increasingly engrossed within the social politics surrounding prostitution, and medical provisions and debate largely determined by contemporary fears over female immorality and vice.[21] The Contagious Diseases Acts, allowing for the coercive detention and medical examination of any woman suspected of being a prostitute in certain sea-ports and garrison towns, had never applied in Scotland. However, within the major Scottish cities similar 'technologies of power' had developed in an attempt to reduce the level of prostitution. Under local burgh police Acts the police had operated a general strategy of legal repression and moral regulation in conjunction with newly established lock wards or hospitals for infected females and with Magdalene and other reformatory asylums.[22] This strategy continued to underpin public order policy within the local state in interwar Scotland. However, measures were increasingly targeted not just upon professional prostitutes but upon young 'sexually active' women in general. They came also to be stigmatised as 'reservoirs' of infection, reflecting in part the prevailing double standard of sexual morality and in part a deeper and more primitive notion of woman as 'polluter'. The 'vicious' habits and unresponsiveness of young women − commonly designated as 'problem girls' − to treatment regimes were viewed by Scottish health officials as both immoral and unclean. Their promiscuity, increasingly depicted within the rhetoric of public health debate as 'amateur' prostitution, was perceived as central to the continuing spread of VD and a serious threat to the health and stability of family and community relationships. Much of the campaign for more stringent VD controls was fuelled by the desire to contain the 'sexual recidivism' of women, and female default due to medical or logistical reasons was often presented as wilfulness or viciousness peculiar to female sexual proclivities. In addition, as eugenic ideology gained currency, women who evaded treatment were increasingly stigmatised as 'moral imbeciles' whose alleged mental deficiency posed a major threat of racial degeneration. Under the 1913 Mental Deficiency Act many were incarcerated for years in Magdalene asylums and mental institutions (as were their illegitimate daughters) in order to cleanse the hereditary taint of immorality. Non-statutory follow-up procedures adopted by health authorities to reduce levels of default and re-infection, such as domiciliary visits and contact tracing, were also highly gender-specific.

As elsewhere in the United Kingdom and Europe,[23] Scottish VD propaganda materials were extremely gendered in their representation of the aetiology and epidemiology of venereal infection. Sometimes, in leaflets and films such as *Deferred Payment*, men's sexual indiscretions were identified as a threat to family and racial health, but, even where male culpability was emphasised, the prostitute or casual good-time girl remained the constant point of reference as the root cause of VD. Men were rarely depicted as wilfully evil vectors of infection. More usually propaganda portrayed the contraction of VD by men as a function of ignorance and misguided susceptibility to the attentions of predatory women, especially when their moral inhibitions were loosened by alcohol. Even when demoralisation of women had been caused by male exploitation, it was the loss of female chastity that was central to the spread of disease.

Social hygiene propaganda therefore reflected and reaffirmed powerful assumptions about the nature and socially desirable boundaries of female sexuality. Women were accorded a limited set of sexual roles. They could either opt for the passive sexuality of the wife and mother, or, as sexual initiator, be stigmatised as a prostitute and the reservoir of disease. There was no acceptable sphere for nonmarital female sexual activity, which was clearly depicted as diseased and pathological, and the sexual health of the single woman was normally accorded a separate identity only as a source and carrier of disease. Similarly, it was conformity by women to the ideals of chastity and maternity that was presented as critical to the preservation of racial health. The assumption that male self-control was problematic, and that their moral behaviour was ultimately the responsibility of their female partners, was frequently aired in VD literature and films. Thus social hygiene lecturers were recommended to close with a slide of the Madonna and 'a few words on the power of womanhood to save the next generation through the purity and good of woman's life'.[24]

Similarly in both World Wars Defence Regulations identified the 'consorts' of servicemen as the critical vectors of disease and singled out for statutory controls the 'amateur prostitutes' or 'good-time girls' supposedly seeking and dispensing unsafe sex, who were deemed to compromise the health and military efficiency of the nation. During the Second World War the introduction under Defence Regulation 33B of notification for named contacts, and penal sanctions for their non-compliance with treatment, was explicitly designed to discipline the 'harpies who prey[ed] on servicemen' and the 'black-out girls whose moral delinquency was threatening the war effort and the national moral fibre'. Predictably the regulation was operated overwhelmingly against women, with infected men being depicted as 'victims' and their female consorts as 'sexual predators'. Female defendants had their alleged promiscuity paraded before the courts and media without any opportunity to establish their innocence beyond submitting to medical examination, while the sexual behaviour and 'hygiene' of male informants went unchallenged. Moreover this double standard was visibly reinforced by the posters and other propaganda materials issued by public health authorities, portraying a demonology of VD from which male figures were notably absent.[25]

A continuing discrimination against women can also be detected in the voluntary system of contact tracing developed after the Second World War as a major strategy for the control of sexually transmitted diseases.[26] During the 1950s and 1960s tracing in Scotland was primarily restricted to female contacts identified by the armed forces, police and public health departments and to identifying the inmates of the more notorious brothels and prostitutes operating in the docks. Thereafter, although more systematic interrogation of infected patients was introduced in most Scottish cities, 'promiscuous female contacts' remained the focus of surveillance and censure. This asymmetry was powerfully reflected in the 'sociological observations' of Edinburgh's Public Health Reports on the sources of infection which still enshrined the concept of women as the proactive polluters well into the 1960s. Thus the sources of infection were tabulated as:

male infection	*female infection*
prostitutes	prostitution
'amateur types'	promiscuous 'amateur' contact
marital partner	marital partner[27]

Clearly the language of public health epidemiology still presented a largely passive role for male sexuality, and the lack of a male analogue to the index of promiscuity of infected female contacts published by Glasgow Health Department during the 1960s and 1970s had arguably similar implications.

Another major feature of the formal and informal controls operating within Scottish VD policy and administration was the desire to regulate the sexual urges of the young. Throughout the twentieth century public health debate surrounding VD has been informed by acute concern at the effect of the apparent breakdown of familial and community controls upon the sexual behaviour of adolescents. Shifts in the lifestyle of juveniles occasioned by changes in income and consumption patterns, and by the onset of new forms of leisure and entertainment such as ice-cream parlours, dance-halls and cinemas, with their appeal to illicit desires, were perceived as a threat to the rational, sober, responsible sexuality expressed within marriage, necessary for social stability and racial health.

Contemporary debate over VD policy was used to articulate such anxieties. To Scottish health administrators, who viewed the First World War as having fractured sexual norms, new control initiatives were imperative to counter 'the lower moral code sapping the vigour of our youth', and a range of policy options including social hygiene education, the endorsement of the vigilante work of purity organisations and the institutionalisation of sexually active minors, were subsequently explored in interwar Scotland. In particular so-called 'problem girls' were singled out for detention in a range of church and remand homes and Magdalene asylums with a view to moral re-education and industrial training. As in France and Germany, new theories of sexual delinquency both reflected and reinforced prevailing anxieties surrounding adolescent behaviour, and propaganda material continued to instil fear of infection in the young as a deterrent from sexual transgression.[28]

The likely impact of the Second World War upon adolescent sexual permissiveness, inflamed, according to public health officials, by 'the "blackout", by boredom and by the lack of emotional control in conditions of stress',[29] revived such concerns. Night curfews and identity cards were proposed for minors as a means of restricting the movement of sexually promiscuous girls, especially in the vicinity of railway stations. There was an escalation in the use of remand homes by the police and health authorities in order to detain juveniles involved in moral offences, and, in Glasgow and Edinburgh, units of the Women's Auxiliary Police Corps were dedicated to the surveillance of the conduct of young girls. In postwar Scotland the discussion of STD prevention and epidemiology, and official nostalgia for the Scottish campaign for controls, continued to be informed by inter-generational concerns and used to stigmatise contemporary youth culture with (in the words of Edinburgh's VD Medical Officer in 1959) its subservience to 'the worst type of American and negro films, booklets, music and dancing'.[30]

Meanwhile, the fear of VD became a potent weapon in the armoury of vigilance and social purity pressure groups seeking to police the social space of the young. A prime example was the regulation of ice-cream parlours. In early twentieth-century Scotland such parlours formed a major focus for youth culture and entertainment in the cities, and their conduct came under increasing attack from community leaders and vigilance societies. The parlours, with their ill-lit, intimate booths and late opening hours, were alleged to be a sinister source of 'venery' and 'moral depravity', encouraging 'gross acts of familiarity' and the spread of venereal infection. Social workers and Poor Law officials regarded them as a major source of recruitment not only for procurers and 'white slave traffickers' but also for the VD wards of the lock hospital. As a result, stringent by-laws were passed imposing a set of moral planning controls. In particular, refreshment areas were not to be partitioned nor connected to any residential area and were to be sufficiently illuminated so that all customers could be distinctly identified from either end of the parlour, especially by moral vigilance officers.[31] A proper study of similar controls for subsequent periods remains to be undertaken, but a cursory survey of the leisure and entertainment regulations administered in the major Scottish cities since 1920 relating to cinemas and dance-halls reveals a similar moral agenda in which social hygiene was never far from the surface.

Arguably the discourse shaping medical practice and policy towards VD in Scotland also enshrined class-specific attitudes towards sexuality and sexual behaviour. Treatment and propaganda were used to articulate essentially middle-class values of self-restraint, abstinence and hygiene as a means of remoralising the poorer classes who attended the clinics.[32] As in Victorian Scotland, immorality remained 'a culturally convenient myth through which to maintain a safe distance between classes'.[33] As David Evans has rightly speculated: 'Even when treatment was effective, the experience of patients may have been stigmatizing and disempowering. Patients were likely to be working-class and may have experienced the treatment and education they received as a form of social control.'[34] As in many European countries, such as France,[35] an assumed correlation between class and sexual 'wantonness' constituted the leitmotif of public health reports until long after the Second World War. It was predominantly working-class sexual behaviour that was scrutinised and appraised (or, more accurately, stereotyped) and, despite the absence of any reliable data on the social distribution of VD, it was the 'libertines' and 'intransigents' within the working class who were identified as the major vectors. As Armstrong has demonstrated, the 'deference' of patients to the medico-moral behavioural prescriptions of middle-class health clinicians and administrators, including the need for 'rational' and 'temperate' sexual habits, was central to the social hygiene of the dispensary.[36] It was entirely consistent that, when venereologists and local authorities came to advance proposals for compulsory notification and treatment for VD, they were content to ignore those patients receiving private treatment (including the highly promiscuous and diseased libertines believed to exist in the very highest echelons of society) and to regulate solely those attending public clinics.

Often class values and assumptions could override or cut across considerations of gender in shaping VD proposals. Thus Scottish middle-class women's groups such as the Women's Citizens Association were in the forefront of the interwar campaign for the surveillance, detention and moral regeneration of the hard core of working-class 'problem girls' who defied middle-class standards of sexual and vocational propriety. Their attempts to control 'sex delinquency' inherited from prewar evangelical rescue work a quintessentially bourgeois view of working-class female adolescent 'promiscuity' as requiring custodial treatment to ensure a material and moral environment in which norms of sexual passivity might be instilled. Similarly, during the Second World War, while ambivalent about DORA 33B, which sought to identify and regulate sexual contacts, women's groups advocated a range of control measures for working-class 'sexual delinquents' who were allegedly harassing servicemen in the Scottish ports and cities. The Scottish Branch of the National Vigilance Association pressed for greater use by the police and social workers of the 1937 Children and Young Persons Act as a means of restraining the 'lower class' of good-time girl. Likewise, the Scottish branches of the Association for Moral and Social Hygiene and the National Council for Equal Citizenship both advocated more women police to discipline 'vicious girls from the lower orders' who were perceived as major vectors of VD, and to patrol 'danger areas' such as stations, camps and parks.

As with the gender and generational aspects of VD regulations, their class specificity both reflected and reinforced a similar asymmetry in the social incidence of other public health or public order controls relating to sexual morality. Thus local authorities strove to introduce legislation to reduce child abuse and prostitution by the regulation of common lodging houses and the so-called 'farmed-out houses' (houses leased from the owners and sub-let or rented for multiple occupancy for limited periods) in which the poorest city dwellers were accommodated. In the press and in the deliberations of the police and of the public health and sanitary departments such housing was a major source of vice and venereal disease. Evidence suggested that they were widely used for the purposes of child prostitution and 'the defilement of young girls'. In the view of the authorities such houses were threatening to become a moral no-go area: 'a great festering mass of humanity, rotten and degraded and obscene, all mixed up together without any control'.[37] In response to this threat of 'racial poisoning' Glasgow and Edinburgh Corporations, backed by the churches and social purity associations, fought a protracted battle in the early decades of the century to smuggle into their routine sanitation Acts controls regulating the age and sex of the inmates and the sleeping arrangements of such properties, and debarring persons convicted of prostitution, procuring or brothel-keeping from keeping and letting lodging premises. However, as with the attempts by Scottish local authorities to legislate for the compulsory notification and treatment of VD, the Law Officers and the Ministry of Health were reluctant to permit local housing statutes to redefine the role of the state in the highly contentious area of sexual behaviour. Civic leaders had to rest content with trying, albeit ineffectually, to implement old bylaws designed to ensure 'sex separation' in the sleeping arrangements of common lodging houses.

Conclusion

However, it would be wrong to view the 'culture of compulsion' surrounding sexually transmitted diseases in Scotland as purely one imposed from above. Many labour organisations favoured more stringent measures regulating immorality and the wilful transmission of VD, and the investigations of Mass Observation in the 1940s revealed that a considerable body of working-class opinion in Scotland approved of compulsory notification and treatment, the penalisation of 'infective intercourse' and conception, and the sterilisation of incurables and habitual offenders; a pattern of social response to be repeated in subsequent postwar moral panics surrounding STDs.[38]

Moreover, in focusing purely upon the discourse surrounding VD controls and propaganda there is a danger of ignoring their arguably limited success in regulating the sexual behaviour of the mass of the population, for the story of VD administration in twentieth-century Scotland is as much a story of sexual 'wilfulness'

THE CULTURE OF COMPULSION

as it is of control. The level of 'sexual recidivism' and re-infection was a constant lament of interwar venereologists and Medical Officers of Health. Similarly a casual disregard for the risks of venereal infection by Scottish youth in practising its alleged 'cult of sexual sensuality' was a leitmotif of post-1950 public health reports. Likewise, more recently, despite the best efforts of a ministerial task force in Scotland to counter HIV and AIDS by inducing 'necessary behavioural change', surveys on sexual attitudes have revealed limited change in the pattern of heterosexual behaviour.[39]

Notes

I am indebted to the Wellcome Trust, whose financial assistance made possible the research upon which this chapter is based.

1 See, for example, L. Bernstein, *Sonia's Daughters: Prostitutes and their Regulation in Imperial Russia* (Berkeley, University of California Press, 1995); L. Bland, '"Cleansing the Portals of Life": The Venereal Disease Campaign in the early Twentieth Century', in M. Langan and B. Schwarz (eds), *Crises in the British State, 1880–1930* (London, Hutchinson, 1985), chapter 9; R. C. Bolea, 'Venereal Diseases in Spain during the Last Third of the 19th Century: An Approach to the Moral Bases of Public Health', *Dynamis*, 11 (1991), pp. 239–62; A. Corbin, *Women for Hire: Prostitution and Sexuality in France after 1850* (London, Harvard University Press, 1990), chapter 6; J. Forrai, 'Prostitution at the Turn of the Century in Budapest', in J. Forrai (ed.), *Civilisation, Sexuality and Social Life in Historical Context: The Hidden Face of Urban Life* (Budapest, Semmel University of Medicine Institute of the History of Medicine and Social Medicine, 1996), pp. 55–62; A. Mooij, *Out of Otherness: Characters and Narrators in the Dutch Venereal Disease Debates, 1850–1990* (Amsterdam and Atlanta, Rodopi Press, 1998), chapter 1; C. Quétel, *History of Syphilis* (Cambridge, Polity Press, 1990), chapters 6–7; L. Sauerteig, *Krankheit, Sexualität, Gesellschaft: Geschlechtskrankheiten und Gesundheitspolitik in Deutschland im 19. und frühen 20. Jahrhundert* (Stuttgart, Franz Steiner, 1999); P. Weindling, *Health, Race and German Politics between National Unification and Nazism, 1870–1945* (Cambridge, Cambridge University Press, 1989), chapter 3.

2 See, for example, F. Mort, *Dangerous Sexualities: Medico-Moral Politics in England since 1830* (London, Routledge & Kegan Paul, 1987), part 4; R. Davenport-Hines, *Sex, Death and Punishment: Attitudes to Sex and Sexuality in Britain since the Renaissance* (London, William Collins, 1990), chapter 7.

3 R. Davidson, '"A Scourge to be Firmly Gripped": The Campaign for VD Controls in Interwar Scotland', *Social History of Medicine*, 6 (1993), pp. 213–35.

4 R. Davidson, 'Fighting "the Deadly Scourge": The Impact of World War II on Civilian VD Policy in Scotland', *Scottish Historical Review*, 75 (1996), pp. 72–97.

5 R. S. Morton, 'Some Aspects of the Early History of Syphilis in Scotland', *British Journal of Venereal Diseases*, 38 (1962), pp. 175–80.

6 T. Lundquist, *Den disciplinerade dubbelmoralen: Studier i den reglementerade prostitutionens historia i Sverige 1859–1918*. Meddelande fran Historiska institutionem i Goteburg, 23 (1982), pp. 435–48.

7 A. Blaikie, *Illegitimacy, Sex and Society* (Oxford, Oxford University Press, 1993), chapter 7; K. M. Boyd, *Scottish Church Attitudes to Sex, Marriage and the Family* (Edinburgh, John Donald, 1980), pp. 4–12.

8 D. McCrone, *Understanding Scotland: The Sociology of a Stateless Nation* (London, Routledge, 1992), pp. 36–9.

9 C. G. Brown, *The People in the Pews: Religion and Society in Scotland since 1780* (Dundee, Economic and Social History Society of Scotland, 1993), pp. 44–5. There are strong parallels here with the influence in the Netherlands of 'confessional blocks' on public morality. See H. Oosterhuis, 'The Netherlands: Neither Prudish Nor Hedonistic', in Franz X. Eder, Lesley A. Hall and Gert Hekma (eds), *Sexual Cultures in Europe, 1: National Histories* (Manchester, Manchester University Press, 1999).

10 *Proceedings and Reports of the General Assembly of the Church of Scotland* (1944), pp. 280–1.

11 E. M. Clive, *The Law of Husband and Wife in Scotland* (Edinburgh, W. Green & Son, 1982), p. 452.

12 Faculty of Advocates, *An Analytical Digest of Cases Decided in the Supreme Courts of Scotland 1868–1922* (Edinburgh and Glasgow, William Hodge, 1924), p. 1095.

13 D. Buchan (ed.), *Folk Tradition and Folk Medicine in Scotland: The Writings of David Rorie* (Edinburgh, Canongate, 1994), pp. 100–1; *Report of Departmental Committee on Sexual Offences Against Children and Young Persons in Scotland*, Parliamentary Papers, 1926 (Cmd. 2592), XV, p. 15.

14 R. Davidson, 'Venereal Disease, Sexual Morality and Public Health in Interwar Scotland', *Journal of the History of Sexuality*, 5 (1994), pp. 267–94.

15 Blaikie, *Illegitimacy, Sex and Society*, pp. 161–6; I. Levitt, *Government and Social Conditions in Scotland 1845–1919* (Edinburgh, Scottish History Society, 1988), pp. xxii–xxiii, 51.

16 Weindling, *Health, Race and German Politics*, chapter 5; P. Weindling, 'Sexually Transmitted Diseases between Imperial and Nazi Germany', *Genitourinary Medicine*, 70 (1994), pp. 284–9; Corbin, *Women for Hire*, chapter 6.

17 Deference to medical expertise in local government and the courts was also regarded as playing an important role in the success of VD controls in Denmark; see Ministry of Health, *Report on Anti-venereal Measures in Certain Scandinavian Countries and Holland* (London, HMSO, 1938), p. 7.

18 Weindling, *Health, Race and German Politics*, pp. 289–90.

19 Mort, *Dangerous Sexualities*, p. 199.

20 Ministry of Health, *Report on Anti-venereal Measures*, pp. 16–18. In Denmark a special section of the police force known as the 'Morality Police' liaised with public health authorities in the enforcement of VD controls.

21 See, for example, W. Tait, *Magdalenism: An Inquiry into the Extent, Causes and Consequences of Prostitution in Edinburgh* (Edinburgh, P. Richard,

1840); W. Logan, *The Great Social Evil: Its Causes, Extent, Results, and Remedies* (London, Hodder & Stoughton, 1871).

22 L. Mahood, *The Magdalenes: Prostitution in the Nineteenth Century* (London, Routledge, 1990).

23 See, for example, F. L. Bernstein, 'The Politics of Gender in Sexual Enlightenment Posters of the 1920s', *The Russian Review*, 57 (1998), pp. 191–217; Mooij, *Out of Otherness*, chapter 3; A. Kuhn, *The Power of the Image: Essays on Representation and Sexuality* (Routledge & Kegan Paul, London, 1985), chapter 5.

24 Edinburgh City Archives, Public Health Department 15/1, text for slide show, 1926.

25 Davidson, 'Fighting "the Deadly Scourge"', pp. 72–97.

26 Davidson, '"Searching for Mary, Glasgow": Contact Tracing for Sexually Transmitted Diseases in Twentieth-century Scotland', *Social History of Medicine*, 9 (1996), pp. 195–214.

27 *Annual Reports of Edinburgh Public Health Department* (1955–62).

28 Quétel, *History of Syphilis*, p. 193. For German concern over the sexual culture of youth and its vulnerability to the scourge of 'sexual bolshevism', see Weindling, *Health, Race and German Politics*, pp. 212–14, 381.

29 *Annual Reports of the Medical Officer of Health for Dundee* (1941–5), p. 114; *Annual Report of Edinburgh Public Health Department* (1940), p. 18.

30 *Annual Report of Edinburgh Public Health Department* (1959), pp. 142–3.

31 Glasgow City Archives, C1/3/47, Glasgow Corporation, Minutes of Magistrates Sub-committee, 1912; F. McKee, 'Ice Cream and Immorality', in *Proceedings of the Oxford Symposium on Food and Cookery: Public Eating* (London, Prospect Books, 1991), pp. 199–205.

32 For a similar interpretation of VD measures elsewhere, see for example, Mooij, *Out of Otherness*, chapter 2.

33 A. Blaikie, ' "The Map of Vice in Scotland": Victorian Vocabularies of Causation', in Forrai (ed.), *Civilization, Sexuality and Social Life*, p. 129.

34 D. Evans, 'The Creation of the Venereal Diseases Treatment Centres in Early-twentieth Century Britain', *Social History of Medicine*, 5 (1992), pp. 413–33.

35 In France syphilis was regarded as 'the plague of the lower classes'. See Quétel, *History of Syphilis*, p. 204.

36 D. Armstrong, *Political Anatomy of the Body: Medical Knowledge in Britain in the Twentieth Century* (Cambridge, Cambridge University Press, 1983), pp. 7–18, 103–9.

37 Glasgow City Archives, D-HEW 1.2 (20), 'Immoral Houses and Venereal Diseases', Minutes of Joint Conference, 3 February 1911; A3/1/237, Glasgow Corporation Order, 1914 proofs.

38 Mass Observation Archives, Sussex University, file report 1599; respondent letters DR2568, 2741, 2932, Boxes DR59–60; DR 2799, 3263, Box DR61.

39 *Scotland on Sunday*, 3 March 1996. In the sixteen to twenty-nine age group, 'more than 40% admitted that they had done nothing to change their sexual lifestyle' although aware of the risks.

Stigmatised sexualities

4

Same-sex relations among men in Europe, 1700–1990

Gert Hekma

This chapter offers a general introduction to a history of European homosexuality, and focuses mostly on western Europe, as its history is best researched. Most sources come from Germany, France, Britain and the Netherlands, which is the country of my own expertise. The perspective is constructionist: every period and culture has produced its own forms of same-sex desires.

Sodomy

Sodomy was the name, taken from the Bible, for an unmentionable sin that was defined as any lustful act which could not result in procreation within marriage. From the thirteenth century, it was not only a sin but also a capital crime. Sodomy included extramarital heterosexuality, non-vaginal sexual acts, all forms of same-sex behaviour, bestiality, masturbation and so forth. The best-known examples of persecution of sodomy were directed against males having anal sex with other males. In some countries, such as Sweden, there were severe prosecutions against young men copulating with animals. Criminal cases of heterosexual sodomy, lesbianism or onanism have been rare in early modern Europe. The same has been in general true also for persecutions of male–male sodomy, but in some cities or states in certain periods many men have been sentenced for it. Examples are Italian cities just before 1500 and Spanish cities thereafter, and in the eighteenth-century France, England and the Netherlands.[1] For the Dutch Republic and its predecessors, thirty-two capital punishments for homosexual sodomy are known for the period 1233–1679 and twelve for 1680–1729.[2] After 1729, there were about two hundred such executions, the last being in 1803.[3] It is amazing to see that the eighteenth-century countries normally considered the most enlightened, such as the Netherlands, England and France, saw such a harsh persecution of sodomites. The revolt against absolutism derived some of its fervour by opposing the sexual digressions of the noble class, but this does not explain the rise in sodomy cases concerning mostly men of the lower and middle class. Just before 1700 King William III of England, stadtholder of the Dutch Republic, and Philippe d'Orléans, brother of the Sun King, had the reputation of being sodomites.

There has been a spirited discussion on the history of sodomy, especially concerning the eighteenth century, to explain the rise of prosecutions and changes in representations. Many authors have claimed that the model of sodomy as a sinful act was replaced by a model of the sodomite as a sexual identity at that time. Traditional male sodomy was the anal penetration of a young boy by an adult man; the new sodomites were men of equal age. The traditional sodomite seduced both women and boys, and was considered to be masculine. The new sodomites had an exclusive interest in their own sex, and were considered to be effeminate. As the 'fop', the promiscuous womaniser, had been the example of the feminine man before 1700, the sodomite replaced him as deviant in gender and sexual roles. A concept of sexual identity replaced a concept of unbridled lust and unmentionable sin. In the major cities of north-western Europe, this sexual identity expressed itself in subcultures with their own meeting places, languages, customs and so forth.

The 'model of the queen' as a sexual identity, it is argued, took over from the model of sodomy as a sexual act. Randolph Trumbach is the strongest promoter of this perspective.[4] To support his thesis, he points to similar changes taking place at about the same time. Thomas Laqueur discovered a gender revolution just before the French Revolution,[5] Roy Porter and Lesley Hall saw the emergence of sex education literature around 1700,[6] onanism became a topic of heated debate and strict repression about 1750, and recently Isabel Hull has uncovered major legal changes taking place in Germany around 1800.[7] Trumbach assumes there to have been a major cultural revolution around 1700, including a gender transformation and sexual transformation. According to him, the gender regime and sexual regime that came into being at this time still define our beliefs and behaviours. Gay men are still queens.

There are several major problems with this thesis. In the first place, it remains unclear when this new sexual identity came into being and whether it has not undergone major transformations. Both the late seventeenth and eighteenth century have been given as the birthday of the queen. Another problem is why, according to Trumbach, the 'sapphists' got a sexual identity a century later than the sodomites. Third, the other changes did not take place at the same time as the queen was born. Trumbach gives 1700 as his birthday, but the debate on onanism and Laqueur's gender revolution took shape only after 1750. Some things changed about 1700, but what exactly, and in which periods, remains under scrutiny. Moreover, different models can be operative at the same time. Boy-lovers continued to exist next to queens and sodomites.

There are several points on the sexual desire of the queens that need to be analysed. In the first place, there remains the question of how exclusive the sexual object-choice of the sodomites was. Many of them were married and seemed to have had intimate relations with their wives. If the queen is a modern figure longing for equal and exclusive relations with other men, marriage should no longer be an option for him. But for most, it was. In the second place, the question of the sexual object should be settled. It seems likely that most queens desired the 'normal' men who were available for sex in large numbers: manservants, sailors, soldiers, messenger-boys. But as long as queens had these desires, their relations did not have the mutuality which characterises contemporary gay relations and so differed from them in an important way.

Myriam Everard has suggested, in a study on eighteenth-century lesbianism, that it was not the object of desire but its measure that mattered before 1800.[8] All people should restrain their desires, and not indulge in them. Tribades (as lesbians were called) were persecuted for their unbridled indulgence in pleasures, and not so much for their object-choice. This was very different from the soulmates and amazons who felt love for women, but who controlled their desires, were not prosecuted and thus belonged to a very different category. Subsuming all these women-identified women into the same category of lesbians is, according to Everard, a mistake because the relevant point of comparison was the measure of lust, not the choice of object. None of the types she discusses may according to her be equated with the late nineteenth-century lesbian as psychiatrists defined her.

The sexual regime of Europe was also exported by its leading empires to other continents. Persecution of sodomy made its ravages among the native people of the Americas, as Trexler has documented,[9] but would also have taken place elsewhere. On the other hand, less repressive attitudes towards same-sex and gender-deviant behaviours among indigenous peoples of other continents became known in Europe, and were used by the *philosophes* as an argument to support decriminalisation of sodomy and other so-called sexual crimes. If 'natural' people had such lenient attitudes in sexual issues, it meant that culture had corrupted European morals. Nature became an important touchstone in moral discussions on sexuality.

The French Revolution

The harsh persecutions of sodomy were used by the *philosophes* of the Enlightenment as an example of what was wrong with the absolutist *ancien régime* and the alliance of state and Church. Montesquieu stated that the most severe punishments were meted out for the most obscure crimes which were difficult to prove: witchcraft, heresy and sodomy. The philosophers proposed decriminalising sodomy and replacing criminal prosecution with social prevention. There was a strong ambivalence among enlightened philosophers regarding same-sex behaviours, as they still wanted to prevent them. Few authors endorsed pederastic loves as wholeheartedly as did Sade. He invited the enlightened authors to support hedonism in all its forms, from sodomy and prostitution to incest and rape, because these lusts are in nature and should know no social barriers. The argument of a biological instead of a divine nature directed thinking about sex from the late eighteenth century, as the examples of gender and onanism also indicate.

After the French Revolution, sodomy was indeed removed from the law books in line with enlightened philosophy. Napoleon's penal code included only articles against public indecency and the corruption of minors. Both articles were regularly applied against same-sex acts. This major change in France had ramifications for many countries as they followed willingly or unwillingly the French example. Belgium, the Netherlands, Spain, Italy, the French cantons of Switzerland and Bavaria all decriminalised sodomy (however it was defined) in the early nineteenth century.

Sodomy was removed from the criminal code, and public indecency entered it. As Hull has emphasised,[10] arguments about sexual privacy did not exist before the late 1700s. Before, sexuality was a public matter of families, villages and the state. The Enlightenment brought a separation not only of state and Church but also of public and private. The state and its institutions were responsible for the public realm, and the *paterfamilias* for the private home where ideally the state should not interfere. Every citizen had the right to an unperturbed private life. Quite clearly, most men interested in same-sex loves and acts had no access to private places and were more or less obliged to resort to such hidden corners in public space as toilets, alleys and parks. Thus they were liable to criminal prosecution for public indecency. In the Netherlands, most cases of public indecency involved homosexual acts, whereas exhibitionism appeared before courts only in the late nineteenth century. Homosexual cases were then punished twice as harshly as exhibitionism, and four times more severely than heterosexual cases.[11] In the early nineteenth century, Dutch courts persecuted same-sex acts under the new laws regarding public indecency as if they were still cases of sodomy.[12]

The Enlightenment altered criminological insights. Punishments after the fact should be replaced by prevention before the facts had come about. Sodomy might be decriminalised, but same-sex desires should nevertheless be curbed by the promotion of heterosexual relations, in particular marriage. The state took as one of its aims propagation of its population. Marriage ought to be made easier for the lower classes in order to prevent unrestrained promiscuity of the young, while on the other hand the libertinism of the higher classes was denounced. The most clear case of sexual disciplining that started around 1800 was the politics of masturbation. Young men should restrain themselves from self-stimulation and reserve their sexual energy for marital coition.

The French Revolution turned out to be a great disappointment for all those who had believed in its slogan of *liberté, égalité et fraternité*. But in the beginning it spurred the hopes also of same-sex lovers. Some even wrote what might be called homosexual emancipatory tracts, such as Sade's *Français, encore un effort* (1795), but there were other apologias for sodomy and buggery. These works had a highly ambivalent character, and were always anonymous. Pleas for equal rights for same-sex desires were based, for example, on the argument that men should be allowed to have sex with each other as long as prostitutes had too wide vaginas or were dangerous because of venereal diseases. Such apologias were typical of the social transformations wrought by the French Revolution, and would not see the light of day afterwards for a very long time. Sade was sent to an asylum in 1801 and his works were banned for the next century and a half.[13]

The sexual changes brought about by the French Revolution had a major impact not only on the countries under French rule but also on others. France became synonymous with social and sexual disorder, and the French novel with pornography. The enemies of France began to uphold a strict morality that stood in stark contrast with the lewdness alleged to have led to all the excesses and abuses of the French Revolution. England and Prussia were the prime examples of this moral strictness, but, starting with Napoleon, France itself began to impose a sterner morality. In the Netherlands, the example of the presumed sexual excesses of the French Revolution and the subsequent popular uprisings that haunted France after 1815 remained a standard staple of sexual-political discourse until the beginning of the twentieth century.[14]

The death penalty remained on the English law books until 1861, and the last execution of a sodomite took place in the 1830s. Many German states removed the crime of unnatural lewdness from their penal laws during the nineteenth century, but, with the unification of Germany in 1871, the Prussian criminal code was the model for the German one. This retained what became the infamous article 175. Russia introduced a new law on sodomy in 1835. The early nineteenth century was a period of regression and repression for same-sex desires. The liberal revolution of 1848 brought a major change.

Sexual sciences and homosexual emancipation

According to Trumbach and Van der Meer, the sodomites of the eighteenth century had already experienced a form of sexual identity which coincided with a gender inversion. This was elaborated into a theory, first by the forensic psychiatrists C. F. Michéa in 1849 and J. L. Casper in 1852, and more systematically by K. H. Ulrichs from 1864 onwards. Michéa argued that *philopedes* were often effeminate men, whose gender inversion might be explained by the recent discovery of the rudiment of a female uterus in some males. His physiological explanation replaced older theories that same-sex acts were a result of sexual excess or onanism. The causal chain was changed. Earlier, a mental state led first to sexual acts and second to diseases that resulted from those sexual acts. Onanism led to enervation, exhaustion, blindness, suicide and so forth. Michéa now found physiological explanations for mental states and sexual inclinations. In older theories, sexual acts led to physiological changes, and in the new theories physiological anomalies induced sexual desires. In the same vein, Casper considered pederasty to be a mental hermaphroditism. For Ulrichs, uranism (his neologism for what would be named homosexuality in 1869) had to be explained as a 'female soul in a male body'. He came up with a kind of hormonal explanation: uranism developed in the womb in the early weeks of pregnancy in the same way as physical intersexual states.

Homosexuality was a result no longer of cultural defects but of bodily changes or innate capacities. The first important question now became how often it was inborn and how often learned. The balance moved slowly in the direction of physiological explanations. The second main question became that of whether it was a regressive or normal state. According to most medical specialists, it was a form of degeneration, fitting in very well with Morel's theory of degeneration of 1857.[15] But for Ulrichs uranism was natural and normal and should not be punished in the Prussian or German laws. Most psychiatrists followed in his steps and advocated decriminalisation of unnatural fornication. But on the other hand they also proposed pathologisation of sexual perversion. Perverts should not be imprisoned but hospitalised. The cure was, however, still a problem. In the early days of sexology, the bath and work cures that were used against sexual excess and onanism were considered to be fitting for homosexuals as well. Later on, the best psychiatry had to offer was a change in sexual object-choice, but few psychiatrists believed in this. The second-best option was to help homosexuals to restrain themselves from homosexual acts. These cures were psychological, as there were no physical means to get rid of homosexual desires.

The main proponents of the psychiatrisation of homosexuality were to be found in Germany, France and Austria. Richard von Krafft-Ebing with his *Psychopathia Sexualis* (1886) was the leading expert on sexual perversion. His book was subtitled 'with special attention to sexual inversion' (which included both homosexuality and gender inversion). Many other authors had paved the way for him, in the first place Ulrichs, and also medical men from Germany, France and Russia such as Westphal, Virchow, Moreau, Gley,

Lacassagne, Lasègue, Binet, Ball, Chevalier and Tarnowsky. *Psychopathia Sexualis* became in its successive ameliorated and enlarged editions the standard work of the new science of sexology. It differentiated between qualitative and quantitative forms. The first included homosexuality, sadism, masochism, fetishism and exhibitionism, all new names devised by the new science. The second included nymphomania, satyriasis (excessive lust in males) and lack of desire. Most theories combined physiological and psychological elements in the explanation of perversion. The best example is Binet, who coined the term 'fetishism'. All perversions were according to him forms of fetishism. They originated in a degenerative bodily structure and got their specific forms through, as he himself framed it, an accidental association of ideas: a strong impression combined with lust. Schrenck-Notzing used such psychological explanations to propose therapy for sexual perversion. But most psychiatrists stressed the importance of inborn factors to explain sexual perversion.

Ulrichs used this theory to struggle against the criminalisation of homosexuality, but his fight was without result in the short term. Germany based its criminal law on the Prussian model, and homosexuality remained a crime. In 1897, only after Ulrichs's death, Magnus Hirschfeld and others founded the world's first homosexual movement in Berlin.[16] Hirschfeld would become the main champion of the homosexual cause for several decades, until Hitler's rise to power. His theory was a more elaborated version of Ulrichs's, and he also saw homosexuality as an inborn capacity of a minority of the population. He replaced Ulrichs's terminology of a female soul in a male body with a more enlarged theory of sexual intermediaries (*Zwischenstufen*). Hirschfeld's organisation and theory did not remain uncontested. In France, Marc-André Raffalovich developed a theory in which he stressed the masculinity and the capacity for sexual restraint in uranians, and in Germany Elisar von Kuppfer, Adolf Brand and Benedict Friedländer opposed Hirschfeld's theory because he made the virile uranians they had in mind into miserable half-breeds. Sigmund Freud suggested alternative psychological explanations.

Theorising about homosexuality was part of a larger discussion on sexuality. It started with public health, where the prevention of venereal diseases induced the medical regulation of prostitution. This policy was promoted by physicians and liberals, but it was opposed by Christians, women and socialists. It resulted in a debate on relations between men and women, on pornography, incest, child abuse and homosexuality. Another background for discussions about sexuality was the evolutionary theory of Darwin, which placed procreation and heterosexuality at the centre of science and sparked off a political feeling for the need to promote heterosexuality. The movement for eugenics was an example of such sexual politics. In these perspectives homosexuality should be curbed, as the German sexologists Max Dessoir and Albert Moll suggested. Learned homosexuality was to be combated and persons with inborn homosexual inclinations had to learn to restrain their desires.

An important result of all these discussions was a much enlarged visibility of homosexuality. The homosexual scandals of the turn of the century – including those concerning Oscar Wilde in England in 1895, d'Adelswärd-Fersen in France in 1903,[17] Jacob Israël de Haan in the Netherlands in 1904, and (the biggest one), Eulenburg in Germany in 1907–8[18] – in particular contributed greatly to the notoriety of homosexuality. Both Wilde and Eulenburg's friend, Kuno von Moltke, initiated the court cases which led to their downfall. Homosexual men went to court to file a complaint that homosexuality was attributed to them, and had to face as a result the fact that such accusations were grounded. After them, no man, however peripherally involved in homosexuality, would file such a complaint as it would always be lost. This greater visibility made homosexually inclined men much more vulnerable. The scandals also made it quite clear that homosexuality was still something scandalous and abject.

Homosexuality not only became a topic of the media and psychiatry; it was also lived in the streets and bars of the large urban centres. Everywhere in Europe, homosexual subcultures flourished in the late nineteenth century as never before. In Paris and Berlin, drag balls attracted hundreds of homosexuals. Berlin may have harboured two dozen gay bars; in Amsterdam the police had a list of about six (although very simple) bordellos for 'sodomites'. Everywhere street life was the most important part of gay life, with public toilets and parks as the spots where sex was found and consumed. Information from psychiatric and legal records makes it quite clear that same-sex desires were easily satisfied everywhere in Europe. In Amsterdam, such crowded male places as railway stations and news centres harboured rich possibilities. A Dutch naval officer's autobiography was published in a psychiatric journal, making it clear that he had never lacked sexual partners, either on board or on land.

In all big scandals, male prostitution with a generous supply of soldiers, male servants, college boys and messenger-boys played a role.

The medical discourse of homosexuality acquired its most important material by way of forensic medicine from this subculture. Arrested homosexual men formed the mainstay of the psychiatric literature. Ulrichs was often quoted, because of his intimate knowledge of the uranian world. The medical discourse relied on this microcosm, but added meanings to it and enhanced its reputation by making it public and more respectable than ever before. Although the general trend was pathologisation, the medical endeavours nevertheless meant an acknowledgement of homosexual desires. And thanks to the efforts of Ulrichs, Hirschfeld and others, a homosexual movement could offer a spark of hope for homosexuals who often had the feeling of being alone in this world.

Cultural life

At the same time homosexuality was becoming a hot topic in cultural life. First French authors such as Balzac, Baudelaire, Huysmans, Verlaine and Rimbaud wrote about same-sex desires, and later Oscar Wilde in England, Willem Kloos and Louis Couperus in the Netherlands, Stefan George and Thomas Mann in Germany and the circle around Diagilev in Russia took up the same theme. The period of 1890–1930 has been discussed as a gay time in culture,[19] because after this first series of authors and artists, many others followed. Never since classical antiquity had homosexuality been so ubiquitous and central in culture, and its representation was strongly influenced by the decadent movement. The concept of decadence was again very akin to that of degeneration. But whereas degeneration implied pathology and cultural decline, decadence implied exploration of all senses and cultural refinement, bending the negative theory of degeneration to more positive uses.

The literary examples of those times must have sent out to the reading public a supportive message of homosexual inclinations.[20] Certainly authors such as André Gide started to write unremitting apologies for homosexual desire. But this literature was of course not without critics, and some of these authors were strictly isolated. The fate of Wilde was something everyone wanted to prevent. E. M. Forster refused to publish his gay novel, fearing the homophobia of the English literary establishment, but elsewhere authors faced fewer problems. Prime examples were Kuzmin in Russia, De Haan in the Netherlands and of course Gide and Proust in France. They set the examples many minor writers and poets followed.

There was some interaction between literature, sexology, the homosexual movement and society. Some authors based their approach on medical models of a third sex, as did Proust and Couperus. Others took the more virile and pederastic version, as did Gide. Society reflected back at the authors, some of them becoming implicated in homosexual scandals, such as Wilde and d'Adelswärd-Fersen. Scandals were again the subject matter of novels, and both Wilde and Eulenburg became characters in gay fiction. The homosexual movement used literature again as a way to promote its ideas, by reviewing the works of gay artists as gay literature, and sometimes by writing justifications in the form of novels. Eeckhoud in Belgium and Exler in Holland are examples.

Travelling up and down

Already in the eighteenth century, the 'grand tour' provided a possibility for northern Europeans to become acquainted with the sexual pleasures of southern Europeans. The tradition of castratos and of boy-love made the south attractive for men from the north. Winckelmann left Germany and found enough joys in Rome never to regret too much the departure from his home country. A little later the poet August von Platen fled Germany and found similar pleasures in Italy. Ulrichs also lived his last years in Italy, and the photographer Von Gloeden established himself in Taormina, where he made nude pictures of the local youth. Like Capri, this Sicilian town became a centre for homosexual exiles. Wilde visited both places, and d'Adelswärd-Fersen built a villa on Capri. Until the Second World War, Italy had a reputation as a sexual paradise for homosexual men from the north.[21]

In the first place, this is of course a place myth, a result of cultural geography giving Italy a name of sexual freedom. Italians would later seek sexual freedoms in the north that they could not find at home in Scandinavia, Amsterdam and London. But this sexual reputation had also to do with poverty and a different structure of sexual desires and gender relations. Most young and unmarried men in Italy, and specifically in southern Italy, seem to have been inclined to sexual pleasures of all kinds. For them, it was not a question of identity but of a desire that could be expressed irrespective of gender. They had few qualms about sexual pleasures, as the guilt culture of the north had so many more.

This culture of sexual pleasures, where sexual identities are not declared, exists to this day along the shores of the Mediterranean. It makes 'coming out' less important, and a gay movement is next to non-existent. Gay men remain part and parcel of their families, who will know about the sexual proclivities of their sons but will not speak openly about it. Officially, gay sex is a scandal, but privately it belongs to nature and nobody cares too much as long as the rules of secrecy and reserve are respected. Many men will be involved in sex with other men or 'third genders'. As long as Anglo-Saxon culture sets the tone, such perspectives on sex will be defined as backward or old-fashioned, and have little chance to survive because they also miss the support they need to continue to develop. What in the end is probably a more sexually repressive system, the Anglo-Saxon, will replace in the long run other systems that are less inhibitory.

Another important question regarding sexual exchange has been raised by Ann Stoler.[22] Focusing on Europe has made us forget, she suggests, that the leading countries were colonial empires, which may have influenced their handling of sexual perversion. She surmises that the theories of degeneration and sexual inversion were based not only on the acquaintance with sexual and criminal subcultures at home but also with 'primitive' people in the colonies. The models of psychiatry could well have been influenced by colonial expertise, and the sexual politics at home reflected the disciplining of 'exotic' tribes.[23]

Repression of homosexuality

It took some time before the countries that had abolished the crime of sodomy reconsidered sexual crimes. Major changes took place only in those countries that still had sodomy laws and where there continued to be a discussion on the abolition of the crime or on the penalties. In Britain, the law was not abolished, but in 1861 the death penalty was replaced by penal servitude.[24] Some German states abolished this crime, such as Württemberg in 1839 and Hannover and Braunschweig in 1840, and other states reduced the maximum penalties.[25]

Towards the end of the nineteenth century, both prostitution and its medical regulation came under attack. Now stricter sex laws were enacted everywhere, not only against prostitution but also regarding the age of consent, pornography and homosexuality. The prime example is the English Criminal Law Amendment Act of 1885 (following the suspension in 1883 of the Contagious Diseases Acts regulating prostitution), which raised the age of (heterosexual) consent and increased the penalties for procuration, but also included the so-called Labouchère amendment forbidding all sexual relations between men both in public and in private. The Dutch laws against immorality of 1911 included a similar array of new articles, forbidding at the same time the public selling of contraceptives and pornography and homosexual lewdness between adults (over twenty-one years) and minors, whereas the heterosexual age of consent was sixteen years. This law targeted both sexes. Finland was exceptional in specifically criminalising lesbianism.[26] In England, women were left out of anti-homosexual legislation because women were assumed not to know about perverted sex or to indulge in it.

Not only did laws become stricter, the same was true for the interpretation of the law. Thus the German High Court ruled in the 1880s that not only anal penetration but also sexual acts that were like penetration, such as intercrural intercourse, fell under article 175.[27] In the Netherlands, public indecency was defined in 1886 in such a way that it also covered indecencies committed in private with other persons as unwilling spectators. In France, courts ruled that the article on the corruption of minors, which at first had been used only in cases of prostitution, also criminalised all persons who had sex with minors.

So the sex laws became stricter at the moment the discussion opened. It might be a rule of European sexual history that as soon as moralities seem to loosen up, laws become stricter. It indicates the deep ambivalence, if not anxiety, about sex in European culture. As soon as some freedoms are gained, stricter laws immediately enclose the newly won liberties. But it is clear that in most respects the general trend is towards more freedoms, not only for homosexuals and lesbians but also for straight women and men. Child-loving is the main exception.[28]

Dark ages

The late eighteenth and nineteenth centuries witnessed the emergence of greater sexual freedoms, and so did the Russian Revolution of 1917. Until the early 1930s, most progressive sexologists considered the Soviet Union as a good example of enlightened sexual politics. Indeed, contraception, abortion and divorce became more generally available. But prostitution, and soon also homosexuality, were repressed. In the early 1930s, the Soviet Union changed its sexual politics completely and now stressed the necessity of propagation. Homosexuality and abortion were forbidden again, and divorce and contraceptives became rare again.

The Soviet Union exemplified the new hopes of the 1920s and the disappointments of the 1930s. After the First World War, Europe came back from the trenches and many people had a feeling of 'never again'. Berlin and Paris became cities of pleasure where few people worried about politics. But soon the politics of both the extreme right and left would set the tone, and the spectres of Hitler, Stalin, Mussolini and others would haunt the hedonists of the gay 1920s. Isherwood's and Spender's novels on Berlin clearly describe this ambivalence of dancing on the edge of impending disaster.

There is no doubt that Hitler's rise to power in 1933 set in motion not only the Holocaust but also the most horrific disaster of gay life in this century. Homosexuals were more fervently prosecuted under the Nazis than ever before. Some ten thousand German homosexuals ended up in concentration camps, where about 60 per cent died.[29] The policies regarding homosexuality were, however, not of extermination, as for Jews and gypsies, but of reintegration. German gay men could better be made capable of straight sex and procreation, rather than simply killed. In camps efforts were made to change the sexual orientation of homosexual men. Also many men were prosecuted or killed for other reasons besides homosexuality. Ernst Röhm, the commander of the SA, was killed in 1934 not for his homosexuality (known to Hitler long before) but for opportunistic political reasons. Hitler wanted to get rid of a man who had been helpful with his rise to power but who had become an obstacle to deals with generals of the army and captains of industry. Nevertheless, homosexuality and the sexual abuse of young men made good arguments to legitimate the murder of Röhm, his consorts and others who had nothing to do with Röhm or homosexuality.

The situation for homosexuals was perhaps less dangerous in fascist Italy and Stalinist Russia, but there they had also to fear for their lives and loves. The Soviet Union reintroduced anti-homosexual laws in 1934. Also in other countries in Europe the situation worsened for homosexual men. Not only in Germany but even earlier in Denmark the castration of so-called sexual criminals was made possible. In the Netherlands, some 250 men involved in criminal cases were castrated between 1937 and 1967. They complied with this infraction of the integrity of their bodies to prevent prison sentences. They bought freedom through corporeal violation. Many more men have undergone this operation under pressure from families, peers and priests. In the same period, the number of men prosecuted for homosexual crimes increased and continued to increase until the 1950s, except in the war years when the police had other priorities. In the Netherlands it was said that, for homosexuals, the war had not ended in 1945. The situation started to loosen up only in the mid-1950s. The same was true for other countries. This is very clear for Germany, where homosexual men who had been imprisoned under the Nazis for homosexual crimes had no right to compensation (*Wiedergutmachung*), and remained in some cases imprisoned after the war had ended. Liberalisation would come in most countries only shortly before or during the 1960s.

Castration was not the only means to combat homosexuality. In these years, a repressive psychiatry also tried to change the sexual orientation of gay men, and supported the claim that homosexuality could be cured. In the Second World War, psychiatry started to be used for military selection. Not only insane men but also homosexuals were refused entry to the army. The idea that homosexuality was a disease made major inroads in the general population. For some gay men this might have been a consolation, but in general it offered not much progress because the medical model of disease did not replace the older models of sin and crime. The effect of psychiatry did not counter but added to the effect of religion and justice. Many gay men of this generation were obliged to see a doctor or a psychiatrist, which certainly did not help them in coming to terms with their sexual orientation, to say the least.

Suicide has always been a *topos* accompanying homosexuality. The typical gay novel of the early twentieth century has a main character who starts with innocent feelings for his own sex, and slowly discovers the social disapproval of same-sex desires. In some cases, he comes across medical texts or homosexual apologies that explain to him what homosexuality is about. In most cases, this sets the stage for his downfall through criminal prosecution, blackmail or other forms of social rejection. In many cases the end of the story is suicide. The first gay movie, *Anders als die Andern* (*Different from the*

Others) (1919), follows closely this plot. But suicide was also a real occurrence for many gay men, starting with 'Fighting Mac[Donald]' and Krupp, and continuing with René Crevel, Alan Turing and many others. It is still contemplated by many contemporary gay and lesbian young people.

With minor exceptions, the period 1933–55 was a dark age for homosexuals everywhere in Europe. Only Sweden, remaining outside the Second World War, liberalised its anti-homosexual laws in 1944. Spain and Portugal had become fascist at the end of the 1930s, and remained so into the 1970s. This closed off the little space that existed for homosexuals in Spain in the early 1930s when Federico García Lorca wrote plays and poems on homosexual love. The start of the Cold War soon after the war saw the rise of anti-communism in the west, and, although communism itself was highly anti-gay, anti-homosexuality was part and parcel of anti-communism and McCarthyism.

Gay liberation

The Swiss organisation the Circle (Der Kreis) was the only movement to survive the Second World War. Shortly after 1945, new homosexual movements started in the Netherlands (COC, 1946), Denmark (Forbundet, 1948), Sweden, Germany (1951) and France (Arcadie). In the 1950s, a short-lived international organisation existed, the International Committee for Sexual Equality. The task these movements had to face was enormous, as they had to struggle against both criminal laws and social prejudice. But with the sexual revolution of the 1960s, the homosexual emancipation movement had smaller and greater successes everywhere in western Europe. Many countries abolished anti-gay legislation, and the visibility of homosexuality in the media increased enormously. Many psychiatrists no longer saw homosexuality as a disease but recommended accepting it on an equal basis with heterosexuality. It started in some cases with the economic argument that curing all homosexuals would be too expensive, and the chance of successful therapy was small.[30]

A major influence came, however, from social sciences, and from across the Atlantic. Europe had set the tone for the discussion on homosexuality for a long time, but after the war the main contribution came from the United States. Kinsey did the first comprehensive survey of the sexual life of American males and females,[31] from which it appeared that 4 per cent of the males had an exclusive sexual orientation towards their own sex, and 33 per cent of the males had experienced homosexual sex. These numbers came as a shock for both American and European public opinion. These data were used both for and against homosexual emancipation. Kinsey himself made it very clear that anti-homosexual legislation was out of date and failed to restrain the high level of homosexual activity among men. In the United States, his work came just before an anti-sexual backlash of which he himself became a victim: he lost his research grants.

In Europe, Kinsey's work contributed to a liberalisation of sex laws. First in Britain, and later in the Netherlands, government committees discussed the laws on prostitution and homosexuality and came out in favour of partial decriminalisation, especially for consenting relations between adults, in 1967 and 1971, respectively. Interestingly, in England the number of men prosecuted for homosexuality increased after the abolishment of some laws; apparently the police more actively pursued men for remaining crimes such as public indecency and soliciting. Other countries also began to decriminalise homosexuality to some extent. The German Democratic Republic did so in 1969, and the Federal Republic of Germany followed two years later. France had witnessed a new anti-gay law in 1961, as senator Calvet introduced an article against the so-called 'social plague' (*fleau*) which was directed against homosexuality. Only with the rise to power of the socialists in 1981 were most anti-gay laws abolished in France. Spain did the same after Franco's death in 1975 and the subsequent democratisation.

A main question has been: what could explain the sudden success of gay emancipation and, more broadly, of the sexual revolution? It has been argued that a humanistic mental health approach made it easier to accept sexual diversity, especially where the churches joined this movement, as was the case in the Netherlands. Here it was precisely Catholic and Protestant mental health specialists who liberalised sexual attitudes with regard to masturbation, premarital sex and homosexuality: not sinning could be very unhealthy.[32] It has been argued that the gender and sexual revolution of the 1960s was made possible by a change from a culture of production to a culture of consumption. The amount of free time increased rapidly, and there was more money to spend on leisure activities. With regard to sex, the availability of the pill and other contraceptives and of penicillin as a solution for venereal diseases made the sexualisation of society easier. The obligation of virginity became a harassment. The explosion of a youth culture in the 1960s, a result of a birth peak after the Second World War, helped considerably to promote the sexual revolution. Gays immediately picked up the chances they got to liberate and amuse themselves.

With the successes of the 1960s and 1970s, the homosexual equal rights movement was replaced by more radical gay liberation movements. The main argument against equal rights was that this presumed still the normativity of heterosexuality. 'The faggot is not perverted, but the society that represses him' ran a German slogan, which was the title of a movie directed by Rosa von Praunheim. In the Netherlands, the homosexual movement struggled for integration in society. But the meaning of integration changed. Whereas it had earlier meant that homosexuals should follow in the steps of heterosexuals, later it stood for the acceptance of homosexuals as they were. It brought up the question of what an unrepressed gay man looked like, which was as impossible to answer as the similar question of feminism: what does a woman want? The politics of integration were replaced in a large part of the gay movement by a politics of sexual difference under the influence of Parisian philosophers.

Paris had been the hotbed of radical sexual politics in the late eighteenth and nineteenth centuries, and it was once more in the late 1960s and 1970s. Post-structuralism and postmodernism paid lavish attention to gay liberation. Deleuze and Guattari, and their gay follower Hocquenghem, defended sexual transgressions and free-floating desires.[33] Foucault passed from the historical hermeneutics of sex to an eulogy of gay sadomasochism.[34] Their criticisms of the sexual politics of their time were influential in gay movements all over Europe, and were dispersed in a multitude of forms, from gay groups in political parties and at the universities, to gay journals and health groups.

Subcultures

Not only the gay movement but also the gay subculture left its underground world and came into the open. For Amsterdam, the growth of the gay bar culture started in the 1950s, when the first large gay discos were opened and sexual specialisation started with a gay leather bar. This bar culture became possible as homosexuals underwent an identity change. Whereas formerly many homosexual men cultivated their feminine qualities and desired 'normal' men or 'trade', from the 1950s they started to cultivate normalcy and to desire their equals, other gay men. Before, the main hangouts of the subculture had been red-light districts, public toilets and parks, but beginning in the 1950s, bars, saunas and other more private institutions took over. Public space had been the best place to find partners; now these private clubs made it possible to find other gay men for love and sex in a hidden world where no straights were present. From the 1950s, gay culture became in a certain way less integrated, as fewer 'normal' men participated in it. But the gay men who did had more sex because they had more opportunities in gay saunas, bars and discos. The relational model changed from a model derived from the prostitutes' world – a short sexual contact of client and whore – to a model derived from marriage: an enduring loving relation of a couple. Inequality was replaced by an ideal of equality, and the idea that a gay couple should consist of a 'male' and a 'female' partner became ludicrous.[35]

Whereas the social status of marriage diminished, gay men started to aspire to the bonds of a coupled life. Psychiatrists could conclude that the best cure for homosexuals could well be to relinquish a promiscuous life of furtive sex and enter a loving same-sex relationship. They closely followed the changes taking place in the gay scene. But before or besides their coupled life, many gay men continued to enjoy a promiscuous lifestyle. With the development of leather bars, saunas and sex parties this random promiscuity could be easily realised because it was an exclusively male world. Hedonism was on the verge of becoming the basis of the gay lifestyle. Sex and love were separated in gay circles, and a sexy friend for one night did not endanger a long-standing love. Anguish about venereal diseases was removed because of the general availability of antibiotics as a cure, and the worst forms of social rejection that had prevented men from entering the gay world of pleasure had disappeared. In fact, gay men may well have been the group that profited most from the sexual revolution. Gay sex was in many cases still a crime in the 1960s, but in the 1970s all negative labels were reversed: it was no longer a crime, sin or disease. The gay world became a space for sexual pleasure. The straight world did not see a similar development, but was, on the contrary, confronted in the late 1970s with debates on sexual violence, incest and assault with men as perpetrators and women and children as victims. While sex was becoming easy in the gay world, it became increasingly fraught with problems among heterosexuals.

Disease and disaster

But gay men had soon to confront a major disaster. The gay health groups that had come into existence in the late 1970s were a blessing in disguise in the early 1980s when AIDS struck the gay community. AIDS started in the United States, so western European countries could prepare themselves by learning from the first American experiences. But few governments did much to learn lessons from America and its politics, in themselves highly prejudicial and ineffective. Discussion of so-called risk groups (the four h's: homosexuals, Haitians, haemophiliacs and heroin addicts) made clear that little would be done as long as AIDS had made no inroads in the 'general' population. Both the right-wing regime in Britain and the left-wing regime in France did little to prevent the spread of the epidemic. The Netherlands, Denmark and Sweden saw a co-operative effort of the gay movement and medical authorities to combat the disease and to help the patients. In France, not only was the state negligent, but it took some time for the gay movement to see AIDS as a disease and not as a bad trick or a new form of medicalisation of homosexuality that was played out against gay men. Independently of politics, nearly everywhere in western Europe gay men were most afflicted by AIDS. Spain and Italy were exceptions to this rule, having large populations of drug addicts struck by the epidemic.

In the beginning, the most horrifying scenarios were developed, suggesting an annual increase in the number of AIDS cases of 400 per cent. This was of course an unrealistic prediction because it meant the gay population would be wiped out in a few years, notwithstanding the fact that many gay men changed their sexual behaviour shortly after the beginning of the epidemic. Moreover, many gay men did not have to change their sex lives at all because they were not promiscuous or had no interest in unsafe sexual practices. Soon it appeared that the epidemic could quite well be curbed. Because of the quick response of the gay community and medical authorities and the prompt acceptance of safe sex techniques by most gay men, AIDS did not make the major inroads among the European gay world that had been expected. It is an interesting question whether the straight world would have been able to change its sexual behaviours as quickly as gay men were able to do. From the available research, it seems likely that the difficulty of communication about sex between men and women would probably have impeded easy acceptance of safer sex in straight circles.

AIDS has had many results, and an interesting one has come from the sex surveys that have been done because of AIDS. Since Kinsey, the number of gay men has variously been stated as 4 or 10 per cent, depending on how many borderline cases were included. But recent research points to a much lower number of about 1–4 per cent of the male population, and even less for females, with quite a few borderline cases.[36] It had been expected that the growing acceptance of homosexuality should have induced more people to claim gay and lesbian identities, but this has not been the case. The most convincing explanation is that Kinsey's sample was biased, and included too many gay men, as this was a great interest of his. Of course, the latest data are also debatable, although all surveys point to a lower percentage of homosexuals than Kinsey found.

A new *fin de siècle*

AIDS was and is a disaster in the gay world, and has left major gaps as many of its inhabitants have died of AIDS. The development and growth of a hedonistic gay world was impeded for a decade. It helped the creation of a new kind of gay and lesbian movement, in the beginning responsible and prudent, later aggressive and violent. Act Up, with its slogan 'silence = death', paved the way for radical organisations such as Queer Nation. France and Britain especially witnessed this radical development, while the Netherlands completely missed it. In many places AIDS organisations, like the French AIDES, kept their distance from the gay movement, although they consisted mainly of gays and lesbians and offered help mostly to gay patients.

The struggle against AIDS has often been understood as a struggle for monogamy. But civil laws did not include gay relations and offered no possibilities for gays and lesbians to formalise their bonds or acknowledge their familial connections, especially with regard to children from earlier marriages, artificial insemination, adoption and so forth. In the early 1990s all over the Western world gays and lesbians started to demand equal civil rights, especially with regard to marriage. This struggle has been partly successful in

Denmark, Sweden, Norway and the Netherlands, but nowhere have the full rights and duties of marriage been given to gay men and lesbian women. This implies that much is left to be regulated: housing, pensions, insurance, legacies, adoption, and so forth. The value of monogamy has risen and is often promoted because of AIDS, but the group that is most touched by this epidemic has no access to the institution that belongs to monogamy.

The targets of the gay movement did not change in all countries from criminal legislation to civic rights. In Britain, there is still a different age of consent for gays and straights, and soliciting is still forbidden. In 1995, there was a reduction of the age of consent for gay sex from twenty-one to eighteen years. The Labour government elected in 1997, which included not only 'out' MPs but even gay members of the government, voted in 1998 for a further reduction to sixteen, but this was blocked by the House of Lords, the British upper chamber of Parliament. For a decade Britain has also had a law forbidding local authorities to promote homosexuality, or to present it as equal to heterosexuality. Elsewhere, the main struggles are against social oppression and rejection. The disappearance of clear targets has weakened the gay movement, as a comparison between the Netherlands and Britain can clarify. In Britain, there is much wider mobilisation of gays and lesbians for Gay Pride marches and similar events than in the Netherlands. New aims, such as the right to marry or to adopt children, have met in the Netherlands with disapproval for different reasons among large sections of the gay public.

Many gays and lesbians have simply no desire to marry. In the 1990s, the gay world is thriving again, and clubs, saunas, parties and darkrooms cater to a large public that looks for safe, 'vanilla' as well as kinky sex. The institutions of hedonism are visited by gay men, but lesbian women and straight people follow in their steps. Especially the interest and participation of (lesbian) women in 'kinky' sex and 'perversity' means a major shift. Whereas women had little space to play in earlier generations, now they do it and enjoy what the shift in gender dichotomy means. Women can take male sexual positions, and men female. To my understanding, it is still more difficult for men to take female positions than the reverse, as may be clear from clothing habits and drag behaviour.

After the fall of the Iron Curtain, gay and lesbian emancipation very rapidly gained a foothold in eastern European countries. East Germany, the Czech Republic, Russia, the Baltic states, Hungary and

Slovenia saw the development of quite successful movements. The situation in Slovakia, Croatia and Albania remains difficult, while Romania continues to be the only country to have explicit and elaborate anti-gay legislation. In other countries – also, surprisingly, in Russia and Serbia – anti-homosexual articles were abolished. As most nations have become members of the Council of Europe, they will face great difficulties in (re)criminalising homosexuality, as discrimination on the basis of sexual orientation is forbidden.[37] Most countries have also seen a rapid development of a gay subculture in recent years, with bars and journals. The outcome of all these developments is for the moment still far from clear.

Conclusion

Gay men and lesbian women have in most European countries combated ideas that homosexuality is a sin, a crime or a disease with some success. Nowhere is it a crime in itself any more, although the Pope is still clinging to the idea that the behaviour is sinful. Since the AIDS epidemic, few people continue to defend the idea that homosexual ambitions are pathological. But nowhere has equality been reached, and everywhere strong prejudices against gays and lesbians continue to exist. In the Netherlands, considered to be liberal in this respect for decades, half of male adolescents consider male homosexuality as filthy. Nowhere has the normativity of heterosexuality been broken.

Notes

1 M. Rocke, *Forbidden Friendships: Homosexuality and Male Culture in Renaissance Florence* (New York and Oxford, Oxford University Press, 1996); K. Gerard and G. Hekma (eds), *The Pursuit of Sodomy: Male Homosexuality in Renaissance and Enlightenment Europe* (New York, Haworth Press, 1989).

2 D. J. Noordam, *Riskante relaties: vijf eeuwen homoseksualiteit in Nederland, 1233–1733* (Hilversum, Verloren, 1995).

3 T. van der Meer, *Sodoms zaad in Nederland: het ontstaan van homoseksualiteit in de vroegmoderne tijd* (Nijmegen, SUN, 1995).

4 R. Trumbach, 'London's Sodomites: Homosexual Behavior and Western Culture', *Journal of Social History*, 9, 1 (1977), pp. 1–33; 'Sodomitical Subcultures, Sodomitical Roles, and the Gender Revolution', *Eighteenth Century Life*, 9, 3 (1985), pp. 109–21; 'Gender and the Homosexual Role in Modern Western Culture: the 18th and 19th Century Compared', in D.

Altman *et al.* (eds), *Homosexuality, Which Homosexuality* (London, GMP, 1989), pp. 149–69.

5 T. Laqueur, *Making Sex: Body and Gender from the Greeks to Freud* (Cambridge, Mass., Harvard University Press, 1990).

6 R. Porter and L. Hall, *The Facts of Life: The Creation of Sexual Knowledge in Britain, 1650–1950* (New Haven and London, Yale University Press, 1995).

7 I. V. Hull, *Sexuality, State, and Civil Society in Germany, 1700–1815* (Ithaca, Cornell University Press, 1996).

8 M. Everard, *Ziel en zinnen: over liefde en lust tussen vrouwen in de tweede helft van de achttiende eeuw* (Groningen, Historische Uitgeverij, 1994).

9 R. C. Trexler, *Sex and Conquest: Gendered Violence, Political Order, and the European Conquest of the Americas* (Ithaca, Cornell University Press, 1995).

10 Hull, *Sexuality.*

11 G. Hekma, *Homoseksualiteit, een medische reputatie: de uitdoktering van de homoseksueel in negentiende-eeuws Nederland* (Amsterdam, SUA, 1987); G. Hekma, D. Kraakman, M. van Lieshout and J. Radersma (eds), *Goed verkeerd: een geschiedenis van homoseksuele mannen en lesbische vrouwen in Nederland* (Amsterdam, Meulenhoff, 1989).

12 Van der Meer, *Sodoms zaad in Nederland.*

13 M. Lever, *Donatien Alphonse François, Marquis de Sade* (Paris, Fayard, 1991).

14 J. Merrick and B. T. Ragan Jr (eds), *Homosexuality in Modern France* (New York and Oxford, Oxford University Press, 1996).

15 D. Pick, *Faces of Degeneration: A European Disorder, c. 1848–c. 1918* (Cambridge, Cambridge University Press, 1989).

16 M. Hingst *et al.* (eds), *Hundert Jahre Schwulenbewegung* (Berlin, Rosa Winkel, 1997).

17 W. H. L. Ogrinc, 'A Shrine to Love and Sorrow: Jacques d'Adelswärd-Fersen (1880–1923)', *Paidika: The Journal of Paedophilia*, 3, 2 (Winter 1994), pp. 30–58.

18 Hull, 'Kaiser Wilhelm and the "Liebenberg Circle"', in J. C. G. Rohl and N. Sombart (eds), *Kaiser Wilhelm II: New Interpretations* (Cambridge, Cambridge University Press, 1982), pp. 193–220; J. D. Steakley, 'Iconography of a Scandal', *Studies in Visual Communication*, 9, 2 (1983), pp. 20–51.

19 J. Meyers, *Homosexuality and Literature 1890–1930* (London, Athlone, 1977).

20 M. Keilson, *Die Geschichte der eigenen Geschichte: Literatur und Literaturkritik in den Anfängen der Schwulenbewegung* (Berlin, Rosa Winkel, 1997).

21 R. Aldrich, *The Seduction of the Mediterranean: Writing, Art and Homosexual Fantasy* (London and New York, Routledge, 1993).

22 A. Stoler, *Race and the Education of Desire: Foucault's History of Sexuality and the Colonial Order of Things* (Durham, Duke University Press, 1995).

23 Compare also R. Bleys, *The Geography of Perversion: Male-to-male Sexual Behaviour outside the West and the Ethnographic Imagination 1750–1918* (London, Cassell, 1996).

24 J. Weeks, *Coming Out: Homosexual Politics in Britain from the Nineteenth*

Century to the Present (London, Quartet, 1977).

25 H. G. Stümke, *Homosexuelle in Deutschland: eine politische Geschichte* (Munich, Beck, 1989).

26 J. Löfström, 'The Premodern Legacy: the "Easy" Criminalization of Homosexual Acts Between Women in the French Penal Code of 1889', *Journal of Homosexuality*, 35, 3/4 (1998), pp. 53–79.

27 J. Hutter, *Die gesellschaftliche Kontrolle des homosexuellen Begehrens: Medizinische Definitionen und juristische Sanktionen im 19. Jahrhundert* (Frankfurt, Campus, 1992).

28 J. R. Kincaid, *Child-Loving: The Erotic Child and Victorian Culture* (New York and London, Routledge, 1992).

29 R. Lautmann, W. Grikschat and E. Schmidt, 'Der rosa Winkel in den nationalsozialistischen Konzentrationslagern', in R. Lautmann (ed.), *Seminar: Gesellschaft und Homosexualität* (Frankfurt, Suhrkamp, 1977), pp. 325–65.

30 B. D. Adam, *The Rise of a Gay and Lesbian Movement* (Boston, Twayne, 1987); A. Salmen and A. Eckert, *20 Jahre bundesdeutsche Schwulenbewegung 1969–1989* (Cologne, Bundesverband Homosexualität, 1989); J. Girard, *Le mouvement homosexuel en France 1945–1980* (Paris, Syros, 1981); F. Martel, *Le rose et le noir: les homosexuels en France depuis 1968* (Paris, Seuil, 1996).

31 A. Kinsey *et al.*, *Sexual Behavior in the Human Male* (Philadelphia, Saunders, 1948).

32 H. Oosterhuis, *Homoseksualiteit in katholiek Nederland: en sociale geschiedenis 1900–1970* (Amsterdam, SUA, 1992).

33 G. Deleuze and F. Guattari, *L'Anti-Oedipe: capitalisme et schizophrénie* (Paris, Minuit, 1972); G. Hocquenghem, *Le désir homosexuel* (Paris, Éditions Universitaires, 1972).

34 M. Foucault, *Histoire de la sexualité 1: La volonté de savoir* (Paris, Gallimard, 1976).

35 G. Hekma, *De roze rand van donker Amsterdam: de opkomst van een homoseksuele kroegcultuur 1930–1980* (Amsterdam, Van Gennep, 1992).

36 G. van Zessen and T. Sandfort (eds), *Seksualiteit in Nederland: seksueel gedrag, risico en preventie van Aids* (Amsterdam and Lisse, Swets & Zeitlinger, 1991); A. Spira *et al.*, *Les comportements sexuels en France* (Paris, La documentation française, 1993); K. Wellings *et al.*, *Sexual Behaviour in Britain: the National Survey of Sexual Attitudes and Lifestyles* (London, Penguin, 1994).

37 K. Waaldijk and A. Clapham (eds), *Homosexuality: a European Community Issue* (Dordrecht, Nijhoff-Kluwer, 1993).

5

Pornography in Western European culture

Dorelies Kraakman

Not all 'writing about sex' is pornography, as is apparent from the plethora of scientific, pedagogic and moralistic writings on sexuality. Conversely, pornography is always writing about sex, that is if we leave aside visual and virtual representations of sex.[1] Whether this makes pornography a distinct literary genre is a question that needs to be addressed from a historical perspective, as will become clear in what follows. I will first develop the argument that 'writing about sex' has divergent origins in European culture; further that in the seventeenth and eighteenth centuries it partook both in the renewal of the novel and in the making of what Michel Foucault has termed *scientia sexualis*; and thirdly that it did not become a homogenised discourse until the second part of the nineteenth century. At the end of the chapter, the question will be raised whether, in the 1990s, pornography, owing to the diverging of its audiences and to its – often parodic – insertion in art, is once again part of a cultural transformation of sex.

In the 1990s mainstream pornography seems to have come to an artistic standstill. By this I mean that, as a genre, it has not renewed its stylistic, narrative or formal structures for a long time. It has no other intent but to excite its readers' sexual responses and it does so with the help of stereotypical images, characters and storylines. It is hardly surprising then that this overworked pornography is not an object of literary criticism. At the most one finds it in studies of popular culture. In socio–cultural terms, pornography belongs to the lower strata of society. One finds it in the rough areas of town, in the murky interiors of sex shops and in the barracks of enlisted men.[2] It is usually cheap and mass-produced, which means an endless recycling of stories and characters. Pornography, in other words, is low culture, which for many people equals 'no culture'.

Paradoxically, eighteenth- and nineteenth-century pornographic books are being sold and bought in the antiquarian book trade for increasing prices, and the people engaged in this trade belong to the world of high culture. Of course we may consider this business the passion of a small group of amateurs and collectors, and as no different from collectors' mania for all kinds of oddities and rarities. But what to make of expensive facsimile editions or reissues of major and minor pornographic works of the past?[3] Besides, there is a notably growing academic interest, from historians as well as literary critics, in the study of classic pornography. All this raises the question of what pornography's place in culture is, and how it got there.

Pornography has long been a hybrid in Western European literary history, partaking of genres as diverse as medical and paramedical advice literature, drinking songs, political pamphlets and the novel. In other words it did not always exist as a homogeneous genre, a fact well testified by the variety of terms which were used to designate writing about sex. Licentious, lewd, libertine, erotic, bawdy, galant, luxurious, and last but not least philosophical, are some names given to a body of literature that served many purposes. In fact the earliest known use of the term *pornography* signifies almost the opposite of the modern meaning, as is shown by Rétif de la Bretonne's treatise on the necessity of public control and regulation of prostitution which appeared in 1769 and bore the title *Le Pornographe*.[4] Pornography first meant serious writing on the dangers of prostitution. When, somewhere in the middle of the nineteenth century, *pornography* was used as a designation for the kind of literature that carried any of the aforementioned epithets, it was also transmuting into the one-track mind prose of twentieth-century porn stories, with or without dirty pictures.

In the nineteenth century, Western European and American governments issued obscenity laws that criminalised the production and distribution of pornographic material. What had long been a concern of ecclesiastical courts and royal censorship became a public matter with the establishment of bourgeois, democratic governments. Jurisprudence was one of the constitutive factors of the historical construction of pornography until, in the first decades of the twentieth century, the same courts came to the conclusion that defining what was pornography was an impossible task. At the end of the twentieth century, after the abolition of obscenity laws during the 1970s and 1980s, politicians, pedagogues and parents are mainly concerned with the possible damaging effects of pornographic material on children. At the same time, commercial television channels broadcast (soft) porn shows, and tabloid magazines are freely available. In some countries, like the Netherlands, public opinion on the negative influence of television on children addresses violence rather than sex. Whether this will become a trend in other Western countries remains to be seen, of course.[5]

However, as already stated, as an artistic genre mainstream pornography is dead: it will not change very much, for better or for worse, for pornography has lost its vitality. Therefore one could say that it is history. It also 'has a history', as Lynn Hunt put it in her introductory essay to a collection of articles on the history of modern European pornography.[6] This chapter will present some features of this history, with a view to offering some understanding of the complex relationship that exists between pornography and Western culture from 1700 until today. Special attention will be paid to those aspects of Western culture that have shaped pornography and have decided its history: the rise of the novel as the genre par excellence to evoke love and emotions, the will to know and the scientific making of sex and sexuality, the domination of bourgeois culture and the institutionalisation of its moral convictions, and, last but not least, transformations in the sex/gender system. Before elaborating on these interdependent processes, some recent research in the field will be discussed.

Since the late 1980s scholarship on pornography has become quite impressive. For most of what will be presented here as the cultural history of pornography I am indebted to the work of Robert Darnton, Jean-Marie Goulemot, Lynn Hunt, Walter Kendrick, Péter Nagy and Peter Wagner, to name only the most renowned specialists.[7] According to most of these scholars the existence of pornography in Western Europe shows common features, despite national differences. Its chronology is marked by more or less the same highlights, continuities and discontinuities; its moral and legal treatment by national governments runs from an original laissez-faire to legislation, seizure and confinement of the books, back to a gradual return to tolerance and legalisation. What is lacking in these studies, however, is a coherent perspective on the transformations which pornography, as a specific form of writing about sex, underwent in the course of three centuries: from high culture to low culture, from culturally meaningful to absolutely valueless.

Questions that have drawn special attention in most of the recent work on pornography are the relationship between pornography and social and political subversiveness, its concurrence with modernity, the gender bias it produces and the reasons for its social marginalisation. Transgression is a key word in almost all studies on pornography and the assumption that sex is transgressive in and of itself underlies the definition of pornography as a potentially disruptive genre. Not uninterestingly, this definition applies first and foremost to the literature of the eighteenth century.[8] Most of the research in fact deals with the eighteenth century. The golden age of erotic literature ended, at least in France, with the Revolution, and most of the work on eighteenth-century erotic literature does indeed take that historical coincidence as a causal relationship and as an argument for the subversive intent of pornography. France was the uncontested seat of the imaginary republic of letters even though most of its inhabitants went back and forth in exile in a number of European cities, from where they published most of their forbidden works.[9] Eighteenth-century France was also the largest producer of erotica, although, here again, a large part of the titles were published abroad. French novels became almost synonymous with pornography.[10] The preponderance of pre-revolutionary France in studies on pornography is thus hardly surprising. That this poses a problem for an appraisal of the (dis)continuities in the cultural history of pornography will soon become evident.

Polymorphous preludes, revolutionary climaxes

Instead of starting simple and turning complex with the passage of time, pornography seems to have moved in reverse, growing perversely from multiplicity to oneness.[11]

Around 1700 pornographic works were relatively rare. Still we can already discern some genre differences, traditional or innovative. The themes of medieval fables remained the material of much erotic literature of the Renaissance and early modern times, but a distinct prose style was developed by Giovanni Boccaccio, in his *Decamerone* (1349–51).[12] The erotic short story was born, and its innovating feature was that it was written in the vernacular instead of in the official language – Latin – of the literate elite. In France, the first collection of erotic short stories, *Les cent nouvelles nouvelles*, which emanated from courtly circles around the later Louis XI, was published in 1480.[13] The genre of the erotic novella, the *conte galant*, remained popular all through the eighteenth century, as shown by several anthologies that often mix together prose, verse and song. Sometimes they were simply inserted in the novel, as adventures around which a storyline was woven.

Boccaccio belonged to the humanist culture of the Italian Renaissance cities. Most of his fellow humanists did not approve of his vernacular writings, however. They preferred instead to revive the classics and so enriched the European erotic tradition, during the fourteenth and fifteenth centuries, with the works of the Hellenist and Roman poets.[14] Foremost the erotic epigram, with a witty, suggestive one-liner at the end, became the model for erotic poetry in France, such as the seventeenth-century libertine poetry of Théophile Viaux and his Parnasse satyrique. These forms, the erotic tale, the risqué epigram and the classics, all belonged to the elite culture of Italy and France. The style of the latter may have been obscene, the former two were written in a distancing mode. The Renaissance erotic literature of the elite was marked by its elegance and figures of speech. The genres in which we find direct eroticism were the fables as well as farces and bawdy songs of popular culture, in which the elite by the way still had a hand.

Another innovation which has had a tremendous influence upon later developments of the novel presented exactly the opposite of the refined manners and elusive sex of humanism. Pietro d'Aretino's *Ragionamenti* (1534, 1536) is a series of dialogues between courtesans, much after the model of Lucian. For Aretino the prostitute was a suitable character to talk about sex in popular language. The countless imitations in all languages in the centuries that followed its first publication, show how well chosen his main character was.[15] But there was more to Aretino's choice of a Roman prostitute. Through her Aretino also attacked the courtly culture of humanism by evoking not the world of the classics but the public present, all the while showing his knowledge of both. The dialogic form, the language of the marketplace and the representation of the present all make Aretino's writing an experiment in writing about sex in a new genre, that of the social satire. And his mixture of worlds is a frontal attack on the elitism of humanist culture.

At the end of the sixteenth century the first copies of Aretino's work were seen in Paris, and the earliest French translation traced by Pascal Pia dates from 1595.[16] References to Aretino in the erotic literature of France concern his *Sonnetti* rather than the *Ragionamenti*, but his influence cannot be underestimated. In the eighteenth century *memoirs* of women of pleasure became popular novelistic adaptions of the dialogues, in France as well as in England.[17] The best-known example from France, *Margot la Ravaudeuse* (1748), offers a strong satirical critique of the new financial meritocracy in France.

Before the seventeenth century very little erotic prose was produced in France. In the seventeenth century a few works were written that can be seen as prototypical. *L'Ecole des filles* (1655) and *L'Académie des dames* (1680), as well as *Vénus dans le cloître* (1683), were all dialogic prose, in which the new scientific naturalism and materialism were transposed to the realm of the sexual.[18] *Vénus dans le cloître* is also an early example of anticlericalism in the erotic novel. Apparently erotic literature could serve more than one master. We find something similar earlier in the century, and in another genre. Bawdy or galant verse had always been legally published, with 'privilege of the king', but the advent of anti-religious elements in erotic verse was unwelcome to the royal censors of Louis XIV. In the seventeenth century this mixture of erotic and heretic poetry was labelled 'libertine'. In the next century 'libertine' came to mean moral and sexual behaviour that celebrated the pleasures of seduction outside the bonds of love and marriage.

In the eighteenth century the production of erotic literature grew quite rapidly to unprecedented proportions. A chronological inventory shows that, starting in the 1730s – with the libertine novels of Crébillon *fils*, *Les Egarements du coeur et de l'esprit* and *Le Sopha* – the genre proliferated. Additionally erotic poetry and short stories continued to be written in the traditional spirit of *gauloiserie* (bawdiness) which found new expressions in drinking societies and clubs. As might be expected, this expansive growth has drawn the attention of scholars in the field of history and literature.

Of the eighteenth-century specialists Robert Darnton and Lynn Hunt are historians, while Péter Nagy, Jean-Marie Goulemot and Peter Wagner are literary scholars.[19] Darnton, who has been conducting a vast research project into the market of forbidden literature of the eighteenth century over the past twenty-five years, has argued that there are no clear-cut boundaries between pornography and philosophical books, because all were subsumed under the title *clandestine*.[20] Darnton also contends that any causal relation between clandestine literature and the origins of the French Revolution is a matter of a complex understanding of the delegitimating forces the corpus of *livres philosophes* unleashed on the orthodoxies of the old regime. It is not easy to do justice to the immense erudition of Darnton's work, but what is relevant for my perspective is his insistence on the heterogeneity of the corpus and its connection to a spirit of sedition, which achieved its apogee in the Revolution.

Darnton, as stated before, does not differentiate between philosophical and pornographic works.[21] Nagy, whose focus is on libertinism proper, and who also stops short at the Revolution, does make the distinction. According to him, not every philosophical work is a libertine book in that it does not have the generic characteristics of erotic literature. A libertine work, on the other hand, always has a philosophical intent or meaning, over and beyond its generic form. This is where Nagy locates its subversive force. The philosophy and science of the Enlightenment were diffused among a wide audience of avid readers of the new bourgeois novel with its sensuous realism. The whole social edifice of the old regime was thus slowly sapped by the instincts according to Nagy. Transgression is partly a matter of breaking generic conventions. The transgressive aspect of pornography in this sense may have been the disruption of literary expectations that was brought about by the new novel.

Like Darnton and Nagy, Lynn Hunt links pornography to the political, but separates it into political and non-political pornography. Her criteria for distinguishing the two are not very well defined, but her motivation is all the more clear. While Darnton and Nagy close the book on pornography at the outbreak of the French Revolution, leaving the question unanswered of what became of this kind of book in the time after the Revolution, Hunt looks beyond this decisive point. But, wanting to maintain the claim that pornography played a special role in successfully attacking the old regime, she chooses to separate an explicitly political category of erotic texts from all others. Tracing the origin of this 'politically motivated pornography' – which in Hunt's words is pornography that targeted political figures – to the works of Pietro Aretino, she sees it reaching its zenith in France in the 1790s, after which it virtually disappeared.[22] It was replaced by a new genre, in which only social and moral taboos were tested, and even this ferment petered out in the next few decades. In the 1830s pornography became what it is today: a genre that aims solely at producing sexual arousal in the reader.

Without contesting Hunt's observation about the direction in which pornography evolved as a genre, I think there are too many loose ends to its genealogy, precisely as a result of the connection that historians have made between its cultural significance and the French Revolution.[23] Hunt edited a book on the history of three hundred years of pornography, and, in the light of those three centuries, the short period in which pornography was a vehicle for direct, slanderous attacks on leading political and clerical figures seems more like a temporary excrescence than an orgasmic culmination ending in impotence. That there was continuity is moreover granted by Hunt herself, who states that non-political pornography coexisted with political pornography from the very first beginnings and continued to be published even during the revolutionary 1790s.[24]

My own research into a random selection of sixty texts from the *Enfer* (the special department of the Bibliothèque Nationale in Paris in which 'obscene' books were kept), all belonging to the period between 1750 and 1850, shows that if we take subversiveness to mean the uprooting of the foundations of cultural truths and values it is certainly not evident that a clear and concise break exists between pre-revolutionary and post-revolutionary erotic fiction.[25] On the one hand the existence of forbidden literature may very well have signified a calling into question of the legitimate authority of the worldly and religious powers to decide what people could read, and therefore know, regardless of its contents. I cannot but agree with Darnton on this point. But that is, so to speak, judging a book only by its cover. When we look at the meanings the individual texts may have had, on the other hand, it is obvious that, at a time when more and more people were trying their hand at the genre of forbidden books, their intentions and the effects may have been very different.

What is left unanswered is the question of the undeniable boom in erotic literature in the eighteenth century, given the few prototypical examples from Italy and France of the sixteenth and seventeenth centuries. Why did it gain such popularity? What is also left is the question of how pornography lost its political acuity. After all, if in the eighteenth century the French, as Hunt suggests, could for political purposes find a model in the writings of Aretino, could then French revolutionaries of 1830 and 1848 not have harked back to the 1790s, when they had every reason to attack the king, his *juste milieu* and the church?[26] This chapter tries to formulate some possible answers to these questions, in which elements from literary history, the history of sexuality and the history of literary censorship are put together.

Novelties

The boom of eighteenth-century erotic literature cannot be considered separately from the burst of novelistic energy. Starting in the 1740s the new bourgeois novel acquired immense popularity, over and against its reputation as a dangerous genre. The danger was seen to be its realism as well as its imaginative force. The novel was the genre par excellence to represent, in the form of dialogue, the social languages of different people. The emancipatory potentialities for different social groups of this heteroglossia – as it is called by the Russian philosopher and linguist Mikhail Bakhtin – may explain its popularity among the rising class of the bourgeoisie in the eighteenth, and among the popular classes in the nineteenth, century.

In fact the origins of the new novelistic prose are already in sight in the baroque novel of the seventeenth century, with its combination of different literary genres and its encyclopedic structure. This last feature of the baroque novel is important for an understanding of the novel as a source of knowledge for its readers, who found in it information and explanation of the new scientific and philosophical ideas. It also links erotic literature to this encyclopedic aspect of the novel. In other words, writing about sex, in novelistic prose, was closely linked to a more general feature of the novel, its spreading of all sorts of new knowledge and ideas, including ideas about nature, physical love, and sex and gender. The literary form this writing took, novelistic prose, then accounts for its possible sensible effects upon the readers. This is the reason why it is difficult, and sometimes even impossible, to decide whether a novel is just pornographic or whether it is a mixture of different genres and different intents. Or, inversely, whether a book of medical advice about sex is not just a cover for a pornographic intent. However different this may be for modern readers, seventeenth- and eighteenth-century readers most certainly turned to the novel for knowledge and instruction, as much as for entertainment.

Just as important as this development in the literary form of the novel was the explosion of the *will to know*, as Michel Foucault has called it. Foucault has traced the beginnings of the production of sexual discourses to the seventeenth century, and its lasting effects to our days. He denies the West an *ars erotica*, in his emphasis on the medical, hygienic, pedagogic and psychiatric discourses of sexuality. In view of what has just been stated about the novel in general and erotic literature in particular, it can nevertheless be maintained that the experimental and plurivocal form of the novel allowed for the textual insertion in it of the new sex discourses. Regardless of the seriousness of intent on the part of individual authors, we can say that the erotic novel, starting with the earliest examples in France, may indeed contain sexual knowledge written in the style of medical advice literature. Even if parodic, the combination may explain, together with a general cultural production of sexual knowledge, the particular interest of the readers in erotic literature. Because if Foucault is right, that is, if starting in the seventeenth century an incitement to speak about sexuality did appear, then the rise of the erotic novel can be seen as one of the effects of that exhortation.

Just as these simultaneous processes explain the rise of the erotic novel – in combination with more socio-cultural explanations such as the growing literacy of the population and the commercialisation of the book – they serve also as a partial answer to the question of its decline. Because, along with the acquisition of a distinct status by medical discourse due to the nineteenth-century positivism, the re-vitalising power of the hybrid form wore out. In the nineteenth-century erotic novel we can see clearly that its sole intent was to amuse. Vice versa, medical literature on sexuality was developing into a genre that took a 'professional' distance from literary, meaning 'fictional', genres. So the two, erotic literature and serious medical discourse, definitely parted ways in the nineteenth century. Granted, this does not suffice to explain the decline of the erotic novel *per se*. After all, it could have rid itself of its encyclopedic character – as, by the way, the novel did – and developed a poetics of its own. But, as I have already stated, this did not happen. We therefore have to turn to other historical events.

First of all it is necessary to say something about literary censorship. As Darnton has shown, clandestine literature in the eighteenth century existed in a system of royal censorship. The royal censor, representative of the absolute power of the French king, had to grant permission to print any book. Most publishers, printers and authors, well aware of the dangers of falling out of grace, decided to publish their books anonymously, mostly with publishers abroad. The books were subsequently smuggled into the country, where they found their way to the public through different selling points. An additional but no less important reason why authors published anonymously was the fact that novels were long considered an inferior genre. Rousseau, for instance, remarked about *Julie, ou La nouvelle Héloïse* (1761) that he was ambivalent about the fact that it was, contrary to his *Emile, ou de l'éducation* (1761), a novel.[27]

With the Revolution and the dissolution of the monarchical powers, an absolute freedom of the press was installed. This temporary suspension of literary censorship lasted until 1811, when the Napoleonic Civil Code introduced the Laws against Public Vice. From then on publishers were directly responsible. The result was that the demarcation between legally published and illegally published books became sharper. Publishers and printers had to decide for themselves whether a book would constitute a legal offence, and it seems that this stimulated a form of self-censorship. Even if this did not happen all at once, it ushered in a new moral era. On the one hand judicial and police activity in seizing immoral books did not take place systematically before the late 1820s, at the time of the Restoration. Catalogues of so-called *cabinets de lecture*, private commercial libraries, even point to the continuation of a reading of erotic literature, of both the eighteenth and the early nineteenth centuries. On the other hand fewer new erotic novels were written in this period, and the new generation of authors did not take any pride in writing them.[28]

The assemblage of a body of obscene literature was further implemented by the establishment, in national libraries, of special departments where the forbidden books were kept, the *Enfer* of the Bibliothèque Nationale in Paris and the Private Case of the library of the British Museum. The history of the *Enfer* makes clear how its institution, in the 1840s, has contributed to the construction of pornography. What started out as a mere coding of those books in the library that fell under the new obscenity laws gradually turned into collecting and cataloguing them. By the placing of these collections in closed departments the general public no longer had access to these books.[29]

Another event that contributed to the gradual isolation of the erotic novel was the renewal of novelistic prose by the Romantic movement, which concurred with the tightening of bourgeois morals. The clandestine erotic novel with explicit descriptions of sexual encounters did not partake in this renewal, which concentrated on laying bare the inner life and motives of the protagonists' psyches.

All in all, the separation of positivistic discourse from Romantic fiction, the moral censorship and the stagnation of literary eroticism converged into the isolation of a particular body of writing about sex that came to be known as obscene literature, or pornography. And, while it remained for a long time the privilege of rich male collectors, it started also to mirror the tastes of a larger, less prosperous public. Pornography has retained this artistic form and style to this day. It is stereotypical and repetitive, exactly because it wants only one thing, to create a pornographic effect.

When writing about sex reinserted itself into Romantic discourse, during the *fin-de-siècle* Decadence and early twentieth-century avant-garde, this coincided, as it had a hundred years before, with a new medical discourse: sexology. Just like the sexologists, whose case studies sometimes read like short stories, novelists explored human sexuality, and like the sexologists they found possibilities of experimenting with literary forms in the 'perversions', such as homosexuality, sadism and masochism. The obscenity trials that were the answer to this new experimenting with writing about sex show that the cultural meaning of art had changed. Not unimportantly, one of the books that had been banned for almost a century, *Mademoiselle de Maupin* (1835) by Théophile Gautier, released from censorship in 1922, had contained the first Art for Art's Sake manifesto. Gautier had proclaimed the liberation of the arts from (moral) usefulness for society, therewith disclaiming any responsibility of artists for the effects of their work, and renouncing the old ideal of the work of art as educative and entertaining.

The discussions that ensued with the publication of books such as *Lady Chatterley's Lover* (1928) by D. H. Lawrence, *The Well of Loneliness* (1928) by Radclyffe Hall and especially *Ulysses* (1922) by James Joyce demonstrate that the educated public was gradually accepting the view that art is morally harmless because it produces an aesthetic experience, which is something different from the unmediated sensual experience of pornography. The repudiation of the direct, sensuous experience must be seen in the context of an artistic movement that is generally called *modernity* or *modernism*. This historical transformation of the arts between 1910 and 1940 which covers many different trends designates a shift from the emphasis on content to experiments with form. With this modernist aesthetic we are far removed from the eighteenth-century concept of the sentimental reader, who was on the contrary expected to be moved by what he or she read or saw.[30] The modern conception of art resulted in the desensitisation of the aesthetic experience and therewith confirmed the need for changing moral and legal opinions. Writing about sex again could be considered a creative literary process. To be sure, the legal ban on such books was not lifted until the 1960s, when for the first time unabridged versions of formerly censored works were published, as well as new novels that reintroduced obscene language and dialogues in the vernacular.[31] The 1959 Obscene Publications Act opened the way for such publications in Britain, by stipulating among other rules that the whole work should be taken into account when measuring its alleged obscene effects. This confirmed earlier discussions about the intrinsic artistic value of a work of art. Writing on sex therefore can be said to have been part of the modernist renewal of the novel since the early twentieth century. Nevertheless – and this is crucial for my argument – no matter how explicit the sexual scenes have become, they are in general not regarded as pornographic.

Modern pornography is seen as exempt from artistic value. It had already lost its revitalising artistic forces in the course of the nineteenth century, as I have shown. At the same time, it lost its transgressive or subversive force. In the 1960s there was a short revival of this kind of pornography, when radical critics of society turned to explicit sexual representations to shake society out of its stale, bourgeois mentality. But the counter-cultural deployment of pornography failed, partly because of feminist protests against its sexist imagery and mostly because its disruptive artistic potential was lost. Pornography was relegated to low culture.

Back to the future

In the 1990s there are signs that writing about sex which is sexually stimulating is regaining some artistic vigour. This is due to the emergence of pornography in the self-affirmative discourses of sexual minorities. Especially women, who in the nineteenth and twentieth centuries were denied an active desire for sex, have, in the aftermath of the feminist denunciation of pornography as an oppressive and humiliating genre, started to write their own commercial porn. Gay men and lesbian women have also created their own pornography that caters to the whole spectrum of 'queer' preferences. An important difference between these productions and mainstream commercial pornography is that the former are presented in the context of a different generic category. The blurbs of erotic books for women almost invariably announce their content as female pornography that suits a specific feminine erotic sensibility, in contrast to the male-oriented commercial pornography. Feminist and emancipatory discourses thus contribute to the construction of Western female sexuality of the 1990s as different, both from male sexuality and from other or older notions of female sexuality that exclude the active pursuit of sexual stimulation by women.

Lesbian and gay magazines – although the latter to a somewhat lesser extent – exhibit a heterogeneity of textual genres within each issue. Pornographic stories (as well as visually titillating representations) alternate in lesbian magazines like *On Our Backs* (USA), *Quim* (Britain) and *Madam* (the Netherlands) with serious articles on cultural and political aspects of lesbian existence and lifestyles. Because these magazines are advocated as engaged entertainment for the radical and subversive sexual minorities, they can be considered as incorporating once more the eighteenth-century ideal of the arts as pleasurable instruction or instructive pleasure – or, in modern parlance, as personal and political. There is as yet no saying what influence these minority discourses have on developments in the arts, but there are some signs that avant-garde groups of young artists are experimenting with pornography as well as with images from queer sexual cultures. However, we have to turn to other disciplines, such as fashion, photography, music, dance and multimedia events, to find exhortations to be sexy, kinky and feel it. Novelists still seem to hold on to the established boundary between literature and pornography, instead of trying their hand once more at what would be not just a moral transgression but also the creation of a new hybrid in literature: a form of sexual writing that installs in the reader a sexual response which fucks the mind and the body.

Notes

1 Visual artefacts that are rated as pornographic, and (interactive) porn on the Internet, will not be the primary focus of this chapter.
2 During the military peacekeeping actions in the former Yugoslavia it became known that the Dutch government had sent issues of *Playboy* to the Dutch divisions. One can argue that *Playboy* does not fit the definition of pornography: the fact remains that soldiers' lockers are a good place to look for pornography.

3 In France Fayard published seven volumes of *L'Enfer de la Bibliothèque Nationale* (1984–8) with around thirty texts from the seventeenth and eighteenth centuries; in *Romans Libertins du XVIIIe siècle* (Paris, 1993) eleven novels were republished; Éditions Mille et une nuits published, in 1995 and 1996, two collections with ten texts each; Editions Séguier started a collection of four in 1995, in its series 'Carré Chair'. These are just a few examples of re-editions of the classics.

4 Its full title was *Le Pornographe, ou idées d'un honnête homme sur un projet de règlement pour les prostituées propre à prévenir les malheurs qu'occasionne le publicisme des femmes.*

5 In case this should lead to the conclusion that we are finally experiencing the permissive society when it comes to sex, it should be pointed out that this tolerance applies exclusively to heterosexual pornography, maybe with a touch of 'kinkiness' on the side, but always in a heterosexual context: 90 per cent of all commercially produced pornographic material is heterosexual, the other 10 per cent is divided over ever increasing numbers of sexual 'identities'. Pornography which features children is set aside from all other sorts and has come under severe legal and moral attack.

6 Lynn Hunt, *The Invention of Pornography: Obscenity and the Origins of Modernity, 1500–1800* (New York, Zone Books, 1993), p. 49.

7 Robert Darnton, *Edition et sédition: l'univers de la littérature clandestine au XVIIIe siècle* (Paris, Gallimard, 1991); Robert Darnton, *The Forbidden Bestsellers of Pre-Revolutionary France* (New York, Norton, 1995); Jean-Marie Goulemot, *Ces livres qu'on ne lit que d'une main: lecture et lecteurs de livres pornographiques au XVIIIe siècle* (Aix-en-Provence, Alinea, 1991); Hunt (ed.), *The Invention of Pornography*; Walter Kendrick, *The Secret Museum: Pornography in Modern Culture* (New York, Viking, 1987); Péter Nagy, *Libertinage et révolution* (Paris, Gallimard, 1975); Peter Wagner, *Eros Revived: Erotica of the Enlightenment in England and America* (London, Secker & Warburg, 1988).

8 With the works of the Marquis de Sade as exemplary of the radical subversiveness: see below.

9 Elizabeth L. Eisenstein has analysed the impact and meaning of the foreign enclaves for the cosmopolitan republic of letters, where it was not so much the Frenchness of the inhabitants as their being francophone which gave them a right to citizenship. Elizabeth L. Eisenstein, *Grub Street Abroad: Aspects of the French Cosmopolitan Press from the Age of Louis XIV to the French Revolution* (Oxford, Oxford University Press, 1992).

10 Peter Wagner, in his monumental study of erotica in eighteenth-century England and America, admits: 'I indeed have frequently had to ask myself what was genuinely English in, for example, erotic fiction and art. The answer this book gives is that France dominated in almost every area of erotica.' Wagner, *Eros Revived*, p. 3.

11 Kendrick, *The Secret Museum*, p. 2. Kendrick's observation is occasioned by the definitions in the *Oxford English Dictionary* and sums up his overall argument about the historical construction of pornography. I share his view, on the basis of my own research relating to the *Enfer*, which is the special department for immoral books of the Bibliothèque Nationale in

France, that pornography, in the modern conception of the word, as well as in its concrete forms, is a product of the nineteenth century. I therefore distance myself from the view, purveyed by historian Lynn Hunt in her collection of essays on the history of pornography in modern European culture, that 'Pornography came into existence, both as a literary and visual practice and as a *category of understanding* [italics added], at the same time as – and concomitantly with – the long-term emergence of Western modernity.' In my opinion it is precisely the *lack* of categorical understanding that made 'writing about sex' so interactive with modernity before developments of the nineteenth century concurred to separate a particular form of writing about sex from others. Hunt, *The Invention of Pornography*, pp. 10–11.

12 In England Geoffrey Chaucer wrote the *Canterbury Tales* (1386), which were also inspired by the medieval fables, but retained the verse form.

13 A French translation of the *Decamerone* was published at the end of the fifteenth century.

14 Such as Lucian's *Dialogues of the Courtesans*, Ovid's *Ars Amatoria*, Petronius's *Satyricon*, and the obscene epigrams of Juvenal, Catullus and Martial.

15 I am not going even to begin to try listing examples. For the influence of Aretino on the libertine novel in Western Europe see Carolin Fischer, *Education érotique: Pietro Aretino's Ragionamenti im libertinen Roman Frankreichs* (Stuttgart, M&P, 1994).

16 Pascal Pia, *Les Livres de l'Enfer* (2 vols, Paris, Coulet & Faure, 1978) is a complete alphabetical catalogue of all the books in the *Enfer* of the National Library of France. Pia lists thirty editions under *Ragionamenti* in chronological order.

17 For its English adaptions see Peter Wagner, *Eros Revived*, pp. 220–5. Wagner judges the whore biography to be the precursor of the pornographic novel. The essence of the pornographic novel, however, is sexual stimulation of the reader, which was, according to Wagner himself, not a necessary function (or rather effect) of the whore biography, 'Initially meant as satire and bawdy entertainment'. I see therefore no reason to present the pornographic novel as issuing from the whore biography. It rather seems that one development of the whore biography has been its assimilation to a pornographic literary form. A contemporary example is Xaviera Hollander's *Happy Hooker*.

18 See for an extensive and excellent analysis of the materialist philosophy in these and other pornographic works Margaret C. Jacob, 'The Materialist World of Pornography', in Hunt, *The Invention of Pornography*, pp. 157–202.

19 In fact the Hungarian Nagy would have to be excluded from this generation of scholars, given the date of his book *Libertinage et révolution*, originally written in Hungarian, 1971. The French translation – by Christiane Grémillon – appeared in 1975, from Gallimard. Since his approach to the subject ushers in the later perspective though, he will be included in this group.

20 Nevertheless, in his *Edition et sédition*, pp. 172–3, Darnton lists sixty-four books under the 'genre' pornography, by which he understands books that do not primarily have a political intent.

21 But see note 20.

22 Hunt, *The Invention of Pornography*, p. 302.

23 In her article 'The Politics of Pornography: *L'Ecole des filles*', in Hunt, *The Invention of Pornography*, pp. 109–25, Joan DeJean argues along the same lines. She supposes that the French tradition wants pornography to be both political and French and has chosen *L'Ecole des filles* (1655) as the 'original' French pornographic novel, because its publication can be linked to the 'Fronde', as the mid-seventeenth-century aristocratic movement of revolt against the throne is called.

24 Hunt, *The Invention of Pornography*, p. 302.

25 Dorelies Kraakman, 'Kermis in de Hel: Vrouwen en het pornografisch universum van de "Enfer", 1750–1850', unpublished dissertation, Amsterdam, 1997.

26 At least one text that I know of has done just that, albeit in a very monotone voice: *Le Tartufe libertin, ou le triomphe du vice*, which was published anonymously between 1830 and 1845. It has recently been republished by Séguier (Paris, 1996).

27 See Tjitske Akkerman, *Women's Vices, Public Benefits* (Amsterdam, Het Spinhuis, 1992), pp. 77–8.

28 As a possible result of this scarcity of new titles, the years 1860–80 were golden years for new editions of eighteenth- and nineteenth-century works by publishers in Brussels.

29 For a history of the *Enfer* see Annie Stora-Lamarre, *L'Enfer de la troisième république: censeurs et pornographes (1881–1914)* (Paris, Imago, 1990).

30 See Erich Schön, *Der Verlust der Sinnlichkeit oder die Verwandlungen des Lesers: Mentalitätswandel un 1800* (Stuttgart, Klett-Cotta, 1993) for a cultural analysis of the ways reading changed from an experience that involved bodily sensations to a pure fantasmatic activity. 'Uns Heutigen ist die (seither ja noch fortgeschrittene) Eliminierung des Körpers aus dem Lesen und die Dominanz des >inneren< Erlebens selbstverständlich geworden' ('For us today, the – since then only increased – elimination of the body from the reading practice and the dominance of the "inner" experience has become self-evident'), p. 91. The loss of the direct corporeal effect, from which only children seem to have been preserved, is what Jean-Marie Goulemot, in his study of eighteenth-century erotic literature, nostalgically regrets. Goulemot, *Ces livres*, pp. 154–5.

31 I cannot begin to list works which fall into these categories, but some historical examples from Europe and the United States are the publication of works by de Sade, of *Histoire de l'oeil* (1928), in 1967, by Georges Bataille under his own name, the (unabridged) appearance of *Lady Chatterley's Lover* and Henry Miller's *Tropic of Cancer*, as well as of such classics as *Fanny Hill* and *My Secret Life*. New works include Pauline Réage's *Histoire d'O* (1955; the first edition was immediately seized, the book could not be published legally until 1975), and the works of James Purdy and Hubert Selby. In the Netherlands *Ik, Jan Cremer* and *Turks Fruit* as well as other works by Jan Wolkers and the works of Gerard Reve exemplify the literary movement of the 1960s that coincided with the sexual revolution.

6

National responses to sexual perversions: the case of transvestism

Angus McLaren

In November 1931 Augustine Joseph Hull, a man who dressed in women's clothing and had lived for months as the wife of an unwitting unemployed labourer, was sentenced at the Liverpool Assizes to an eighteen-month prison term for gross indecency. For contemporaries the Hull case was a remarkable story of transvestism. For the historian of sexuality the interest of the trial and its aftermath is that they provide a vantage point from which to view some key aspects of the early twentieth-century public discussion of sex and gender. Why was cross-dressing viewed by some as so alarming? Why were others beginning to discount its import? By examining the responses made to the case by magistrates, medical scientists and sexologists one is provided with an insight into the complexities of transvestism and some sense of how the discussion of sexual 'abnormality' in the interwar period served particular professional interests. In addition, by using the trial to highlight the contrasting ways in which reformers and medical experts in England, Germany and France broached the subject of the male perversions, it is possible to gain some under-standing of the differences in European sexual cultures.

To appreciate fully the ramifications of the Hull case one must start by placing it in context. Beginning with the legal side, the first question to be asked is, what was Hull found guilty of? Much of the public assumed that his crime was cross-dressing since that was the focus of the news reports and headlines. In a later, similar case a London tabloid reported that 'a young man in red dance dress and silver shoes accosted two police officers who were patrolling in a motor car on the Great West Road'. The press let it be understood that the man in question was charged with 'masquerading', when in fact he, like most transvestites, was actually charged with committing a homosexual offence. Such confusions were due to the reluctance of newspapers to discuss homosexuality openly.

Trials involving transvestism were always given more coverage than simple cases of homosexuality, but few readers understood the legal status of cross-dressing. Hull's trial judge described the case as 'exceedingly peculiar' and told the jury that they would have to search long and hard to find a parallel.[1] This was obviously true, though one should not forget that in Western Europe there was a long tradition of cross-dressing for purposes of disguises, masquerades, rituals and theatre.[2] English priests, like shamans elsewhere, customarily wore gowns. In earlier centuries cross-dressing was employed at the Feast of Fools, by mummers and frequently by male protesters in skimmingtons, enclosure protests and large-scale confrontations with the authorities as in the Rebecca riots of the 1840s. In Shakespeare's plays the female roles were first played by men and by the nineteenth century comic drag artists emerged and female impersonators had become a popular staple at naval and military celebrations.[3] Indeed the same newspapers that reported the shocking and puzzling events of the Hull case carried the reviews of the traditional English Christmas pantomimes in which Peter Pan was played by a woman and Cinderella's ugly sisters by men.[4] Dame Edna Everage and Danny La Rue in the late twentieth century would embody, each in his own way, long drag queen traditions. Such socially accepted forms of cross-dressing were legitimated because – by being dramatised, ritualised and controlled – they provided the community with safe entertainment free of sexual involvement or danger.[5]

But cross-dressing had an equally long subversive tradition, particularly when employed by women. People disguised themselves to play roles otherwise forbidden to them. In the religious realm in addition to the acceptable 'manly' female saints there were popular memories of the mythical usurper Pope Joan.[6] The most famous female cross-dresser, Joan of Arc, was burnt as a witch. Most women, however, had practical, 'external' reasons for donning men's garb: the pursuit of employment opportunities. In eighty-three of the ninety-three cases of female transvestism traced in seventeenth- and eighteenth-century Holland the woman had passed as a soldier or sailor.[7] The idea that women would seek male powers by donning male attire made sufficient sense to be usually viewed by the public as presumptuous rather than perverse. Cross-dressing women were sometimes punished, but on occasion the valiant Nancys and Pollys who were discovered serving as soldiers or sailors were feted as heroines.[8] In eighteenth-century popular ballads such masquerades were portrayed as momentarily subverting gender order, a theme which was to resurface in twentieth-century films.[9] In nineteenth-century France and Germany the law forbade women to wear male clothing yet permits could be acquired to circumvent such restrictions.[10] In the Victorian age a number of famous women writers assumed men's names – including George Eliot, George Sand and Daniel Stern – for reasons of professional benefit.[11] Female transvestism among the lower classes declined, it has been suggested, because the new medical inspections of the army and navy made passing more difficult. It may have also been related to clothes becoming less bulky and form-concealing. Cross-dressing presumably permitted the expression of lesbian sexual feelings. Some have advanced the unlikely idea that such feelings were more easily expressed in the nineteenth century and therefore female cross-dressing became less necessary.

In the twentieth century the most notorious female transvestite was 'Colonel Barker' – actually an English woman by the name of Valerie Arkell-Smith – who passed for many years as a retired military officer. Not only did she successfully pass herself off as a blimpish military hero and sometime member of the British Fascist Party, she married an unsuspecting woman whom she abandoned three years later. Only the colonel's bankruptcy in 1929 brought the scandal to light.[12] Radclyffe Hall, author of the classic lesbian novel *The Well of Loneliness* which came out the previous year, was appalled by the revelations of Barker's activities, which Hall believed would set back the movement for homosexual rights. She wrote that she would like to see the colonel drawn and quartered. 'A mad pervert of the most undesirable type, with her mock war medals, wounds, etc.; and then after having married the woman if she doesn't go and desert her! Her exposure at the moment is unfortunate indeed and will give a handle to endless people – the more so as what I long for is some sort of marriage for the invert.'[13] Hall, seeing herself as having a masculine psyche, wore male attire and called herself John. Colonel Barker offended her not for cross-dressing but for only having 'pretended' to be a male.[14] Magnus Hirschfeld, the Weimar sex reformer, described the similar case of a German painter who was charged with adultery. The painter, a determined and intelligent woman, had run away from home at the age of fourteen, passed as a man and finally settled down and 'married'. The painter's wanderlust led to the charge of adultery being pressed against 'him', which in turn led to the wife's discovery that her painter 'husband' was a woman.[15]

Late nineteenth-century observers such as Cesare Lombroso fretted that there were some young women who began to exhibit signs of deviancy in their school years by showing an excessive interest in mathematics and chemistry and ended up by opting for short hair and male clothes. Many more men than women were led into transvestism, he lamented, because males were the more excitable, variable and potentially perverse sex.[16] Women's cross-dressing could be rationalised as a practical matter, but most commentators assumed that cases of male transvestism could not because it made no sense for a man to dress like a woman. Only the mentally unbalanced would embrace a role that offered no practical advantages. Nevertheless cases of male transvestism, regarded by doctors as precipitated by irrational 'inner' drives, were increasingly reported after the 1850s.[17] The few cases of male transvestism that came to light in the nineteenth century were regarded by doctors as morbidly dangerous and necessarily linked to homosexuality. Taylor's *Principles and Practices of Medical Jurisprudence* contained one report of an 'Eliza Edwards' whose unclaimed dead body was sent to Guy's Hospital. Edwards, to the surprise of all, including her personal physician, turned out to be a man. Since the age of fourteen he had played the role of an actress. His male organs were perfect, but, noted the doctors with apparent satisfaction, 'The State of his rectum left no doubt of the abominable practices to which this individual had been addicted'.[18]

Sodomy and soliciting by male prostitutes were associated in the public mind with transvestism but the point that cross-dressing was not in itself a crime was made clear in the most famous nineteenth-century exposé of male transvestites, the trial of Boulton and Park.[19] Ernest Boulton, the twenty-two-year-old son of a stockbroker, and Frederick William Park, son of a Master in the Court of Common Pleas, played women's roles in amateur theatricals and often went about in public in female attire. They were arrested outside the Strand Theatre in April 1870 and charged with intent to commit a felony. The felony in question was buggery. The crown produced as evidence many letters in which Boulton and Park announced their affections for male friends, but failed to provide any evidence of sexual relations. The defence reiterated that in England going about dressed as a member of the opposite sex was not a crime.[20] The judge summed up in the accused's favour and the jury found them not guilty. Nevertheless the popular belief that homosexuality and transvestism were inseparable was captured in a contemporary limerick.

There was an old person of Sark
Who buggered a pig in the dark;
The swine in surprise
Murmured: 'God blast your eyes
Do you take me for Boulton or Park?'[21]

Such suspicions were apparently confirmed by occasional trial accounts of individuals who cross-dressed to entrap homosexual clients. Julius Walters, an Austrian (also known as Klara Myer), was on 13 November 1908 sentenced to five months in jail for 'masquerading as a female'. Walters had been similarly convicted in 1896, 1899, 1900, 1904, 1906 and 1907.[22] Walters was, according to the police, a well-known associate of blackmailers who regularly accosted gentlemen in Bloomsbury. At his 1904 trial the judge castigated him as an incorrigible rogue and sentenced him to twelve months of hard labour and twelve strokes of the cat.[23] Masquerading was not a crime as long as no criminal deception was involved, but by law any disguise could be cited as evidence of an intention to commit a crime.[24] The crime in the case of a man dressed as a woman would usually be soliciting. Transvestites were most likely to be charged with importuning for immoral purposes under section one of the Vagrancy Act of 1898, a law applied exclusively to homosexual men.[25]

Aside from female impersonators and male prostitutes men rarely ever cross-dressed – as women did – to gain employment, but a 1930s case reads remarkably like a cross between the scripts of the American films *Some Like it Hot* and *Tootsie*. A Birmingham male saxophonist, unable to get work in an orchestra as a man, thought he might have better luck if, dressed as a woman, he applied to a 'ladies orchestra'. He accordingly borrowed an outfit from his wife, but before he could audition was arrested and charged under section four of the Vagrancy Act of 1824 with being an 'idle and disorderly person found in female attire at the ——— hotel for an unlawful purpose'. Since he had not committed a larceny he was acquitted. A legal expert observed that the situation would have been different if the position in the orchestra had been obtained. 'Had the Birmingham saxophonist succeeded in getting money for playing in a "ladies orchestra" and done nothing except wear his frock and blow his instrument, he would presumably have been convicted of obtaining his wages or salary by false pretences.'[26] In a similar case an ex-officer who obtained work in the 1930s as a parlour maid was jailed, though not for cross-dressing; having provided a false character, he was convicted under the Servants Character Act of 1792.

At the turn of the century experts found the idea of men dressing as women more and more disturbing. Observers who regarded their over-civilised, increasingly 'feminised' world as unhealthy viewed men manifesting 'feminine tendencies' with unprecedented loathing.[27] Self-doubts rather than confidence fuelled the strident Victorian claims that there existed clear-cut male and female roles. To be male was to be assertive; to be female, passive. 'Inversion' was determined to consist of a reversal of such roles. Therefore the homosexual male, it was believed, would necessarily be effeminate and given to wearing women's clothes; the lesbian would be mannish. The rising concern about the purported threat posed by homosexuality was partly a reaction to changing women's roles. With declining fertility rates and women's demands for access to male educational and professional preserves being read as signs of a repudiation of motherhood, social commentators felt obliged to reassert what sexuality was all about. Doctors in the last decades of the nineteenth century accordingly insisted with unprecedented vigour that healthy individuals should demonstrate their heterosexuality by cleaving to an appropriate gender role. Those who failed were deemed to be sick. Richard von Krafft-Ebing initially fell back on degeneration theory to explain the spread of homosexuality, and most late nineteenth-century commentators agreed that it was a sort of insanity.

Even the first defenders of homosexuality who appeared at the turn of the century felt compelled, given the prestige of biology, to base their arguments on theories of physical and psychic hermaphroditism. Edward Carpenter and Magnus Hirschfeld presented the homosexual as an 'intermediate sex' carrying specific somatic or psychological anomalies. Havelock Ellis also believed inversion had, like colour-blindness, some congenital basis, but was a harmless anomaly. Heterosexuality was, according to Sigmund Freud, something that had to be attained, and in such a context he viewed homosexuality simply as a developmental failure.[28] Freud, in dispensing with organic arguments and in suggesting that the hope of

attaining a full understanding of heterosexuality was just as prob-
lematical as deciphering the causes of homosexuality, presented
himself as a daring path-breaker. In fact researchers such as Max
Dessoir and Albert Moll had already noted that the alert researcher
could observe distinct stages in the development of both normal and
abnormal sexual instincts.[29]

The central thrust of the new sexual analyses of the early
twentieth century was to split sexual aims and objects. Experts
increasingly accepted that there was no necessary link between
appearance and desire, and there existed a multiplicity of roles including the masculine type who was homosexual and the transvestite
who was heterosexual.[30] Though doctors might still describe homosexuality as 'abnormal', they now tended to view it as a medical
rather than a moral problem. Medical hegemony was accepted and
the 'sickness' explanation embraced by many homosexuals including
Oscar Wilde, Sir Roger Casement and Goldsworthy Lowes Dickinson.
Reformers such as Hirschfeld and Ellis in some cases advocated self-
acceptance while doctors trotted out 'cures' that ranged from
hypnotism to aversion therapy.[31]

The discussion of transvestism followed a similar pattern. Why
did male transvestism appear to be on the rise in the late nineteenth
century? Foucault has reminded us that the demand to know one's
'true' sex is a recent phenomenon. Hermaphrodites were for centuries
accepted in the Western world as marvellous beings. By the nineteenth century, biology, law and administration insisted that one was
either male or female. Medicine and the state not only restricted
choices, but, intent on making sure that sex and gender matched, set
about tearing off disguises, detecting errors and enforcing 'legitimate' sexual constitutions. Sex, once a hidden attribute, was in the
twentieth century proclaimed by the experts to be the most profound
aspect of an individual's identity.[32] Ironically the rise of male cross-
dressing was probably precipitated by the unprecedented attention
paid to the importance of knowing one's 'true' sex. The unintended
consequence of experts' insistence on sexual polarity was the driving
of men who felt feminine into wearing women's clothing.

Men generally had access to a wider range of social roles than
women, yet this was not to be the case when it came to cross-
dressing. A woman who dressed as a man was not regarded as particularly threatening; her 'disguise', which could be regarded as
functional or provocative or erotic, did not necessarily undermine

her femininity. Sarah Bernhardt and Marlene Dietrich could be lauded for cross-dressing; any man who dared do the same would have been derided.[33] At worst doctors recoiled from transvestites with disbelief or disgust; at best physicians presented the male transvestite as 'sick'. Yet those who confessed to being made nervous or nauseous by cross-dressing were the self-proclaimed 'normal'. The image of masculinity which emerged from such discussions was that of a surprisingly fragile entity which had to be carefully cosseted and protected.[34]

What were the national differences in the responses made to transvestism? Researchers focused primarily on male transvestism. The classic account of transvestism and the coining of the term was provided by the pioneering German sex reformer Magnus Hirschfeld (1868–1935) in *Die Transvestiten* (1910). In the late nineteenth century his fellow countrymen Carl Westphal and Krafft-Ebing had presented the first scientific descriptions of cross-dressing. The pessimistic Krafft-Ebing viewed it as a stage on the road to insanity. Freud in *Three Essays on the Theory of Sexuality* (1905) gave a partial account of transvestism according to which the urge was located in infancy. The child fixated at a certain stage of development on the mother. Fearing her loss, the child refused to move on.[35] The ever-curious and optimistic Hirschfeld became interested in transvestism when assisting two army men who had been arrested for dressing as women.[36] Cross-dressers, he found, were over-represented in the ranks of the military.

Hirschfeld, a homosexual himself, countered the claims of both pioneering sexologists like Krafft-Ebing and the Freudians like Wilhelm Stekel that transvestism was necessarily linked to homosexuality. Only about 35 per cent of Hirschfeld's male sample were homosexual, as many were heterosexual, 15 per cent were bisexual and the rest were 'auto-monosexual'. Of the fourteen female impersonators Hirschfeld interviewed eight were married and of these five were heterosexual. Transvestism was, according to Hirschfeld, a sexual variation in itself that demanded proper investigation. He viewed the transvestite as a sort of androgyne who in cross-dressing displayed his 'true' personality. Effeminacy did not mean homosexuality. Hirschfeld suggested that male clothing had simply lost much of the individualism and expressiveness that it once possessed. Female clothing offered some males a longed-for form of expression. Their mothers and wives tended to be understanding.[37] 'They are apt', reported Max Hodann, a German sex reformer, 'to be very shy and diffident in their general and social attitude, quite apart from sexual matters. Another complexity in their natures is this: they are by no means always homosexuals.'[38]

Hirschfeld also gave examples of individuals who, like Hull, were almost forced by society into cross-dressing. On the one hand a Polish man who lived in Berlin was constantly stared at when he wore men's clothing. On the other the police arrested a masculine woman on seven different occasions on suspicion of her being a cross-dressed man. Such harassment occurred despite the fact that in Germany, though cross-dressing was technically against the law, the police on occasion actually provided permits to allow the practice.[39] Since we inherit traits from both male and female parents Hirschfeld felt it hardly surprising that the boundaries between the sexes were not as firm as respectable society imagined. Transvestism was for him simply a vivid demonstration that in each individual 'there rests the sex that does not belong to it'.[40] This was a sympathetic though obviously not a full-hearted endorsement of such a persona. Hirschfeld, liberal as he was, harboured the fear that transvestites would produce 'degenerate' offspring.[41]

The first short though sympathetic account of cross-dressing in English was written by Edward Carpenter, while in the process of defending homosexuals as normal and healthy.[42] In 'Intermediate Types Among Primitive Folk', which first appeared in the *American Journal of Religious Psychology* in July 1911, Carpenter drew on anthropological accounts of priests and witches adopting the clothing of the opposite sex. He went on to note that the 'enormous delight' that many people experienced through cross-dressing was due to more than either religious inspiration or homosexuality. 'It must also not be overlooked, in dealing with this complex and difficult subject, that the mere fact of a person delighting to adopt the garb of the opposite sex does not in itself prove that his or her love-tendency is abnormal – i.e. cross-dressing does not *prove* homosexuality.'[43]

Havelock Ellis, the British sexologist who devoted his life to the collecting and classifying of variants of sexual behaviour, got around to dealing with transvestism only in the late 1920s.[44] Ellis, like others, began by assuming that transvestism was an annexe of homosexuality; he concluded that it was not necessarily an aspect of sexual inversion nor a fetish or replacement of the sexual object. Though he noted that Hirschfeld was of the same opinion, Ellis went on to critique the German's stress on the significance of the subject's dress or, as Hirschfeld called it, his 'disguise'. Clothing was only part of the syndrome, argued Ellis, and the term 'disguise' was hardly appropriate because it was only when wearing the attire of the opposite sex that the subject really felt *not* disguised. As an example Ellis provided, among his many first-person accounts, that of 'R. L.' who poignantly described the unpleasant sensations of returning to male attire. 'I slipped out into a world that was particularly distasteful to me, my collar choked me, my trousers oppressed me like bandages, my boots felt clumsy, and I missed the clasp of corsets, and the beautiful feel of underwear.'[45] Ellis did not like either the terms cross-dressing or transvestism, both of which he felt paid too much attention to external trappings. In their place Ellis preferred to use the term 'Eonism' after the remarkable eighteenth-century French diplomat the Chevalier d'Eon, an intellectually gifted man who though not an invert desired to wear women's clothing.[46]

Ellis devoted the long opening chapter of the seventh and final volume of *Studies in the Psychology of Sex* to a discussion of 'Eonism'. All perversions were, for Ellis, simple distortions of healthy feelings. Sadism, for example, he viewed as an exaggeration of the enjoyment of the element of pain inherent in the sexual act. Transvestism he similarly presented as due to an exaggerated identification of the young male with his first object of attraction – his mother. Ellis, in seeking to win the public's understanding for the transvestite, shrewdly made the mother – England's icon of respectability – central to his explanation. The subject was presented as motivated not by some base instinct but by an inflated sympathy for and identification with his mother, whom he in effect was 'courting'. 'It is normal for a man to identify himself with the women he loves. The eonist carries that identification too far, stimulated by a sensitive and feminine element in himself which is associated with a rather defective virile sexuality on what may be a neurotic basis.'[47] Ellis noted that the Freudians also viewed cross-dressing as an aspect of the 'persistence of infantile traits'. Wilhelm Stekel in particular attacked Hirschfeld's notion that there was any biological basis to the syndrome. But Ellis observed that the blanket claim of the Freudians that all transvestites – even the heterosexual – were latent homosexuals was not very helpful.[48]

In addition to childhood experiences Ellis believed that hormonal influences, or what he called 'secretions', were important. Cross-dressing's basis could be due to both acquired and innate causes. The transvestite might have an 'erotic empathy' for members of his own sex, but that was not the same as a homosexual passion. Indeed Ellis pointed out that some transvestites found homosexuality as distasteful as any other aspect of masculinity.[49] Although Ellis regarded the syndrome as shaded by tones of masochism and autoeroticism, he found his subjects to be usually highly moral individuals who identified with others. 'It [transvestism] tends to occur among people who are often educated, refined, sensitive and reserved.'[50] They were, he claimed, of 'high character and distinguished ability and normal in other respects'.[51]

Given the fact that the Chevalier d'Eon was Europe's most famous cross-dresser, it comes as somewhat of a surprise to discover that the French paid so little serious attention to transvestism.[52] In interwar Germany men were supposedly on the lookout for sissified weaklings. In America males were reported to be afraid that if they appeared too 'sophisticated' it could reflect adversely on their manhood. In Britain, as Quentin Crisp recalled, 'The men of the twenties searched themselves for vestiges of effeminacy as though for lice.'[53] But the French appear to have failed to take transvestism seriously. Why? Because no citizen of the hexagon quailed at the thought of being too sophisticated? Because the absence of a law criminalising homosexuality between consenting adults defused the issue of cross-dressing? Because the French were just not very good at theorising?

Esquirol made the first psychiatric observations in France of cross-dressing, Binet traced its psychological basis and Magnan looked for its anatomical causes, but, as Dr Agnes Masson made clear in *Le Travestissement: Essai de psycho-pathologie sexuelle* (1935), which provided an overview of the subject from the time of Henri II and the abbé de Choisy to current hormonal theories, the French had little new to contribute to the twentieth-century discussion of the syndrome.[54] The same impression is garnered by a recent spate of works on the subject. Gary Kates in his work on d'Eon presents Havelock Ellis, rather than any French expert, being responsible for 'medicalising' the problem of transvestism. Jann Matlock asserts that the French middle class in the last decades of the nineteenth century – frightened by feminism, declining fertility and rising rates of syphilis and homosexuality – were fixated on the threat posed by cross-dressing. But upon investigation one finds that the French psychiatrists she cites who raised such alarms relied largely upon German cases supplied by Westphal, Moll and Krafft-Ebing. If the French were as worried about cross-dressing as Matlock claims, one wonders why they did not produce their own case studies.

Lenard Berlanstein, in his careful chronicling of the rise and fall of transvestism in the French theatre, reminds us that in fact female cross-dressing enjoyed an enormous popularity in the first part of the nineteenth century.[55] He notes that from the 1880s onwards fears and anxieties concerning sexuality began to undermine the acceptance of such theatrical practices. At the same time he points out that French bohemian circles offered gender ambiguity a tolerance that it found nowhere else in Europe.[56] One accordingly wonders how he can then proceed to assert that France experienced higher 'levels of gender panic' than were experienced in Britain and the United States.

Making cultural comparisons is a task obviously fraught with difficulties, but on the level of public discourse at least it is obvious that the issue of transvestism − like most of the other 'perversions' − was in the early twentieth century less subject to scientific investigation in France than in England and Germany. There were, moreover, in England and Germany public movements supporting sex reform. The Hull case, with which we began this chapter, was discussed at the British Sexological Society on 15 December 1931 and again on 5 January 1932.[57] The public pressure that the Society succeeded in exerting did have some effect. In April Hull was transferred to Wormwood Scrubs and arrangements made for him to attend the Tavistock Clinic for treatment.[58] In Germany Hirschfeld's organisation was equally active in seeking to temper the rigours of the courts.

The French in the interwar period were much less prone to engage in such organisations. Pierre Vachet's account of 'Pierrette', whose life could be usefully compared to Hull's, did not conclude with any call for legal reform.[59] Francophiles might attribute the failure of the French to have much new to say about the perversions to their liberalism, their laissez-faire attitudes towards sexual practices, their sexual sophistication. Such an interpretation could be countered as too charitable given the fact that a publication like *Le Problème sexuel* (1933), which sought to popularise new sexological insights, had to rely heavily on non-French contributors like Norman Haire, Havelock Ellis, Magnus Hirschfeld, Max Hodann and Helene Stöcker. The more pessimistic might argue, as Robert Nye has done, that French sexology was simply tardy; failing to shift its focus as readily as its German or British counterparts from the biological to the psychological underpinnings of deviancy. The French continued at the turn of the century to overlook psychological motivation and search for the stigmata of the pervert. But one might argue that sexology had little impact because the French – longer wedded to Lamarckian models of evolution – were not biological enough; they denied the innateness of the perversions. The Germans and English, in order to defend homosexuals, asserted people were born with particular penchants. Accordingly therapy was likely to have little success, and therefore society had to be tolerant. In France there was no law against adult homosexual practices and so no reforming movements were created.

Such speculations hold out the danger of privileging theory. Overshadowing all discussions of sexuality in France was the fear of depopulation and the 1920 law that outlawed discussions of contraception and abortion. Interwar French sex reform activists like Madeleine Pelletier and Eugène Humbert ended their lives in prison. At the meetings of the World League for Sexual Reform the French had to be represented by the obscure but evocatively named non-entity Madame Stella Croissant.[60] In such a hostile atmosphere it was hardly surprising that French sexology was so cautious. A reading of the *Bulletin de la Société de Sexologie* reveals that its leading experts, like Dr Edouard Toulouse, sought to win public respectability by stressing the need for discipline and direction. Whereas the British Society for the Study of Sex Psychology could publish tracts on sexual variability and the erotic rights of women by activists like Stella Browne and Laurence Housman, the French society focused on eugenics, sterilisation of the feeble-minded, overpopulation and prostitution.

It is important to remember, however, that in the last third of the nineteenth century French researchers such as Binet, Ball, Moreau, Lacassagne, Magnan, Legludic, Raffalovich, Féré and Chevalier could claim that French sexology was as advanced as its German counterpart. Moreover, in the decade prior to the First World War some of the most radical discussions of sexuality in Europe took place in France. The French neo-Malthusian anarchists used the issue of the workers' right to contraception as the basis for cultural resistance to the state. They moved on from birth control to issues such as venereal disease and tuberculosis. Via popular education they egged on their audience to reclaim the body. They particularly addressed women, providing alternative images to those of motherhood.[61] This pioneering movement was effectively silenced by the laws of 1920 and 1923, and subsequent discussions of sexuality, to avoid legal entanglements, had to be carefully tailored.

It is obviously more difficult to determine how sexual practices varied from culture to culture than how specific theorists differed. Even asking why French sexology in the twentieth century appeared to be less innovative than its German and British counterparts reminds one of the pitfalls of the old debates about the causes of French industrial 'backwardness'. If one assumes to know in advance which European cultures were in matters of sexuality 'advanced' and which were the 'laggards' one runs the danger of missing the essential details of each nation's experience. National comparisons can often be enlightening but a review of the early twentieth-century discussion of transvestism serves as a particularly apt example of the futility of seeking to impose a normative standard on either individuals or cultures.

Notes

1 *Glasgow Herald*, 16 November 1931, p. 13.
2 On evidence that many boys use Hallowe'en parties to experiment with cross-dressing see John T. Talamini, *Boys Will Be Girls: The Hidden World of the Heterosexual Male Transvestite* (Scranton, PA, University of Scranton Press, 1982), p. 20; Peter Ackroyd, *Dressing Up: Transvestism and Drag, The History of an Obsession* (London, Thames & Hudson, 1979).
3 On the popularity of female impersonators at American naval bases in the early twentieth century see George Chauncey Jr, 'Christian Brotherhood or Sexual Perversion: Homosexual Identities and the Construction of Sexual Boundaries in the World War One Era', *Journal of Social History*, 19 (1985), pp. 191, 207 n. 14.
4 On how cross-dressing allowed respectable male theatre spectators to relax and with good conscience ogle the 'principal boy's' legs or insult the horrid, old 'dame' see Jane W. Stedman, 'From Dame to Woman: W. S. Gilbert and Theatrical Transvestism', in Martha Vicinus (ed.), *Suffer and Be Still: Women in the Victorian Era* (Bloomington, IN, Indiana University Press, 1972), pp. 20–37.
5 Sharon R. Ullman, '"The Twentieth-century Way": Female Impersonation and Sexual Practices in Turn of the Century America', *Journal of the History of Sexuality*, 5 (1995), pp. 573–600.
6 On the myth that to avoid electing a woman the cardinals inspect the papal candidate and must ritually declare 'Habet duos testiculos et bene pendentes' – he has two testicles, well hung – see Alain Boureau, *La Papesse Jeanne* (Paris, Aubier, 1988), p. 16.
7 Rudolph M. Dekker and Lotte C. van de Pol, *The Tradition of Female Transvestism in Early Modern Europe* (New York, St Martin's Press, 1989).

8 Randolph Trumbach, 'London's Sapphists: From Three Sexes to Four Genders in the Making of Modern Culture', in Julia Epstein and Kristina Straub (eds), *Body Guards: The Cultural Politics of Gender Ambiguity* (New York, Routledge & Kegan Paul, 1991), pp. 122–3; Diane Dugaw, *Warrior Women and Popular Balladry, 1650–1850* (Cambridge, Cambridge University Press, 1989); George S. Rousseau and Roy Porter (eds), *Sexual Underworlds of the Enlightenment* (Manchester, Manchester University Press, 1987).

9 Reinhold Schunze's play *Viktor und Viktoria* became the film *First a Girl* (1935) directed by Victor Saville and later *Victor Victoria* (1982) directed by Blake Edwards. See Patricia Petro, *Joyless Streets: Women and Melodramatic Representation in Weimar Germany* (Princeton, Princeton University Press, 1989), pp. 153–5.

10 We know that in France the painter Rosa Bonheur and Napoleon III's mistress Marguerite Bellanger took advantage of such provisions, but it must have been a question of restricting bourgeois clothing since observers such as A. J. Munby noted that many working-class women in the mining and fishing industries necessarily dressed much like workmen; on the law of 16 brumaire year IX forbidding women to wear trousers or culottes without a medical certificate see Anon., *Code de la femme* (Paris, Editions et Librairies, n.d.), pp. 30–1; Jann Matlock, 'Masquerading Women, Pathological Men: Cross-dressing, Fetishism and the Theory of Perversion, 1882, 1935', in Emily Apter and William Pietz (eds), *Fetishism as Cultural Discourse* (Ithaca, Cornell University Press, 1993), pp. 31–61. On Germany, see Emil Gutheil, 'Analysis of a Case of Transvestism', in Wilhelm Stekel (ed.), *Sexual Aberrations: The Phenomena of Fetishism in Relation to Sex* (New York, Liveright, 1930), pp. 281–318.

11 Susan Gubar, 'Blessing in Disguise: Cross-dressing for Female Modernists', *Massachusetts Review*, 22 (1981), pp. 477–508; Sandra M. Gilbert, 'Costumes of the Mind: Transvestism as Metaphor in Modern Literature', *Critical Inquiry*, 7 (1980), p. 394.

12 The trial reports filled the columns of *The Times* during March and April of 1929. For the argument that the masquerade was employed so that both women could deny their lesbianism, see Vern L. Bullough and Bonnie Bullough, *Cross Dressing, Sex, and Gender* (Philadelphia, University of Pennsylvania Press, 1993), pp. 162–4.

13 Michael Baker, *Our Three Selves: The Life of Radclyffe Hall* (London, Hamish Hamilton, 1985), p. 254.

14 Hall's *The Well of Loneliness*, which seriously defended homosexuality, was seized by the police whereas Virginia Woolf's *Orlando* (1928), which played with ideas of transvestism and transsexualism, was a publishing triumph. 'Different though the sexes are,' wrote Woolf, 'they intermix. In every human being a vacillation from one sex to the other takes place, and often it is only clothes that keep the male and female likeness, while underneath the sex is the very opposite of what is above.' Quentin Bell, *Virginia Woolf: A Biography* (London, Hogarth Press, 1973), pp. 138–9.

15 Magnus Hirschfeld, *Transvestites: The Erotic Desire to Cross Dress*, trans. Michael A. Lombardi-Nash (Buffalo, Prometheus Books, 1991), pp. 95–100.

16 Cesare Lombroso and G. Ferrero, *La Femme criminelle et la prostituée* (Paris, Alcan, 1896), pp. 419–24.

17 On male transvestism in early modern Europe, see Guido Ruggiero, *The Boundaries of Eros: Sex Crime and Sexuality in Renaissance Venice* (New York, Oxford University Press, 1985), p. 136; Alan Bray, *Homosexuality in Renaissance England* (London, Gay Men's Press, 1982), pp. 86–9.

18 A. S. Taylor, *The Principles and Practices of Medical Jurisprudence* (London, Churchill, 1894), vol. 2, pp. 289, 470.

19 Jeffrey Weeks, *Sex, Politics and Society: The Regulation of Morality since 1800* (New York, Longman, 1981), p. 101; Michael Harris, 'Social Diseases? Crime and Medicine in the Victorian Press', in W. F. Bynum, Stephen Lock and Roy Porter (eds), *Medical Journals and Medical Knowledge: Historical Essays* (London, Routledge, 1992), pp. 108–25.

20 William Roughead, *Bad Companions* (Edinburgh, W. Green, 1930), pp. 149–83; and see also the *Times* reports for 1870 and 1871.

21 H. Montgomery Hyde, *The Other Love* (London, Heinemann, 1970), p. 94.

22 Hirschfeld, *Transvestites*, p. 275.

23 *The Times*, 13 April 1904, p. 3; and for a similar case see also *Illustrated Police News*, 18 December 1924, p. 3.

24 W. Norwood East, *Society and the Criminal* (Springfield, IL, Thomas, 1949), pp. 165–6.

25 Weeks, *Sex, Politics and Society*, p. 102. On drag and transvestism in the United States, see George Chauncey, *Gay New York: Gender, Urban Culture and the Making of the Gay Male World, 1890–1940* (New York, Basic Books, 1994).

26 Anon., 'Masquerading', *Justice of the Peace and Local Government Review*, 26 February 1938, p. 135.

27 E. Anthony Rotundo, *American Manhood: Transformations in Masculinity from the Revolution to the Modern Era* (New York, Basic, 1993), pp. 273–7; Sandra M. Gilbert and Susan Gubar, *No Man's Land: The Place of the Woman Writer in the Twentieth Century: Sexchanges* (New Haven, Yale University Press, 1989), vol. 2, pp. 324–76.

28 Sigmund Freud, *Three Essays on the Theory of Sexuality* (1905), in *The Standard Edition of the Complete Works of Sigmund Freud*, trans. James Strachey (London, Hogarth Press, 1953), vol. 7, pp. 136–8.

29 Frank J. Sulloway, *Freud: Biologist of the Mind: Beyond the Psychoanalytic Legend* (New York, Basic Books, 1979), pp. 298–305.

30 George Chauncy Jr, 'From Sexual Inversion to Homosexuality: Medicine and the Changing Conceptualization of Female Deviance', *Salmagundi*, 58–9 (1982–83), pp. 120–30.

31 Weeks, *Sex, Politics and Society*, p. 105.

32 Michel Foucault, *Herculine Barbin: Being the Recently Discovered Memoirs of a Nineteenth-century Female Hermaphrodite*, trans. Richard McDougall (New York, Pantheon, 1931), p. 4.

33 The adoption of androgynous fashion styles by several generations of twentieth-century heterosexual women who wished to appear mysteriously seductive deserves examination. See Martha Vicinus, 'Turn-of-the-century Male Impersonators: Rewriting the Romance Plot', in Andrew

H. Miller and James Eli Adams (eds), *Sexualities in Victorian Britain* (Bloomington, IN, Indiana University Press, 1996), pp. 187–213.

34 Marjorie Garber, *Vested Interests: Cross-dressing and Cultural Anxiety* (London, Routledge, 1992); Judith Butler, *Gender Trouble* (New York, Routledge, 1990).

35 Freud, *Three Essays*, p. 56.

36 During the First World War call-up, reported Hirschfeld, there were several cases of men showing up in dresses at German recruiting offices. Magnus Hirschfeld, *Sexual Anomalies and Perversions*, ed. Norman Haire (London, Encyclopaedic Press, 1952), p. 198.

37 A 1960s study based on the Kinsey Institute files concluded that transvestites suffered at an early age from distorted and confused notions of gender, but noted that such findings were drawn from a self-selected sample of sex offenders who ended up in jail. Little was known of the far larger number of 'masqueraders' who avoided brushes with the law. Paul H. Gebhard, John H. Gagnon, Wardell B. Pomeroy and Cornelia V. Christenson, *Sex Offenders: An Analysis of Types* (New York, Harper & Row, 1965), pp. 410–11.

38 Max Hodann, *A History of Modern Morals*, trans. Stella Browne (London, Heinemann, 1937), p. 48.

39 Hirschfeld, *Transvestites*, pp. 267–73.

40 *Ibid.*, p. 231.

41 Charlotte Wolff, *Magnus Hirschfeld: A Portrait of a Pioneer in Sexology* (London, Quartet, 1986), pp. 107–9.

42 Chushichi Tsuzuki, *Edward Carpenter, 1844–1929: Prophet of Human Fellowship* (Cambridge, Cambridge University Press, 1980), pp. 131–4, 145–51.

43 Edward Carpenter, 'Intermediate Types among Primitive Folk', *Selected Writings, Volume 1: Sex* (London, GMP, 1984), p. 263; and on the Berdache see Walter L. Williams, *The Spirit and the Flesh: Sexual Diversity in American Indian Culture* (Boston, Beacon Press, 1986).

44 See Vincent Brome, *Havelock Ellis: Philosopher of Sex: A Biography* (London, Routledge & Kegan Paul, 1979); Phyllis Grosskurth, *Havelock Ellis: A Biography* (London, Allen Lane, 1980).

45 Havelock Ellis, 'Eonism', *Studies in the Psychology of Sex* (Philadelphia, F. A. Davis, 1928), vol. 7, p. 87. For the similar argument that some women feel at ease only in male clothes and regard themselves as 'transvestites' when forced to wear dresses, see Holly Devor, *Gender Blending: Confronting the Limits of Duality* (Bloomington, IN, Indiana University Press, 1988), p. 129.

46 A further sign of the growing interest in the subject was the appearance of M. Coryn's *The Chevalier d'Eon* (1932), hailed as a 'skilful biography of a pathological specimen' in *Week-end Review*, 20 August 1932, p. 216.

47 Ellis quoted in Hodann, *History of Modern Morals*, p. 49.

48 Ellis, 'Eonism', p. 102.

49 For a similar claim that 'true' transvestites were not homosexual, see East, *Society and the Criminal*.

50 Ellis, 'Eonism', p. 29.

51 Havelock Ellis, *Views and Reviews: A Selection of Uncollected Articles, 1884–1932* (London, Harmsworth, 1934), vol. 2, p. 219.

52 Gary Kates, *Monsieur d'Eon is a Woman: A Tale of Political Intrigue and Sexual Masquerade* (New York, Basic Books, 1995).

53 Quentin Crisp, *The Naked Civil Servant* (New York, New American Library, 1983), p. 21.

54 Dr Agnes Masson, *Le Travestissement: essai de psycho-pathologie sexuelle* (Paris, Editions Hippocrate, 1935); and see also H. Legludic, *Notes et observations de médecine légale: attentats aux moeurs* (Paris, Masson, 1896), pp. 169–73; Eugene Wilhelm, 'Publications allemandes sur les questions sexuelles', *Archives de l'Anthropologie Criminelle*, 27 (1912), pp. 301–9.

55 Lenard Berlanstein, 'Breeches and Breaches: Cross-dress Theater and the Culture of Ambiguity in Modern France', *Comparative Studies in Society and History*, 38 (1996), pp. 338–69.

56 For a 1899 story of a bohemian who falls in love with a grisette who turns out to be a baker's boy see Michael Wilson, '"Sans les femmes, qu'est-ce qui nous resterait": Gender and Transgression in Bohemian Montmartre', in Staub and Epstein, *Body Guards*, pp. 195–222.

57 *Week-end Review*, 19 December 1931, p. 787; 2 January 1932, p. 10; and on the make-up of the Society, which went under a variety of names, see Lesley Hall, '"Disinterested Enthusiasm for Sexual Misconduct": The British Society for the Study of Sex Psychology, 1913–1947', *Journal of Contemporary History*, 30 (1995), pp. 665–86.

58 For the journal's expression of its appreciation for Sir Herbert Samuel 'in mitigating by sympathy and science the rigours of the system which he finds himself responsible for administering', see *Week-end Review*, 16 April 1932, p. 475.

59 Pierre Vachet, *La Psychologie du vice: I. Les Travestis* (Paris, Editions Grasset, 1934).

60 World League for Sexual Reform, *Sexual Reform Congress* (Copenhagen, Levin & Munksgaard, 1929), p. 22.

61 Elinor A. Accampo, 'The Rhetoric of Reproduction and the Reconfiguration of Womanhood in the French Birth Control Movement, 1890–1920', *Journal of Family History*, 21 (1996), pp. 351–71.

7

Keeping their fingers on the pulse: lesbian doctors in Britain, 1890–1950

Emily Hamer

Unlike the mass of women who had female partners during the period 1890–1950, there *is* information about a fascinating group of pioneering women doctors in Britain: there are biographies and auto-biographies, appearances in contemporary reminiscences and surveys of successful women, obituaries and entries in the *Dictionary of National Biography* and *Who's Who*. These particular women – Louisa Martin-dale, Louisa Aldrich Blake, Flora Murray, Octavia Wilberforce and their partners – formed a relatively cohesive group united by their common profession of medicine and by geographical location, social class, and strong ties of friendship and respect.[1] However, while there is a relative profusion of material charting their lives, its emphasis is on their professional, rather than their personal, lives. It is these women's careers as doctors, the hospitals in which they worked, the practices they built up, the research articles that they wrote, in essence the contri-bution that they made to medicine, that is the locus of interest.

Even autobiographies and biographies tend to be impersonal. For professional women of this period auto/biographical writing was a far more formal affair than it is today. Its aim was to justify and legitimate the nonconformist lives lived by its subjects, and to encourage other women to follow them into the male world of well-paid and interesting work. As Mary Scharlieb, another early and much-lauded woman doctor, noted in her autobiography published in 1924, 'I have not written my story for my own sake, not even for the joy it has brought me ... my objective is to convince medical women that a successful, happy, and useful career can be and ought to be the guerdon of their toil.'[2]

Thus, while the lives of successful women in the first decades of the twentieth century are documented, the intimate detail of these lives has to be teased from a dry and earnest formal record. This is true of women who had conventional private lives as well as those who did not. While Mary Scharlieb mentions her marriage, children and the death of her husband, in total these references add up to scarcely more than two pages. Women who were not married, and therefore did not have easy public terms of reference with which to frame their private lives, often provided even less clear-cut detail about their personal lives.

However, perhaps surprisingly for modern readers, lesbians in the first decades of the twentieth century did not simply conceal or deny the reality of their affections. Today the pre-1950s history of lesbianism in Britain is read through the trial of *The Well of Loneliness* in 1928 and through the life of its author, Radclyffe Hall. While Radclyffe Hall remains perhaps England's best-known lesbian, she actually lived a life which was enmeshed within a large and close-knit lesbian community. Hall's subsequent elevation to the personification of British lesbianism would have horrified and infuriated almost all her lesbian peers, friends and enemies alike. For after all she was just one lesbian amongst many, and moreover unusually rich, leisured and flamboyant.

Historians of early twentieth-century British lesbianism have tended to treat Radclyffe Hall's public persona and her novel of lesbian despair and frustration as a simple reflection of the broad reality of lesbian life in the period between 1890 and 1950. However, the political agenda behind *The Well of Loneliness* is complex: Hall wanted to show how lesbians needed and deserved greater public tolerance and compassion. In this context the lesbians she wrote about had to have their lives blighted by social antipathy to homosexuality. As I will show, Hall's actual lesbian contemporaries were neither uniformly oppressed by psycho-sexual analyses of their inversion nor impelled towards suicide or lives of dejection and self-loathing.[3]

The reality of British lesbianism

It is a necessary antidote to the cult of Radclyffe Hall as the British lesbian made flesh to examine the lives of other British lesbians in this period. The experience of British lesbians has differed from that of other European lesbians for a multitude of reasons. Culturally there has been a divide between women's experience in Mediterranean Catholic counties and Protestant Anglo-Saxon countries.[4] In Britain,

Germany and the Scandinavian countries women's access to higher education and the suffrage, divorce and professional careers that was achieved by the late 1920s led to *de facto* change in how a significant minority of women were able to live their lives. For women in other European countries formal rights did not translate into a cultural acceptance of women actually exercising those rights; women in Portugal gained the suffrage in 1911 but this did not produce a significant mass of professionally active independent women.

Again it was in Germany and Britain that psychoanalysis and sexology were established as legitimate areas of study and where a new discourse around sex, gender and desire was developed which sought to be neutrally scientific not morally coercive. Although Paris had some importance as a centre for psychoanalysis and sexology, it lacked the economic and political framework which had liberated women in Britain and Germany. The famous lesbians of Sapphic Paris were largely expatriate British and American women; indigenous French lesbian life, with the exception of that of prostitutes and the aristocracy, remains veiled even to this day.[5]

Homosexuals in Germany were campaigning politically from the turn of the century for more acceptance and the repeal of oppressive legislation. This campaigning was not mirrored in Britain for two important reasons: the trial and imprisonment of Oscar Wilde for sodomy in 1895 had terrified a generation of previously rather flagrant gay men into silence, and British lesbians historically had suffered no legal oppression. While in Germany lesbianism was explicitly proscribed and women could be prosecuted for wearing men's clothing, in Britain lesbians faced no legalised repression.

Education, political activism, professional opportunities, cultural liberalism and a non-interfering church and state provided a space for British lesbians in the period between 1890 and 1930 to build their own lives. The late 1920s probably marked the high point for British lesbians and lesbianism before the new possibilities produced by the gay liberation and women's liberation movements of the 1970s. For in those years a number of classic lesbian novels were published: Elizabeth Bowen's *The Hotel*, Rosamund Lehmann's *Dusty Answer* and Virginia Woolf's *Orlando*, as well of course as *The Well of Loneliness*. The trial and banning of *The Well of Loneliness* marked the end of the British indifference to lesbianism, but for the generation which had grown up and come out before this watershed the new disapproval just came too late.

In this chapter I will examine the very different autobiographical legacies of Louisa Martindale, Flora Murray, Louisa Aldrich Blake and Octavia Wilberforce, all women with well-established lives before 1928. None of these women appears to have ever had a male lover or to have had any interest in acquiring one. Instead they loved other women, and it is how this love was articulated both privately and publicly that I want to explore here. None of these women was a public lesbian in the mould of Radclyffe Hall yet neither has their love for women been expunged from the record.

Louisa Martindale

The most straightforward description of this love is illustrated by Louisa Martindale (1873–1966) in her autobiography, *A Woman Surgeon*, published in 1951. Louisa Martindale met the Hon. Ismay Fitzgerald, daughter of Lord Fitzgerald of Kilmarnock, at a dinner party in 1910. Louisa sums up their relationship briefly but concisely: 'She was, I thought, very unusual looking and beautiful ... I invited her to come to me for a fortnight, with the result that she stayed thirty-five years.'[6] While *A Woman Surgeon* was first and foremost a professional autobiography, Louisa Martindale highlighted Ismay's place in her life by devoting an entire chapter of it to Ismay. This chapter is hard to miss – it is called 'Ismay Fitzgerald'.

Ismay died in 1945 and Louisa was devastated, for it was with Ismay that she had found her 'full share of love and friendship'.[7] This may not provide us with intimate details of their relationship but it is a clear and unequivocal statement by Louisa Martindale that it was Ismay, a woman, who fulfilled her; a beautiful woman with whom she made a home and shared not just friendship but also, and primarily, love. This kind of autobiographical directness is uncommon for women who spent their lives loving other women in this period, even more so in a book published in the conformist and heterosexualist 1950s.

But then Louisa Martindale was an unusual woman. She came from a family of tough, eccentric, successful feminists who had little interest in men. Her mother, Louisa senior, was an intimate friend of Minnie Benson (widely identified as a lesbian), and her sister Hilda was a high-flying civil servant who never married. Louisa Martindale made no attempt to dissemble or gloss her life and her loves for public consumption. Her nonconformism did not apparently result in professional difficulties: she became a Companion of the Order of the British Empire in 1931 and a Fellow of the Royal College of Obstetricians and Gynaecologists in 1933, and she was also President of the Medical Women's International Association.

Martindale was knowledgeable about sex both as a mechanical procreative coupling and as an orgasmic source of pleasure; she notes in her autobiography that she took great pleasure in explaining to young couples how to have more enjoyable sex lives. Freud was known to her social circle, and there was no possibility that Louisa did not 'know' about lesbianism. Louisa Martindale did not write so openly about her love for Ismay out of naivety about how it might be read; she wrote about it because it was a source of pride and joy to her, and as she approached eighty she did not care what people might think about their relationship.

Louisa Aldrich Blake

Louisa Martindale was no doubt supported by the fact that, in the social and professional circles in which she moved, love such as she and Ismay had shared was common. One of Louisa's friends was Louisa Aldrich Blake (1865–1925); the two Louisas had shared lodgings when they were both studying at the London (Royal Free Hospital) School of Medicine for Women in the 1890s. Both women were to become successful surgeons and they were to remain friends and colleagues; in 1919, for instance, they spent six weeks travelling around America together lecturing and visiting hospitals. Louisa Aldrich Blake was a family friend, for Ismay knew and trusted her enough to choose her as her surgeon.

Louisa Aldrich Blake's biography was written by Lord Riddell just after her death, and it was a paean to a great surgeon. Aldrich Blake had won numerous prizes at medical school, graduated with first class honours and in 1895 became the first woman in England to qualify as a master in surgery. She was one of England's premier woman surgeons and she was to win establishment accolades; Louisa Aldrich Blake was elected a Fellow of the Royal Society of Medicine in 1910 and created a Dame in 1925.[8] It is this medical success story that Riddell focuses on and his biography is a discreet and dry book.

Riddell knew Louisa Aldrich Blake but, as he states, he was not a close friend, and this is a biography where personal detail takes up little space. That said, certain interesting facts do emerge. Riddell notes that at the age of sixteen Louisa 'struck school-mates as above all things "manly"' and that by her early twenties this was confirmed; 'intimates called her "Harry" and were proud of her gentlemanly appearance'.[9] It was not just a gentlemanly appearance, for she was a proficient cricketer and boxer, and was to become an enthusiastic motorist and mechanic.

Lord Riddell writes of Aldrich Blake that 'so far as I can discover she never had a love affair. I once asked her why she never married. She laughed and was about to reply. Unhappily someone came into the room and interrupted the conversation.'[10] It is tempting to see Aldrich Blake's laughter as amusement at Riddell's naivety, and this does seem plausible. Riddell obviously feels that the apparent lack of love in her life is problematic, for he insists in the next paragraph that Louisa Aldrich Blake 'never aped the man, and never wished to be regarded as mannish. Indeed she strongly objected to mannish women. Her friends were mostly of a feminine type.'[11]

This attempt to de-lesbianise Aldrich Blake is rather problematic. Being called Harry, not an obvious abbreviation of Louisa, would seem to be rather 'mannish', and even Riddell describes Louisa as 'virile'.[12] In 1915 Octavia Wilberforce described Louisa Aldrich Blake as 'a tall, massive individual who wore a stiff collar and a tie like a man's ... [a friend] looked upon her as the "sheep in wolf's clothing", as she was sure she was a man'.[13] Louisa did not become a butch fifty-year-old by accident or as the result of indifference, for, as Riddell notes, she had been perceived as butch since adolescence.

Louisa Martindale, while writing about living at College Hall in the 1890s, mentions Louisa Aldrich Blake's special friend, 'an art student, who one day astonished us all by coming back from being presented at court, looking perfectly lovely in her feathers and train'.[14] This was clearly a feminine friend, and it seems likely that this was Rosamund Wigram. Rosamund Wigram was an artist who worked in a variety of fields: she exhibited at the Royal Academy in 1906 and during the First World War she taught wounded soldiers how to make needlework pictures.[15] She went on to set up house with Aldrich Blake in London in 1915 and lived with her until Louisa's early death in 1925.

Although Riddell acknowledges Rosamund Wigram's help in his introduction to the biography, she is almost entirely absent from the story of Louisa Aldrich Blake's life that he recounts. Rosamund, who was not to die until 1958, must have had significant control over how Riddell recounted Louisa's life.[16] Riddell states that he had almost no personal papers to work from, and suggests that this was because few were written; however, it is just as likely that Rosamund censored Riddell's access to Louisa's correspondence and to the detail of her personal life.

Certainly there is no mention in this biography of Aldrich Blake's long-standing friendship with Louisa Martindale and Ismay Fitzgerald, nor of her friendship with 'Micky' (Naomi) Jacob, who was to become one of England's most notorious lesbians after the Second World War. Rosamund chose not to enable Riddell to provide a context in which to place Louisa Aldrich Blake's and Rosamund Wigram's love; the social networks in which they lived their lives are not discussed. The only intimate description of Louisa and Rosamund's relationship that Rosamund was to allow Riddell to quote was a letter where Louisa had written, 'Rosamund's presence in the house is an abiding joy.'[17] In the main, however, Louisa Aldrich Blake's love of women was, by her lover's choice, allowed to die with her.

Flora Murray

The relationship between Louisa Aldrich Blake and Rosamund Wigram was so long-standing that they presumably met either through a family friendship or at school. Ismay Fitzgerald and Louisa Martindale met when they were in their thirties; they were brought together by a mutual friend who knew that they shared a mutual commitment to the women's suffrage movement. Flora Murray (1869–1923) and Louisa Garrett Anderson (1873–1943) also met each other through involvement with the women's suffrage movement.[18] However, they went on jointly to head the Women's Hospital Corps (WHC) in France during the First World War, and it was there that their relationship was cemented.

Many women doctors went from Britain to work in hospitals throughout Europe during the First World War. Louisa Martindale and Louisa Aldrich Blake both spent periods in France, where they worked as part of the medical team of the Scottish Women's Hospital unit at Royaumont Abbey. Flora Murray was a physician and Louisa Garrett Anderson a surgeon, and together they established the WHC, which ran women-staffed hospitals in Claridges Hotel in Paris and then at Wimereux near Boulogne. After the British authorities had seen the success of the WHC hospitals Garrett Anderson and

Murray were invited to return to London to establish a military hospital in Endell Street. This invitation was unprecedented and was of great symbolic value to women generally, indicating that they were as competent as men: it was particularly encouraging for women doctors.

Louisa Garrett Anderson had also trained as a doctor at the London (Royal Free Hospital) School of Medicine for Women in the 1890s, qualifying in 1906, and she too was to be elected a Fellow of the Royal Society of Medicine. Flora Murray had trained in Scotland and it was here that she had her first serious lesbian relationship with another doctor, Elsie Inglis, who went on to found the Scottish Women's Hospital and who died following a gruelling time in Serbia in 1917. The establishment of two potentially competing teams of British women doctors during the First World War may well have been due to the personal and professional awkwardness of Flora Murray and Elsie Inglis working together after their relationship had ended.

The only written record that either Flora or Louisa Garrett Anderson appears to have left of their lives together is *Women as Army Surgeons*, which recounts the history of the WHC. Although it is Flora's name that is on the cover, the book is written in the third person and refers to the two women as an inseparable entity: 'Dr Garrett Anderson and Flora Murray'. As the third-person style suggests, this is an explicitly unintimate record of an organisation rather than of the lives of Flora Murray and Louisa Garrett Anderson. Only a few scraps of personal information can be retrieved. The book's dedication strikes almost the only personal note in the entire volume: 'To Louisa Garrett Anderson / "Bold, cautious, true and my loving companion".'

Both women were supporters of the militant wing of the suffrage campaign, and were members of the Women's Social and Political Union and admirers of Mrs Pankhurst; Flora had been Mrs Pankhurst's personal doctor. Louisa, as the niece of Millicent Fawcett and the daughter of Elizabeth Garrett Anderson, was born into a suffrage dynasty. Flora and Louisa and many of their staff explicitly linked their war work with feminism: 'Endell Street [hospital] represented work for the country and work for the woman movement combined.'[19] Flora and Louisa were clearly flamboyant suffragettes: flags and bunting were displayed at Endell Street when women gained the partial suffrage in 1918.

Flora Murray has a dry wit which she occasionally allows to surface, for instance when she writes that 'rumour in the main office had it that the Doctor-in-Charge [Murray herself] disapproved of mothers and of marriage'.[20] This rumour is slightly qualified but certainly not condemned. The most entrancing revelation concerns fancy-dress staff parties at Endell Street: 'Colonel and Mrs Dug-Out – the one exuberant in kilt and plaid, with fierce red whiskers; the other clinging and elegant, in lace cap and mittens – received the guests and joined in the dance.'[21] If the Colonel and his lady were the most important people present and the hosts of the evening it seems likely that they were Murray and Garrett Anderson, with the Scottish and 'boyish' Flora Murray taking the butch role with the whiskers and the kilt and Louisa that of the clinging and elegant femme.[22]

After the Endell Street hospital closed in 1919 Flora Murray and Louisa Garrett Anderson went to live in Penn in Buckinghamshire, where they worked in private practice. They were successful middle-class women and presumably lived comfortably until Flora died following an operation in 1923 at the age of fifty-four.[23] Her obituary filled the front page of *The Vote*, the leading suffrage and feminist paper of the period, and in it Beatrice Harraden, an old friend from Endell Street, recounts Flora's successes *vis-à-vis* the medical profession and the sexism of the British army.[24] Louisa did not move from Penn, and died in 1943 at the age of seventy. While Louisa and Flora did not leave a straightforward account of their love, Flora certainly seems happy to have acknowledged it to a knowing lesbian audience.

Octavia Wilberforce

The fourth in this quartet of women doctors is Octavia Wilberforce; Octavia was to leave a much more detailed and apparently more personal account of her life, *The Eighth Child*, than any of the other women in this group. Octavia Wilberforce was of a younger generation than Martindale and Aldrich Blake but she came to know them through medicine and through her older lover Elizabeth Robins: Elizabeth, Louisa Aldrich Blake and Louisa Martindale were all involved with the establishment of the Lady Chichester Hospital for Women and Children in Brighton in 1912.

Octavia Wilberforce's autobiography was not published in her lifetime, and it appears to be an intimate and private account of her life. However, this is deceptive: the typed manuscript of *The Eighth Child* was donated by the heirs of Wilberforce's estate, along with a small selection of her letters to Elizabeth Robins, to the Fawcett library after her death. It is not clear how much editing of the manuscript and letters was carried out posthumously by her estate: an edited version of *The Eighth Child* with a commentary has been published under the title *Octavia Wilberforce: The Autobiography of a Pioneer Woman Doctor*.

Octavia Wilberforce (1888–1963) met Elizabeth Robins (1862–1952) in the summer of 1909 when Octavia was twenty-one and Elizabeth was forty-seven. At this first meeting at a luncheon party Octavia noted Elizabeth's beautiful deep-set eyes that were the colour of speedwell, her charming grace, her unforgettable voice and her enthralling and witty talk.[25] This meeting Octavia describes as 'a turning point in my life ... It was a case of hero-worship at first sight.'[26] The potential for hero-worship in the circumstances was clear: Octavia was an almost uneducated middle-class girl living at home before marriage, occupying her time with gardening and golf; Elizabeth was a well-known and accomplished actress and writer famous for her radical and unconventional views.

Octavia's life had been curtailed and shaped by the expectations of her class and her family. Almost all her desires were met with disapproval and resistance from her family. They did not like her playing golf as her mother 'had heard that these golfing women were ravening wolves and corrupted the young. I learned that a friend of Dolly's had said that they smoked and drank and even called each other by their surnames!'[27] Meeting Elizabeth led Octavia to determine to do something with her life, and small fights about the suitability of golf were soon replaced with larger ones.

Octavia's family, although impressed by Elizabeth's fame and eminent friends, were very anxious about her pernicious influence over Octavia. Their anxiety was wholly justified: with Elizabeth's support Octavia turned down a good offer of marriage, started to receive coaching in secret from mistresses at Roedean and determined to train as a doctor. She and Elizabeth also fell in love, or, as Octavia put it with clear lesbian precision: 'I want you *always*, whether I make an awful muddle of things, or – whatever happens, to keep a finger on me at all times and in all places.'[28]

The relationship between Octavia and Elizabeth was not unproblematic: Elizabeth appears to have been a slightly reluctant and worried older lover. Moreover, Octavia does seem to be worried about what people will make of her love for Elizabeth. This in essence is what makes *The Eighth Child* such a complicated document to interpret for, while it celebrates the importance and centrality of Octavia's love for Elizabeth and suggests that their love glorifies everything that they do, it also fights shy of naming their love. The difficulty for Octavia-the-writer does seem to be the anxiety that Octavia-the-lover will appear to be a lesbian and hence amoral and degrading, and thus that Octavia-the-lover will devalue Octavia-the-doctor.

Although this was an issue for all the women I have discussed, it does seem to have been especially difficult for Octavia, as her autobiographical writing makes clear. Octavia clearly believed that it was her love for Elizabeth that enabled her to be a good doctor: in a letter dated 22 July 1918 she wrote:

> [I] can only concentrate utterly on two things; one, the health of the world, essentially impersonal, and one, essentially personal – my love for you. Darling, don't you see that it's heaven sent for me to have this relationship? You see, nobody was ever born with such a store, a wealth of caring as your Sussex Child. Consequently, nobody could be more easily lonely if I'd never known you … Since I have you, nobody is more satisfied up to the hilt, more lavished in affection, more continuously pouring at your feet every drop of love in my whole being as this your devoted child. So see how completely blessed am I. And in consequence what a good doctor I will be. Everything is interwoven, dependent on my caring for you, which is the end and aim of my life.[29]

This letter ends with a postscript: 'Will you answer this letter, my darling? Because it isn't often I let as much affection as this get into a letter.'[30]

Octavia's overt anxiety means that much of her autobiography appears incoherent. For instance, she states that at the age of twenty-eight 'of homosexuality I knew nothing'.[31] It seems extremely unlikely that this was simply and unproblematically true, for by the time Octavia was twenty-eight she was living in London, at medical school and knew well both Louisa Martindale and the butch Louisa Aldrich Blake.[32] The circles she moved in were the same as those of infamous bohemian lesbians like Edy Craig and Christopher St John.

However, it is possible that she knew nothing of a homosexuality which was expressed as an objectified and purely physical desire for another woman. For the lesbians Octavia knew were all engaged in relationships of mutual love, where erotic desire was tied to a particular lover. This reading fits with the context in which Octavia brings up the issue of homosexuality. Another medical student, dubbed X. Y., had made sexual advances towards Octavia when she was living in digs in London. Octavia wrote that 'It is not surprising that X. Y.'s behaviour, and the guarded explanations of what I had taken to be mental derangement, came as a considerable shock to my innocence.'[33]

The shock seems to have been that X. Y. would not stop pursuing Octavia even when Octavia made it clear that she was not interested. Octavia eventually complained to the Dean of the medical school about this harassment. The Dean was none other than Louisa Aldrich Blake, who Octavia said 'was sympathetic but doubted if she could put a stop to her pestering me; besides the girl was well connected and she did not want to antagonise her parents. Occasionally, she reassured me, there were queer girls who behaved like that but they got over it.'[34] The *queerness* of these girls is not their erotic love for other women *per se* but their ability to pursue this desire when it has been clearly rejected by the woman in question.

Octavia writes that:

At that period I was completely ignorant of one side of behaviour. I had accepted the fact that many girls had devoted friendships, which were both normal and healthy, as in fact I had with Joan and Phyllis. But this obsession on the part of X. Y., as I will call her, suddenly struck me as something, ugly, alarming, unhinged. What did it mean?[35]

Elizabeth, in America during this crisis, had her own suspicions about what it meant − 'she thought I must have been encouraging the girl'.[36] It is interesting that Octavia omits Elizabeth's name from a conversation about normal and healthy and commonplace devoted friendships.

The language of love

As is apparent from the quotations I have used, Octavia and Elizabeth often used the language of mother and child together; indeed Octavia describes asking Elizabeth 'if she would allow me to look upon her as my adopted mother'.[37] This language of mother and child when it occurs between two women is often invoked to show that the relationship is not a lesbian one, but literally like the loving but unsexed relationship of a mother and daughter. This is, I think, a mistake. A sexual relationship between two women, particularly with a significant age difference, may well have felt to the participants as having more similarity to that of mother and daughter than to that of husband and wife. This is perhaps even more likely when men as a sex and in their sexual dealings are not seen as laudable and when marriage as a relationship is perceived as a financial contract. Elizabeth and Octavia, who were both explicitly feminist and saw, in the words of their friend Cicely Hamilton, 'marriage as a trade', are clearly part of this grouping.

In a letter to Elizabeth describing how she had received a proposal of marriage Octavia writes:

> I suddenly felt so revolted at what it all meant from *my* point of view. I was so staggered at the horror of such thoughts that (I didn't tell you this before) to prevent the sleeve of his coat touching mine I walked in the ditch! If I have ever grown up it was at that moment. Anyhow I suddenly saw a great many things horribly realistically and it completely took my breath away. And among other things I felt on the same level as an animal.[38]

Pat Jalland, the editor of *The Eighth Child*, argues that this shows that

> Octavia Wilberforce was reserved and physically undemonstrative ... [this] illustrates Octavia's innocence, immaturity and inexperience at the age of twenty-three. It also shows how powerful her revulsion was at the 'physical prospect' of marriage, which evidently overwhelmed her by its horror.[39]

I would agree that it does show that Octavia felt no engagement with Charlie's sexual desire for her and had no desire more generally for sexual engagement with men. Perhaps more significant is that she accuses herself not Charlie as being like an animal: this indicates that this encounter with Charlie made Octavia recognise or reconceptualise some of her own erotic desires and actions, and perhaps see them for the first time as part of a continuum of sexual activity and desire. Octavia frequently contrasts marriage and what it entails with female friendship and its concomitants. Marriage, a relationship possible only between a man and a woman, was found lacking.

After describing her proposal of marriage to Elizabeth, Octavia wrote:

> Some people are cut out for marriage; they are made for it and would be most happy in it. Perhaps people are made differently, but I am *not* cut out for it. Everybody I know would be shocked and horrified by that statement and at this: the very thought of it makes me shudder and it revolts me. This will not be said to anyone else if I retain my senses.[40]

It was not physical or emotional intimacy *per se* that repelled Octavia but the fact that in marriage this intimacy was necessarily with a man.

In a letter to Elizabeth, Octavia writes: 'Kiss me, you said tonight & my heart went out to you in a flood … At the back of my mind I shall be kissing you all yr voyage across & you can't mind that because it will only be in my mind, not the contacts you don't like.'[41] We can speculate about the 'contacts' that Elizabeth did not like – perhaps it was a particular sexual practice such as penetration or oral sex, or perhaps it was a new post-menopausal sexual difficulty – but this letter clearly places Elizabeth and Octavia's relationship within a sexual continuum.

Unlike the other partnerships that I have examined here, Octavia and Elizabeth's was not life-long – unsurprising perhaps given the difference in their ages and Elizabeth's longevity. From the late 1920s Octavia appears to have become intimate with Marjorie Hubert, a fellow doctor who was only seven years her senior, who displaced if not entirely replaced Elizabeth in Octavia's affections. Angela John describes Elizabeth's return to England at the end of the Second World War thus:

> At first, simply being back and having Octavia near, gave Elizabeth a 'kind of suspended happiness'. The previous year she had written that Octavia was the best that she had met 'on the long road'. Octavia returned the compliment, 'day in, day out I always refer my thoughts to you … You've been the beacon, the searchlight, the inspiration over all the years … And you must feel

this always – distance makes no difference'. On the envelope Elizabeth added later 're-read in sadness 24 March 1946 but kept in hope'.[42]

It seems that Marjorie and Octavia's relationship had solidified during Elizabeth's absence in America, much to Elizabeth's misery.

By the time Elizabeth died in May 1952 at the age of ninety, Octavia and she had had a relationship that spanned over forty years and which for both of them was absolutely foundational. Elizabeth supported Octavia both financially and emotionally as she struggled to qualify as a doctor. They did not always live together, Octavia following training and jobs around England and Ireland, and Elizabeth spending time with her family in America. But significantly they were perceived by their contemporaries to have done so. Sybil Thorndike, a close friend of theirs, described them uncomplicatedly as having shared a home in Brighton.[43]

Lesbian community

These four couples – Louisa Martindale and Ismay Fitzgerald, Louisa Aldrich Blake and Rosamund Wigram, Louisa Garrett Anderson and Flora Murray, and Octavia Wilberforce and Elizabeth Robins – were contemporaries and professionally and personally close. They all lived in south-east England with the professional focus of their lives centred on London and Brighton. In the small world of women doctors they were women, and women with female partners, who loomed large. Their lives were focused on women: women-run hospitals, at home and abroad; women's health; the suffrage movement; the women who they lived with; and the network of women who found each other and learnt to support each other in their efforts to build new ways of living.

Louisa Aldrich Blake and Louisa Martindale knew each other as students and remained friends until Aldrich Blake's death in 1925; Octavia Wilberforce was the student and friend of both of them. Louisa Martindale and Ismay, and Octavia and Elizabeth were all involved closely with the New Sussex Hospital. Louisa Garrett Anderson and Flora Murray knew Elizabeth Robins and Rosamund Wigram, who both performed volunteer work at the Endell Street hospital. Louisa Aldrich Blake had worked at the Elizabeth Garrett Anderson Hospital, where she had presumably come into contact with Louisa, the female doctor in the family. They all shared mutual friends such as Beatrice Harraden (1864–1936) and Cicely Hamilton (1872–1952).[44]

The complexities of writing about their lives or giving other writers access to their lives are illuminatingly illustrated by the auto/biographical legacies that they have left us. What they have chosen not to tell us is as informative, about the experience of living lesbian lives in long-term partnerships in this period, as what they do tell us. It is as a group of women who knew each other that the piecemeal information that has survived becomes coherent. I would argue that lesbian history can be compiled only by examining such micro-histories: in essence 'lesbian history' is no more than the sum of lesbian lives.

The lives of this group of lesbians are revealed by the networks of friends and interests which connect them. Although all of them left specific and chosen records of their lives, none of these provides transparent access to the reality of those lives. In particular I have tried to show the different ways women from this group approached biographical and autobiographical writing with regard to articulating their love for other women. It is by considering this biographical and autobiographical material as parts of a patchwork that a more substantive and resonant sense of these women's commitments and identities emerges.

Notes

1 For an explanation of why I am confident in naming these women as lesbians see Emily Hamer, *Britannia's Glory: A History of Twentieth-century Lesbians* (London, Cassell, 1996), chapter 1.

2 Mary Scharlieb, *Reminiscences* (London, Williams & Norgate, 1924), p. 22.

3 For further detail on Radclyffe Hall and her contemporaries see Hamer, *Britannia's Glory*, chapters 2–5.

4 I include the experience of Irish lesbians with that of English, Welsh and Scottish lesbians as in this period British legislation was in force in Ireland; obviously the experience of Irish lesbians lies between these two extremes.

5 See for example, Shari Benstock, 'Paris Lesbianism and the Politics of Reaction, 1900–1940', in Martin Duberman *et al.*, *Hidden from History: Reclaiming the Lesbian and Gay Past* (New York, Meridian, 1990) and Catherine Van Casselaer, *Lot's Wife* (Liverpool, Janus, 1986).

6 Louisa Martindale, *A Woman Surgeon* (London, Gollancz, 1951), p. 228.

7 *Ibid.*, p. 228.

8 Entry for Louisa Aldrich Blake by R. Strachey, in J. R. H. Weaver (ed.), *Dictionary of National Biography, 1922–1930* (Oxford, Oxford University Press, 1937).

9 Lord Riddell, *Dame Louisa Aldrich Blake* (London, Hodder & Stoughton, 1926), p. 15.
10 *Ibid.*, p. 24.
11 *Ibid.*, p. 24.
12 *Ibid.*, p. 32.
13 Octavia Wilberforce, *Octavia Wilberforce: The Autobiography of a Pioneer Woman Doctor*, ed. Pat Jalland (London, Cassell, 1989), p. 74.
14 Martindale, *A Woman Surgeon*, p. 34.
15 *Dictionary of British Artists 1880–1940* (London, Antique Collectors Club, 1976), p. 545, and Flora Murray, *Women as Army Surgeons: Being the History of the Women's Hospital Corps in Paris, Wimereux and Endell Street September 1914–October 1919* (London, Hodder & Stoughton, 1920), p. 192.
16 Obituary, *The Times*, 20 May 1958.
17 Riddell, *Dame Louisa Aldrich Blake*, pp. 72–3.
18 They certainly knew each other from 1909. Sylvia Pankhurst, *The Suffragette Movement* (London, Virago, 1977), p. 204.
19 Murray, *Women as Army Surgeons*, p. x. This introduction was written by Beatrice Harraden, novelist, suffragette and librarian at the Endell Street hospital.
20 *Ibid.*, p. 204.
21 *Ibid.*, pp. 226–7.
22 Flora Murray is described thus in *The Vote*, 10 August 1918, p. 1.
23 Louisa Garrett Anderson's estate was valued at £113,540 when she died. *The Times*, 8 April 1944.
24 *The Vote*, 10 August 1918, p. 1.
25 Wilberforce, *Octavia Wilberforce*, pp. 14–15.
26 *Ibid.*, pp. 14–15.
27 *Ibid.*, pp. 32–3.
28 Octavia Wilberforce to Elizabeth Robins, *c.* August 1911. *Ibid.*, p. 38.
29 *Ibid.*, pp. 92–3.
30 *Ibid.*, p. 93.
31 *Ibid.*, p. 74.
32 The London (Royal Free Hospital) School of Medicine for Women.
33 Wilberforce, *Octavia Wilberforce*, p. 74.
34 *Ibid.*, p. 73.
35 *Ibid.*, pp. 73–4.
36 *Ibid.*, p. 73.
37 *Ibid.*, pp. 73–4.
38 *Ibid.*, p. 28.
39 *Ibid.*, p. xxiii.
40 *Ibid.*, p. 28.
41 Angela John, *Elizabeth Robins: Staging a Life, 1862–1952* (London, Routledge, 1995), p. 199.
42 *Ibid.*, p. 236.
43 Sybil Thorndike, 'Elizabeth Robins as I Knew Her', in Octavia Wilberforce (ed.), *Backsettown and Elizabeth Robins* (Brighton, privately published, 1952), p. 29.
44 See also John, *Elizabeth Robins*, p. 199 and Martindale, *A Woman Surgeon*, p. 173.

Sex and reproduction

8

Falling fertilities and changing sexualities in Europe since *c.* 1850: a comparative survey of national demographic patterns

Simon Szreter

Introduction: an historical demography of heterosexuality

As Michael Mason has clearly argued and expounded at length, if we want to construct a history of sexuality (understood as a collective plural noun), then we have to start by recognising that it has an irreducibly significant physical and behavioural side, upon which and around which its individual imaginings and cultural codes are dialectically premised.[1] The changing behavioural contexts, in which the cultural negotiation of sexualities occurs, are a vital part of the full historical account.

We do not, of course, possess any abundance of direct historical evidence documenting popular patterns and varieties of sexual activity in the European past, although some early modern historians, such as Jean-Louis Flandrin for France and Martin Ingram for England, have made ingenious use of somewhat more indirect sources generated by both the Catholic and Protestant churches' self-appointed roles as guardians of family morality.[2] However, we can examine in considerable detail, and with a reasonable degree of confidence in the validity and representative nature of the evidence, what might be termed the demographic basics of the modern history of heterosexuality in Europe.

As will be shown here, thanks to the work of demographic historians, we do possess for most European countries a reasonably comprehensive and robust modern historical record of the most relevant aspects of their changing patterns of heterosexual behaviour, in the form of empirically derived estimates of national trends in marital fertility, and of associated changes in marriage patterns and in illegitimacy rates. Indeed in the case of most European countries it is possible for the period since the mid nineteenth century to study the relationship between these three demographic basics of sexuality in much greater detail than will be presented in this brief, exploratory presentation, since the information is often available for the different provinces of each country, for various social groups or according to an urban versus rural differentiation.

Of course, for any survey of the relationship between demographic change and sexuality in Europe during the period since the mid nineteenth century, the dramatic fall in marital fertility which has occurred during that period constitutes a dominating feature of the landscape in every single case. Indeed it is very possible that cultural historians may have tended to discount the potential of this process, or even of demographic change in general, to offer a significant contribution towards our understanding of what it is that is special and unique about the history of sexuality in a particular society precisely because of the extreme generality of the phenomenon. Such cultural historians may therefore be interested to hear that although social scientists continue to refer to 'the fertility decline' or 'the fertility transition' as if it is a generic phenomenon, over two generations of scientific study have failed to identify much that is general about the way that fertility fell. Just as all the nations of Europe (except Albania) have experienced 'industrialisation' at some time during the nineteenth and twentieth centuries, but each in its own entirely distinct way, so, too, falling fertility has occurred in each of these countries during approximately the same span of time, and in each case in a quite distinct way.

The evidence which the following discussion is based upon is tabulated in the Appendix. This reproduces, in highly abbreviated form, some of the enormous databank of such indices for all the nations of Europe compiled by a number of researchers working during the 1960s and 1970s on the European Fertility Project under the direction of Ansley J. Coale, Director of the Princeton Office of Population Research.[3] It should be noted that there have been a number of important criticisms made of these Princeton indices. Their utility is certainly much more limited and their validity much more culturally circumscribed than their progenitors, A. J. Coale and his colleagues, originally believed to be the case. In particular the notion of 'natural fertility', which underwrote the Princeton methodology, has been exposed as incoherent.[4] Nevertheless, despite their conceptual and methodological shortcomings, the Princeton indices can legitimately be used in the broad descriptive manner in which they are deployed here, so as to provide robust, if rather crude, comparative indicators of the modern historical trends in the three main components of each European nation's changing fertility patterns: its marital fertility (Ig), its non-marital fertility (Ih) and the proportion of women married within the fecund age-range of fifteen to forty-nine years (Im). Some further relevant data, from different sources, will also be introduced to illuminate the discussion for the most recent period of the 1980s and 1990s, as there has been some very interesting further change in this most recent period, which is not covered by the historical data compiled by the Princeton project.

A preliminary word of explanation is in order, as the indices in the Appendix may appear somewhat off-putting and uninterpretable to the uninitiated. To measure and compare changing fertility in the past is not a straightforward matter. This is because even if it were possible to hold all non-biological influences absolutely constant, the fertility characteristics of any population of women vary substantially with respect to age, principally because of a changing incidence of sterility.[5] As a result, the fecundability (theoretical ability to conceive, holding all other influences constant) of any group of women will exhibit a pattern of increase through teenage to a maximum level in the early twenties, which thereafter tails off – slowly at first, but more rapidly in the later thirties. It is necessary in comparing the fertility characteristics of actual historical populations to take this non-linear pattern of age-specific fecundability into account. The three Princeton indices take the form of decimal fractions, calibrated against a notional 'standard' of 'absolute' or 'natural' fertility recorded by the Hutterite Anabaptist community of North America in the 1920s. These decimal fractions are the figures recorded in the Ig (marital or legitimate fertility) and Ih (non-marital or illegitimate fertility) columns for each of the nations of Europe. Thus the first line of the Appendix shows a value for Ig of '0.686' for England and Wales in 1871. This tells us that the rate at which married women in England and Wales were bearing children corresponded to 68.6 per cent of the rate of childbearing among Hutterite women in the 1920s.

The third index, Im, is a measure of the extent to which women spend their most fertile childbearing years within marriage. In European countries, where the convention of entry into the state of marriage has historically been strongly associated with the commencement of a woman's reproductive activities (so that overall non-marital fertility was always much lower than marital fertility, as comparison of Ig and Ih demonstrates), this has been an important, second and independent aspect of the way in which the fertility of a population might vary, apart from the question of the rate at which childbearing occurs within marriage.[6] The importance of the Im index for the purposes of this chapter is that it provides a genuinely comparable measure of the incidence of marriage among women in the different national populations in question across the period since the mid nineteenth century. The nearer to 1.0 the value of the decimal fraction for Im, the greater the incidence of marriage during the fertile years, which tends to equate to a younger typical female age at marriage.

Thus the figure for Im in the first line of the Appendix shows that the prevailing pattern of marriage among English women in 1871 meant that they were spending only just over a half (50.9 per cent) of the fecundity-weighted years of their collective lives in a state of marriage and therefore 'at risk' of contributing to the nation's marital fertility rate. By multiplying 0.686 by 0.509, we can produce a figure of 0.349, which expresses the fact that the number of births being produced by married women in England and Wales in 1871 was 34.9 per cent of the number which would have been produced had this been a Hutterite community with universal marriage from age fifteen in the 1920s. The comparable figure for 1911 is 22.4 per cent (0.467 multiplied by 0.479 equals 0.224). This means, therefore, that there was a 36 per cent absolute fall in marital fertility across the four decades, 1871–1911, composed mainly of a reduction in fertility within marriage (by 32 per cent, from 0.686 to 0.467), but also partly due to a decline in the proportion of their fecund years women were spending in the married state (a fall of 6 per cent from 0.509 to 0.479). Finally there is an Ih value at the end of the first line of 0.041 for non-marital fertility. This indicates that the very substantial number of unmarried, yet fecund women aged fifteen to forty-nine in the population of England and Wales at this time were producing only just over 4 per cent of the births that they would have produced had they been reproducing at Hutterite rates of fertility. As can be seen by looking at Ih for the earliest dates in the columns for the other countries, non-marital fertility in England and Wales – although nothing like as low as in Ireland, the Netherlands and Greece – was towards the lower end of the range for Europe as a whole.

The two polar opposites: England and France

Thus, according to these measures, while marital fertility in England and Wales fell by 32 per cent between 1871 and 1911, non-marital fertility, or illegitimacy, actually fell significantly faster, by 54 per cent (from 0.041 to 0.019). As marital fertility continued to fall further in England and Wales to 1931, so, too, did illegitimate fertility; but over this subsequent period it was marital fertility which fell rather more than non-marital fertility (37 per cent and 26 per cent, respectively, across these two decades). Meanwhile, the Im index indicates that women were spending a decreasing proportion of their fecund years within marriage over the first four decades to 1911, and were still proportionately 'less married' between the ages of fifteen and forty-nine in 1931 than they had been in 1871. (For technical demographic reasons the Princeton measures actually slightly under-estimate the extent to which marriage was still being postponed in the interwar years.)

The unusual relationship between falling marital fertility and a decreasing incidence of marriage is of great potential importance. In fact this is a primarily English, rather than Welsh, phenomenon. The relationship holds for all of the forty-five 'county' units into which the Princeton project disaggregated the data for England and Wales, with the sole exception of South Wales, where, quite to the contrary, nuptiality actually became more popular as marital fertility fell. Principally because of the importance of the Glamorgan coalfield, by 1911 fully three-quarters of the population of Wales lived in the six southern Welsh counties (although, of course, relatively few of them were Welsh-speaking and a large proportion were not ethnically Welsh because of the weight of English, and Irish, as well as north Welsh, immigration into the coalfield). Therefore this pattern of falling fertility accompanied by reluctance to enter marriage cannot be claimed as a Welsh characteristic. Indeed, the Welsh appear to have behaved more like the French, the antithesis of the English model.

However, the English model does seem to have characterised an important part of the Scottish population. This is despite the fact that the figures recorded in the Appendix for Scotland do not show any particularly strong relationship either way between falling marital fertility and nuptiality, reflecting the fact that in many of the thirty-three Scottish county units distinguished in the Princeton study there was no strong relationship between the two variables.

But in the two most populous, adjacent, lowland counties, in which 40 per cent of the 1911 Scottish population lived, there was, indeed, an unambiguous 'English' pattern, with falling marital fertility accompanied by increasing deferment of marriage. These were the two urban counties of Midlothian (Edinburgh and the area to its south) and Lanarkshire (Glasgow and its southern hinterland), with their strong historical, economic and cultural links with their southern neighbour.

Throughout England and lowland, urban Scotland, therefore, it would seem that the relationship between falling marital fertility and relative reluctance to enter marriage was positive until the First World War. The relationship seems to have entered a new phase sometime thereafter. John Hajnal dated the beginning of a fall in the average age at which first marriages were contracted as occurring from the late 1930s.[7] Early marriage gained in popularity enormously after the Second World War, until the 1960s. Marital fertility remained low and fairly unchanged during this latter period, and yet non-marital fertility began to rise strongly. After 1961 a third distinct phase is evident, with marriage once again declining in popularity from the peak of the early 1960s. Meanwhile marital fertility had also apparently entered a further episode of substantial decline, while non-marital fertility offered a partly compensating increase. The latter reflects the phenomenon of the post-1960s rise of cohabitation, consensual partnering and both voluntary and involuntary single parenthood in many Western societies; but also, antedating this, there was an increasing boldness in sexual experimentation before marriage among the young from the 1950s onwards, reported in sex surveys of the period.[8] These developments have drawn forth a substantial and an increasingly interesting literature.[9] England and Wales and Scotland have all participated in this most recent trend in the demography of changing sexuality; but they are by no means the leading examples. It has been Sweden and Denmark (followed by Norway) which have clearly led the world from the late 1960s onwards in adopting this new form of social behaviour, such that by 1990 almost 50 per cent of all births registered in these two countries were non-marital and, of course, the incidence of marriage had fallen to an historical nadir in all three countries.

In earlier work I have been able to explore the implications of the gross national trends in demographic indices in much greater detail in the case of England and Wales. Primarily this has been through an analysis of the relationship between birth control within marriage and the timing of marriage among 195 (male) occupational subdivisions of the married population of England and Wales in 1911. These 195 occupational categories were further subdivided according to the date at which couples married and the age of the wife at marriage, thus resulting in a relatively high degree of socio-demographic resolution.[10] On this basis it was possible to show that in the decades before the 1911 census was taken there was a strong positive correlation between delaying marriage and birth control after marriage. Those occupations recording the lowest marital fertility in 1911 were also those in which the greatest proportion married older brides (those aged over twenty-five years old); and this was true both among the cohorts marrying in the 1870s and 1880s and among those marrying in the years 1901–5, shortly before the 1911 census. It was also feasible to verify this relationship even more precisely. The latter marriage cohort had been married on average only 7.5 years in 1911. By comparing the average number of children born in that short space of time to those marrying brides aged twenty to twenty-four years old, as against those aged twenty-five to twenty-nine years old, it was possible to show that within each of the 195 occupational categories it was in almost every case the older marrying sub-set of couples who had already begun to space out their births to a greater extent than the younger-marrying sub-set, the former recording a significantly lower marital fertility over the first 7.5 years of marriage.[11] It can be shown that this relationship obtains also if the fertility characteristics of the married populations of the approximately one hundred county boroughs and urban districts of England and Wales in 1911 are examined in the same way.[12]

From the point of view of the history of sexuality, important interpretative implications flow from having established the ubiquity and strength of this particular relationship between these two key demographic variables in the English case. As inspection of the Appendix shows, this strong positive relationship is not exhibited by most of the sixteen other west European countries listed there.[13] This is not surprising, since it has always been considered that, once effective techniques of birth control within marriage had become an established practice in any European society, this would logically obviate the social need for the fertility-restraining function of traditional delayed marriage, the north-west European institutional mainstay of many generations past.[14] Hence the Appendix shows that in most west European countries, unlike England and lowland Scotland, there is either no relationship or a negative relationship evident between falling marital fertility (Ig) and steady or rising nuptiality (Im), indicating that most national populations abandoned late marriage as they became competent in methods of birth control within marriage.

Certainly France is the outstanding example of this, exhibiting a pattern of marital fertility falling steadily from 1831 while age at marriage and proportions married both increased, a relationship which has also been rigorously demonstrated to prevail at the disaggregated level of the eighty or so *départements*.[15] France, in particular, therefore, represents the most marked polar opposite to the pattern exhibited by England and lowland Scotland. What can this signify for their differing sexual cultures? In the case of France, at least, there is something of a consensus among its historians that extraordinarily low marital fertility already in the mid nineteenth century was achieved with the aid of a relatively sophisticated and widely diffused positive and hedonistic culture of both marital and non-marital sexuality. This countenanced, if not positively encouraged as norms, the sexual initiation of young men with prostitutes and their subsequent patronage even after marriage, the practice of *coitus interruptus* and a range of non-coital sexual activities within marriage, and possibly a certain popular moral indulgence towards the sin of coveting thy neighbour's wife, or at least so the gentle tone of *Clochemerle* would have us believe.[16] On the limited but consistent historical testimony that is available, it seems, therefore, that the French may well have enjoyed the first national culture of positive sexual control in the Western world: a popular culture which was sensually self-indulgent but managed this in a remarkably controlled fashion, at least with respect to births within marriage. Certainly the relationship between the demographic indices of sexuality tabulated in the Appendix, and the more disaggregated evidence reported by van de Walle and Weir, is entirely consistent with this proposition. As French people, in the various *départements*, increasingly became accustomed to the effective control of births within marriage, so they were prepared to marry earlier and earlier, without any rise in either the marital fertility or the non-marital fertility rates suggesting any faltering in their techniques of control.

By contrast, the relationship of the demographic indices for England and lowland Scotland and for the former's component occupational and urban categories, indicates that most couples who successfully restrained the rate at which births appeared after marriage (and they were not controlling the flow to anything like the same extent as the French until the interwar period) had begun by delaying marriage as long as they could, a trend which actually increased throughout the first four decades during which marital fertility fell. Indeed, the first piece of research seriously to propose that sexual abstinence might have been an important method of birth control used by married couples was a detailed, micro-demographic and qualitative study of a section of the professional bourgeoisie of Edinburgh in the late nineteenth century, completed by Debbie Kemmer in 1989.[17] This means that, quite to the contrary of the French, this was not a popular culture, either among the middle or the working classes, exhibiting confidence in its capacities to restrict fertility after marriage. Those wishing most earnestly to avoid the burden of a large family or of too many births too fast, began by remaining for as long as possible in the state of sexual abstinence which we know to have been the traditional convention for several centuries for premarital adults waiting to marry in British society.[18]

There is plenty of corroboration for the proposition that late nineteenth- and early twentieth-century English society was a society with little knowledge of the more effective methods of birth control within marriage, while even basic knowledge of sexual anatomy was commonly withheld from the premarital, young adult generation wherever possible, especially young women.[19] Parental and institutional, community control over courtship was tightening among both middle and working classes. The markedly falling illegitimate fertility rate throughout the period is consistent with a culture of abstinence and prudence among young adults coming to be increasingly embraced by the populace at this time. There is also a range of cultural evidence to support this thesis of increasing preoccupation with sexual restraint and its psychological implications: the new concern over 'neurasthenia' and male deficiency in sexual functioning;[20] and the considerable upsurge in popular anxiety, to a great extent orchestrated both by the increasingly vigorous feminist movement and by some within the medical profession, over the dangers and degrading nature of venereal disease.[21] Of course this was an important political vehicle for the negotiation of gender relations in general.[22] But it is also significant in the present context because it can be seen as a discourse of fear, expressing

anxiety over lack of control in the sexual domain and an un-
comfortable relationship towards sexuality.[23] By contrast, Quétel has
argued that in France public disquiet over the dangers of syphilis
was much more in evidence in the interwar decades, after the
appearance of reasonably effective prophylaxis, and finds that public
concern there was very much the expression of an organised, semi-
official campaign sanctioned by the French medical establishment.[24]

Thus, as I have argued at length elsewhere and with supporting evidence drawn from the period's few surviving sources of direct
testimony regarding methods of birth control and frequencies of
sexual intercourse, there was an important functional aspect of the
famed code of inhibited 'Victorian' sexuality, which the respectable in
all ranks of British society aspired to throughout this period and,
indeed, well on into the interwar and even post-Second-World-War
years.[25] A. J. P. Taylor could write of the English at the end of the
1930s as a 'frustrated people', hung up about its sexuality.[26] Unlike
in France, prostitution had only sordid and clandestine connotations
of shame and disease in English culture.[27] Indeed anything 'French'
in sexual matters was synonymous with depravity in English popular
and highbrow currency throughout the last quarter of the century.[28]
The English drew upon and extended their traditional culture of
sexual abstinence for young adults throughout most of the period
during which they successfully reduced their marital fertility. The
principal methods of birth control, used within marriage as without,
until the merciful appearance of cheap and aesthetically acceptable
latex condoms from 1930 onwards, were a combination of attempted
sexual abstinence, reduced sexual activity, withdrawal when the will
failed and the resort to abortion when that failed, too. The
contrasting demographic indices of sexuality in France are testimony
to a burgeoning culture of sexual control and institutionally transmitted competencies over a range of sexual practices (probably partly
through the custom of prostitute sexual initiation considered acceptable as a *rite de passage* for young men), as opposed to the culture of
sexual evasion, silence and fear which prevailed across the Channel.

Furthermore, we can examine the behaviour in these terms of
one important element of the British diaspora. Australia and New
Zealand were, of course, predominantly settled by the English, and
by Scots and Irish. As the Appendix shows, both of these countries
share in the 'English' pattern of the demography of 'Victorian'
sexuality.[29] It seems therefore, that these expatriate communities,

including one which had been infamous for its casual liaisons and consensual marriage at the beginning of the nineteenth century when it was composed principally of male convicts, had by the beginning of the twentieth century so thoroughly endorsed codes of 'Victorian respectability' in matters sexual as to have become almost indistinguishable in sexual demography from the English.[30]

If there is a spectrum or range of variation in the cultures of sexuality among the different national populations of Europe, it may be that the English and the French constitute the two polar opposites. Certainly their tabulated indices in the Appendix are starkly in contrast to each other. But also, in both of these cases, further detailed and disaggregated studies of some of the relevant aspects of their social, demographic and cultural history have been adduced in the discussion above, appearing to confirm that the inferences which it appears can be made from the relationship between the demographic indices at the national aggregate level are, indeed, valid.

Other European patterns: a demographic typology of sexualities?

Apart from the two polar opposites of France and England, along with the two other nations of Britain which have already been discussed, the remaining twenty-one European countries whose demographic indices are reproduced in the Appendix seem (with the exception of Ireland) to fall either into the French or English pattern or else into one of four additional categories or types.

The uniqueness of Ireland's fertility and nuptiality history in the wake of the Famine's devastation is well known and this is certainly reflected in the indices for 1871–1911 in the Appendix, which show an unusual combination of extremely low illegitimacy combined with very low and falling nuptiality and yet relatively high fertility within the markedly reduced number of marriages contracted. However, if the twentieth-century pattern is examined, a case could almost be made out that Ireland's demography of sexuality resembles quite closely, but a century later, its larger Catholic and similarly peasant-agriculture-dominated cousin, France. As fertility within marriage fell from 1911, so the proportions entering marriage rose, while non-marital fertility declined slightly, too. However, it should be pointed out that the levels of marital fertility prevailing in Ireland, even by 1980, were substantially above those that had been found in France since before the beginning of the twentieth century. On balance it seems most correct to view Ireland as a unique entity in terms of its demography of sexuality, a case *sui generis*.

Outside the British Isles there is a single other 'western' European country which seems to follow very closely the English model. This is Finland. The timing of its demographic change is somewhat different, with its marital fertility falling only a little before the First World War; but the relationship between the three demographic indicators is almost identical to the English case, with an even more marked reluctance to enter marriage accompanying the first four to five decades of birth control within marriage, while at the same time illegitimate fertility dropped unmistakably. Just as in England and lowland Scotland, the popularity of marriage recovered between 1930 and 1960, while marital fertility continued an uninterrupted fall; and since 1960 falling marital fertility has once again been accompanied by a new disinclination to marry, but this time in the context of strongly rising non-marital fertility. In the absence of any further historical evidence, this demographic pattern would predict for Finland since 1880 a history of 'Victorian' sexuality, embracing a 'culture of abstinence', which may not have begun to 'thaw out' among the members of the younger generations until the 1960s and 1970s, perhaps a decade or so later than in England's case. However, only detailed cultural and social research can show whether or not the Finnish statistical behavioural patterns can, indeed, be explained by an essentially similar history of sexuality to that of the 'English' model.

The three Mediterranean countries of Italy, Spain and Greece provide an example of apparent similarity masking enormous substantive differences. Their demographic indices display the same initial pattern as the English model, with marital fertility and nuptiality both falling together to 1931 (to 1951 in Greece's case), after which fertility continued to fall but, as in England, marriage began to rise in incidence. However, the superficial similarity with England and lowland Scotland during the earlier period in fact belies very substantial and historically long-established differences in the demography and culture of marriage and sexuality between the two sets of societies. The Mediterranean cultures were characterised by a centuries-old pattern of wide age-differentials between older grooms marrying relatively young brides. This differentiated Tuscany from England, for instance, as far back as the fourteenth century, when our earliest reliable records begin.[31] In the Mediterranean societies long-standing, land-based marriage arrangements were gradually being displaced from the late nineteenth century onwards by the increasing proportion of the population composed of young migrants moving to the growing industrial cities, no longer drawing their livelihood from the land and consequently enjoying an increasing independence from the customs and interests of their parents, including in the selection of marriage partners.[32] Owing to the manner in which the Princeton fertility indices were constructed, so as to measure attributes of the female population only, the falling nuptiality indices in the Appendix cannot discriminate between an increasing bilateral disinclination to marry young on the part of both sexes, as in Britain, as against a progressive closing of age differentials, as in the case of the Mediterranean populations in this period. With patriarchal sexual exploitation decreasing and companionate, freer choice of marriage partners increasing, it is interesting to note the illegitimate fertility rates also falling markedly throughout the whole period in these countries, both during the initial phase when female marriage age was rising and in the more recent period when female age at marriage has been falling again.[33]

Indeed, the extremely low non-marital fertility of these three Mediterranean countries in the most recent period in the table, 1960–80, underlines the continuing distinctiveness of their demography of sexuality, relative to virtually all other European countries. Elsewhere this most recent period has seen a pronounced rise in non-marital fertility, reflecting the increasing popularity of consensual unions and also a substantial rise in the related option of single parenthood (which sometimes reflects positive choices but more often second-best expedients) as a familial context for child-rearing. This reiterates the point made earlier about the variety of demographic regimes, despite the common pattern of falling marital fertility. Although they have experienced a radical reduction in marital fertility like all the other national populations of Europe, the Mediterranean countries have emerged from this common historical experience with a distinctively different culture of family formation and demography of sexuality, logically implying that the process of falling fertility itself happened in an entirely distinct way and for different perceived reasons from those which motivated it elsewhere. Hence it is considered here that these three Mediterranean countries should be classed together as a third distinctive 'type' (after the

171

'English' and 'French' types) of sexual culture, according to the evidence of their demography of sexuality.

The strong contrast between this Mediterranean group and a further group which can be distinguished, the three western Scandinavian countries of Sweden, Denmark and Norway, is also instructive and worth pursuing. Indeed there seems to be evident a Franco-Scandinavian model of sexual demography. During much of the initial period of rapidly falling marital fertility the countries of this western Scandinavian group all exhibited, like France, an increased propensity to enter marriage, accompanied by little net change in either direction in their relatively high levels of illegitimate fertility. The similarity between the three Scandinavian countries in the most recent period since 1960, as leaders of a wider, international trend towards cohabitation, consensual unions and single parenthood, in place of formal marriage, has already been remarked upon (with Norway slightly lagging in this respect). It is France, among all the other European countries, which follows most closely behind the western Scandinavian countries in this trend.

Portugal should probably be added also to this Franco-Scandinavian group. Certainly the historical falling marital birth rate was accompanied by a rising popularity of marriage in Portugal. Sweden's non-marital birth rate actually rose slightly during the initial period of falling fertility; and in Portugal's case, where illegitimacy in the 1860s was (with Germany) the second highest in Europe (after Austria), non-marital fertility actually climbed substantially further throughout the first four decades during which marital fertility fell, from 1890 to 1930. Indeed Portugal was unique in this characteristic throughout Europe. Although by the 1960s Portugal's non-marital fertility had finally fallen to about half its 1930s peak level, certainly a case could be made, on these grounds of the anomalous behaviour of its non-marital fertility index, for allocating Portugal to its own category, rather than including it with the Franco-Scandinavian group. However, the recent period again displays much similarity with the other members of the Franco-Scandinavian group, though with a slightly later phasing: by the 1980s the popularity of marriage in Portugal was in decline, having peaked in 1975; and non-marital fertility was once again rising substantially, having doubled by 1990 from its 1975 nadir.[34] On balance, therefore, Portugal can perhaps be allocated to the Franco-Scandinavian 'type', rather than left on its own as a second 'isolate', like Ireland.

The three southern European populations have shown fewer signs, even in 1990, of participating in these last two developments.[35] Yet these features have been claimed by some as a universal, historically novel trend towards family formation outside marriage.[36] Popenoe sees this development as due to the nuclear family's supposed incapacity to accommodate an egalitarian trend towards greater individualist, self-fulfilment goals for women. This, of course, fails to realise the implications regarding flexibility of the extent to which 'the nuclear family' has always historically been associated with a range of caring adults in addition to the mother, such as fathers, older siblings, grandparents, other mothers and older sisters in the community, and even non-related individuals and couples (often termed 'friends') throughout much of British history (due to the practice of centuries during the early modern period, whereby young teenagers left home for service and apprenticeship while residing in households in other parishes).[37] Indeed the short period, from the 1930s until the 1960s in most Western societies, of very small families, universal formal education, increasing mechanisation of housework and low levels of married female participation in the workforce, has been an historical anomaly, during which mothers have been expected to perform, alone, most of the family's child-rearing activities from birth to late teenage. A change back towards a more 'mixed economy' of caring between a greater variety of agents and institutions is, therefore, the more likely typical outcome in most of these European societies due to the acquisition, once again, of a wider range of additional goals beyond that of childcare alone, by adult females with children (rather than the progressive 'abandonment' altogether of the nuclear family, as in Popenoe's prognosis).

It seems most likely that the western Scandinavian countries' apparent 'lead' over other developed societies in this respect primarily reflects their interrelated historical inheritance of a high degree of both practical and formal, legal and constitutional, female independence; allied to early and generous funding of a comprehensive welfare state, and a dominant, popular political value system which has been liberal and collectivist, rather than libertarian or conservative, with the corresponding implications that alternative family forms to those sanctioned by tradition are not merely passively accepted (as in the libertarian, Anglo-Saxon polities of England and the USA) but positively supported by the state. This analysis would therefore predict that such alternative family forms as consensual union and single parenthood may not become particularly popular among the more socially and morally conservative societies, such as those of the Catholic and Greek Orthodox south in Europe (or, perhaps, it may be more specific – although possibly tautological – to refer to these as more family-centred societies, in which the institution of the family is more culturally pervasive in its hold over individuals' loyalties and senses of self-identity).[38]

If the western Scandinavian countries have a relatively similar, collectivist and at least implicitly 'feminist', pro-welfare-state historical inheritance, it is certainly true that it is Sweden and Denmark which have been particularly marked in this respect. Although Sweden's welfare state has often been considered the leading model of generous, collective provision, it has been well established that many of the key features were first developed and applied in Denmark, so that it is really both of these two states which have pioneered these forms of civil society during the late nineteenth and early twentieth centuries.[39] Hence it is understandable that Norway's demography of sexuality should appear as a less marked version of its two Scandinavian neighbours, the two leaders in this historical development.

Given the similarity between France and the west Scandinavian states, the position of the two geographically intermediate 'Low Countries' of the Netherlands and Belgium is of considerable interest. In both of these cases, while young people increasingly entered marriage in greater numbers and at younger ages as marital fertility control was achieved – just as in the Franco-Scandinavian model – illegitimate fertility also fell very markedly (after a brief initial rise in Belgium), quite unlike the 'French' model and more like the completely different 'English' model. Also quite unlike the Franco-Scandinavian group (or, indeed, the 'English' model) – but rather like the Mediterranean group in this respect – the non-marital fertility of both Belgium and the Netherlands has recently remained at rather modest levels of no more than 10 per cent of total births still in 1990, in the context of much reduced entry into formal marriage. In both sets of cases and in all five countries this constitutes an interesting historical echo of the relatively low levels of illegitimate fertility prevailing in their pasts, before the dramatic reduction in marital fertility. As in the Mediterranean societies, consensual union with children is apparently not viewed as an especially attractive option in the Low Countries today. In these countries pregnancy apparently results in either marriage or abortion, whereas in most other north-west European societies continued cohabitation is a third option often exercised. The Low Countries probably differ from the Mediterranean countries in the extent to which premarital cohabitation is acceptable. The Low Countries, therefore, are similar to their north-west European neighbours in viewing cohabitation as a relatively normal state of affairs but do not extend the acceptability of this unmarried state to encompass also a childrearing context.

An obvious contrast with the Low Countries, which is also consistent with this thesis of long-term general continuities in sexual demography, is provided by their neighbours to the south and east, the two countries of Germany and Austria. It is argued here that these form, together, a 'Central European' group or type. As in the Franco-Scandinavian group, marriage became more popular as marital fertility fell among the two principal German-speaking peoples. But their twentieth-century fertility history has been quite distinctive, with marital fertility actually rising substantially in both cases between the 1930s and 1960s. Furthermore, their non-marital fertility patterns are very different from those of the Franco-Scandinavian group. These two populations exhibited (along with Portugal) the highest levels of illegitimate fertility in the late nineteenth century; and, while such non-marital fertility gradually declined alongside the fall in marital fertility, it remained at comparatively high levels throughout the period. By contrast with most other cultures, and especially with the Mediterranean and the Low Countries, non-marital fertility seems always to have been something of an option in German-speaking society from the mid nineteenth century through to the present day.

However, it is all the more intriguing in view of this that the two Germanic nations do not share with the west Scandinavian countries (which also exhibit a consistent historic pattern of comparatively high non-marital fertility) a leading role in the late twentieth-century movement towards very high rates of childbearing outside formal marriage. If the interpretation offered above is on the right lines, this suggests the importance of the very different contexts of the political economy of gender and childrearing in the two different groups of countries as accounting for this divergence in the late twentieth century in their relative attachment to formal marriage. Although both sets of countries have developed comprehensive, collectivist welfare states since 1970, Germany and Austria have exhibited relatively low participation rates of women in the formal workforce, whereas the Scandinavian states have recorded the highest levels.[40]

Indeed it may well be that the historic high illegitimacy rates of women in Germany and Austria reflect an ideologically and politically constructed position of institutionalised dependence for women, reflected in these statistics relating to the labour and marriage markets in those societies. In Scandinavia, however, a similar statistical phenomenon may have resulted from a more positive range of options and the cultural acceptability of a stronger bargaining position for women. Certainly it is well documented that, throughout much of Norway's fishing and transhumance economy, the law and customs of the country recognised that husbands necessarily delegated much of their economic authority to wives, and this may have applied more generally throughout the western Scandinavian societies.[41] This may also, incidentally, be part of the explanation for Portugal's rather unusual demography of sexuality: another heavily maritime culture exhibiting high non-marital fertility.[42] However, a quite distinct, alternative approach to explaining this difference between the Franco-Scandinavian and the German-speaking populations might be to examine instead the very different experiences of the two sets of countries in the two world wars of this century, with an eye to the socio-sexual and demographic implications of these divergent experiences. In particular the rising marital fertility of the period 1930–60 indicates a unique response among the German people to the catastrophic destruction and decimation of the male population, which their support for the Nazi regime brought upon their country.[43] There is also the issue of responses in the popular culture of sexuality and gender relations to the unusual conditions and disruptive circumstances of total war and its aftermath.[44] Clearly, more detailed knowledge is needed to adjudicate among these speculative possibilities.

Switzerland presents a rather complex picture, comprising several distinct phases. The initial prolonged period of decline in marital fertility from 1860 to 1910 occurred in the context of a substantial rise in the popularity of marriage and a complementary fall in what was already a very low illegitimacy rate. The latter continued to fall to very low levels in 1930, despite something of a marked retreat from marriage during the second and third decades of the new century. Thereafter, with marital fertility remaining relatively stable, both marriage itself and non-marital fertility rose together to 1960. Since 1960 marital fertility has once again fallen significantly while nuptiality has both fallen (to 1975) and recovered a little (to 1990), whereas non-marital fertility has remained (to 1990) relatively unchanged at about the lowest level in Europe, equal to Italy and only a little higher than Greece.[45] Overall the most salient feature of Switzerland's sexual demography is the consistently extremely low level of non-marital fertility. Superficially this would place Switzerland with its southern neighbour, Italy, in the 'Mediterranean' category, and it certainly debars Switzerland from being considered part of the 'Central European' German-speaking group. But quite unlike the Mediterranean group, nuptiality rose during the initial period of falling fertility. In fact, the behaviour of the Swiss demography of sexuality indices is most similar to the lowland countries pair of Netherlands and Belgium, duplicating their patterns in every respect with the exception of the temporary but nevertheless pronounced episode of retreat from marriage between 1910 and 1930. Switzerland has therefore been placed in the same category as the Low Countries, although a case could certainly have been made for its retention on its own. Furthermore, considering the complexity of this politically and linguistically heterogeneous society, it would be remarkable if more detailed research did not uncover a variety of sub-national patterns in its sexual demography.

There remains only to consider the data for Russia plus the six eastern European countries, each of which fell under the aegis of at least two different occupying empires (Imperial Russian, Soviet Russian, Austro-Hungarian, Nazi and Ottoman) throughout most of the period under review. In consequence of their politically turbulent histories, the statistical sources for the calculation of demographic indices are much more fragmentary and unreliable in all of these cases and for many of them time-series data for a constant territorial extent do not really exist, except for the period of Soviet rule. As a result I will confine myself only to a few rudimentary comments in these cases. To the extent that the early figures are at all reliable, they appear to show in all cases, except Bulgaria, an 'English' pattern of falling marital fertility accompanied by both declining incidence of marriage and falling non-marital fertility to approximately 1930 (to 1959 in Russia's case). If the data were robust, this would license the inference that falling fertility in these societies occurred in the absence of a popular culture of sexual control and competence, and was achieved primarily through the range of non-appliance methods adopted within a regime of attempted sexual abstinence: reduced coital frequency, *coitus interruptus*, forms of the rhythm method and lactational abstinence, perhaps abortion and infanticide. Thereafter, with marital fertility continuing to fall, the popularity of marriage rose until the 1960s or 1970s in all cases, indicating an increased sexual competency from the interwar period onwards and the adoption of a range of the more efficient, co-operative appliance methods of contraception; non-marital fertility has also tended to rise slightly in most cases since 1930, especially since 1975. Bulgaria, the exception to this general pattern for eastern Europe, shows a simple, linear trend corresponding to a more 'Franco-Scandinavian' pattern: strongly rising nuptiality and non-marital fertility alongside falling marital fertility throughout the period from 1905 to 1990 (while the incidence of marriage has recently fallen somewhat from its peak in 1975).[46]

Thus, the twenty-five European countries (counting England as separate from Wales, following the discussion in the text above) whose historical demographic indices are tabulated in the Appendix appear to comprise six broad types of sexual demography (plus one 'solitary': Ireland). They could be arranged in the following order, between the two historical poles of 'English' abstinence and 'French' pro-sensualism:

1) 'English'   England, (lowland) Scotland, Finland
2) 'East European'   Czechoslovakia, Poland, Hungary, Romania, Yugoslavia, Russia
3) 'Mediterranean'   Italy, Greece, Spain
4) 'High & Low Countries'   Netherlands, Belgium, Switzerland
5) 'Central European'   Germany, Austria
6) 'Franco-Scandinavian'   France, Sweden, Denmark, Norway, Portugal, Wales, Bulgaria
7) Ireland

Conclusion: patterns of persistence in the demography of sexuality

Of course the foregoing exercise may be viewed as stretching the spirit of Weber's heuristic notion of ideal-types to its acrobatic limits. It must be recalled that the data displayed in the Appendix here offer only national aggregate trends in the three basic demographic indices of heterosexuality. These are simply the most historiographically accessible bare bones for providing a comparative historical demography of national sexual cultures over the last century and a half.

It would be fatuous to suppose that the study of this particular sub-set of sexual phenomena could, in and of itself, give us any interpretable information of great value about the history of changing sexualities. However, it would be equally absurd to proceed in our studies of sexuality in the past as if information of this kind and on these aspects of sexual behaviour could make no helpful contribution. The main hope for intellectual progress in this difficult field, where evidence typically remains idiosyncratic, sparse and allusive, would seem to be through the integration of as many relevant sources of evidence as possible. Thus, where the foregoing analysis has had most to offer, as in the case of England and France, it has been through the mobilisation of the fruits of other kinds of relevant historical research, in order to contextualise the meaning of the demographic indices.

Ideally the data of the sort presented here for each nation would be disaggregated into sub-national measures relating to those 'communication communities' which actually constituted the distinct social groups or contexts which exhibited significant differences in fertility and sexuality.[47] The three dimensions addressed in the indices in the Appendix should be supplemented by time-series evidence on abortion rates, infanticide, incidences of prostitution, premarital conception rates, coital frequencies and extra-marital sexual behaviour. Although some of this superior bank of evidence will no doubt be hewn and won at the cost of great effort by future historians, I fear that the archival lodes are not of sufficient quality that we will ever be able to achieve more than a partial knowledge. Nevertheless, something at least can be done with the incomplete evidence deployed here, interpreting fragmentary survivals being the staple of the historian's art.

It is therefore important to remind ourselves of the further complexities lurking beneath the surface of the national patterns and their allocation into the above groupings. The national figures tabulated in the Appendix themselves offer hints of further divergences within the 'groups' identified here. Within the Mediterranean group, for instance, the Greek Orthodox nation of Greece could be considered a case *sui generis* because of the uniquely low level of non-marital fertility, which shows no sign at all of altering, according to the figures for 1990, even though female first marriage rates in

Greece were down in 1990 by 30 per cent on their early 1970s peak.[48] In other words the stigma of non-familial childrearing remains sufficiently strong in Greece that, while young couples are once again postponing formal marriage, they are taking great care, presumably through either refraining from premarital coitus or through effective contraception, or possibly through abortion (I have not found a report of any official figures for abortion in Greece), to avoid illegitimate births.[49]

Like Greece, Italy and Spain have seen very similar recent declines in marriage, since the late 1970s, which also have not been accompanied by a rush into childbearing outside marriage. However, it could be said that Spain, quite unlike Greece, shows distinct, if incipient, signs of moving towards the more northern European pattern, while Italy lies exactly between the other two in this respect. Thus there is a clear, graded spectrum visible inside the 'Mediterranean' group, indicating that further detailed research should uncover important differences between them, despite their similarities when viewed within a broader comparative perspective. Nevertheless, the Mediterranean countries are very similar in sharing (with the Netherlands) the lowest female workforce participation rates in the OECD, as measured in 1984. It is interesting that this is something in which Portugal again confirmed itself as a quite distinctly non-Mediterranean country, with a relatively high female participation rate in 1984. In this Portugal was intriguingly like all the other European historical 'maritime' economies, which headed the list of OECD female economic participation rates in 1984 – suggesting, perhaps, that the experience in these economies, with institutionalised male absence, of necessary reliance for centuries on female economic discretion over the household, has enabled women to negotiate national cultures more respectful of their relative autonomy.[50]

One additional relevant statistic can be cited which also tends to reconfirm that what the three Mediterranean countries share in common is more significant than the differences between them. In 1985 and again in 1990 Italy and Greece both recorded by far the lowest divorce ratios in Europe: no more than twelve divorces per hundred marriages (I could find no figures for Spain and, given the Irish constitution's prohibition on divorce, there are no figures available there, either). Measured in this way only Albania recorded ratios this low, with Poland, another great Catholic population, next, at about fifteen divorces per hundred marriages. All other European countries recorded divorce ratios varying between about twenty and forty-five per hundred marriages for both years, 1985 and 1990. There was a tendency for the western European populations (except France) to be found towards the upper end of the range, particularly the Scandinavian populations, including Finland, and also England and Wales; while eastern European populations, especially the Greek Orthodox of Bulgaria, were at the lower end of the range.[51] France's difference from the Scandinavian countries on this count is, of course, highly significant, indicating that, for all their similarities, there are certainly important differences between the Gallic and Scandinavian sexual cultures.

Overall the highly general patterns of the demography of evolving national sexual cultures discussed here reveal intriguing broad consistencies across the modern period, despite the fact that this was an era of epochal transformation in the fertility of marriage. As a result it has been possible to place most of the countries of Europe into one of six broad categories (although both Switzerland and Portugal could, like Ireland, be considered cases *sui generibus*). Undoubtedly when examined in detail the histories of the sexual mores of each European nation show themselves to be unique, composed of a range of sub-national 'variants' and continually subject to culturally negotiated change. Yet, and despite this, the highly general, comparative perspective deployed here indicates that there are also certain patterns of persistent difference between national or even trans-national, regional entities over long durations.

These enduring differences, although far from clear-cut, *may* be interpretatively highly significant. They bespeak very long-term, historical continuities which are indicative of differences between each of the various blocs or types identified here, in their respective ethical dispositions, concerning the morally correct way and the appropriate institutional environment in which to rear children. This would necessarily be something which would be strongly associated with systemic differences between these cultural blocs in how their individual members construct their social identities, loyalties or codes of honour, which in turn are fundamental in endowing their social worlds with morally evaluated meaning – the shared language which all individuals are crucially dependent upon for social life.[52] If it were true that European societies, and the national polities according to which most of them have been organised for at least the last two centuries, 'carry' these distinctive codes of evaluation and

honour, then 'new' sexual mores, including even those of 'the permissive society', may be more correctly seen not only as culturally
dynamic but also as intrinsically *socially* conservative. This is because
the deployment in each society of a range of these new forms of
sexual behaviours may be viewed as a means by which they continue
to express their culture's distinctive approach to childrearing and to
parental responsibilities, but adapted to the new and changed,
relatively affluent socio-economic circumstances in which they find
themselves.

The point, therefore, is that, without a comparative as well as
an historical perspective, in studying recent developments in
sexuality and the family in each country alone, we may be placing
too much emphasis upon the significance of the novel arrangements
of post-industrial society, such as cohabitation, consensual unions,
the increased popularity of 'Icelandic' marriage (in Iceland it was
traditionally normative for marriage to follow rather than to precede
the birth of the first child) and single parenthood. We may be
deceived into considering these new forms of behaviour to betoken
an absolutely new form of trans-national, 'modern' society, relatively
uninfluenced by more nationally and sub-nationally inflected historical
patterns. We may be too impressed with the supposedly more
universal cultural imperatives of economic and political liberalism,
secular rationalism, individualism and consumerism, and the new
options made available by the social support system of the welfare
state. Although all these relatively new or growing influences are,
indeed, important, the argument here is that it is equally important
to recognise that the new arrangements are *adaptations:* between the
inherited practices and values of the cultural blocs and the new
conditions in which those traditional goals have to operate in order
to manifest themselves.

The strange patterns of large-scale persistence in the
demography of sexuality indicate that it is important to appreciate
the extent of the functional, social continuities that are involved and
the enduring powers of certain, distinctive moral and ethical
positions. In all of these different European cultures, heterosexual
(and, indeed, very interestingly, many homosexual) individuals
continue to value highly reproduction, childrearing and parenting,
and they apparently also continue to construe these activities in a
manner which is distinctive according to the particular way in which
they themselves were brought up. The evidence for this is the

persistence or consistency of patterns discussed here, which indicate that the vast majority within each bloc continue to understand the meaning of childrearing in a way that is shared more closely with their own parents' distinctive construction of it than it is with individuals from a different region of Europe with a different inheritance in this respect, who happen to share the same income level or occupation.[53]

As Jane Lewis and Kath Kiernan have helpfully clarified, the postwar era in many post-industrial societies such as Britain has witnessed at least two highly significant, related transformations in the orthodox ideology surrounding the demography of sexuality and marriage.[54] First, with the public availability of the pill and the relatively secure separation for women of sexual expression from conception, there has been an acknowledgement, even in the established church's teaching, of the separation of sex from marriage. Second, there has been an acknowledgement, ultimately even in law, of the separation of formal marriage from parenting, as consensual marriage, separation and single parenthood have all become more frequent occurrences. However, the present perspective would additionally emphasise, as of equal importance, the *persistence*, in these much changed circumstances, of the majority of the population's continued wish to form sexually mutually exclusive dyadic relations, albeit of shorter durations than previously (this being a matter of outcome, rather than necessarily of typical intention, however), and the continued strong association of this goal and form of behaviour with the wish to have children and to be a parent.

In attempting to reconstruct the intensely negotiated history of changing sexualities and gender relations in Europe's different states, there needs, therefore, to be full recognition of these powerful regional differences of cultural practice and belief, in terms of family life and childrearing, along with the other most relevant and closely involved institutions of society such as the social security system and the legal and ecclesiastical systems.[55] These inherited historical forces are in a dialectical relationship with the evolving discourses of sexuality, out of which are negotiated changing sexual codes: behaviours and attitudes. New trends in sexual relations, such as cohabitation for instance, which may appear to be absolute novelties if taken in relative isolation, may be more correctly interpreted as adaptations facilitating functional continuities, in terms of these longer-term priorities of each society, whereby distinctive meanings of childrearing and parenting are in fact substantially preserved but in much changed economic and socio-political contexts.

The value of the comparative demographic approach to the history of sexuality, therefore, is to insist on placing its historical reconstructions in the context of the encompassing institutions of society with which it is most intimately related. So far in European history this has predominantly meant the range of institutions involved in social reproduction. It is a truism to observe that contraception has removed a logical link between sex and reproduction, and also that between marriage and childrearing. However, in view of this it is all the more remarkable how much heterosexual behaviour appears to remain interpretable in terms of the perpetuation of socially conservative motives and goals, regarding the establishment of durable dyadic relationships and the rearing of children, as two central sources of adult identity. A comparative demographic perspective may therefore act as an important complement to the work of cultural and social historians in helping to make sense of this paradox, which signals the importance of the more enduring side of the dialectics of changing sexualities in European history.

Appendix: Princeton fertility indices for selected dates for the countries of west and east Europe, 1830–1980

	Date	Ig	Im	Ih
England & Wales	1871	0.686	0.509	0.041
	1911	0.467	0.479	0.019
	1931	0.292	0.503	0.014
	1961	0.289	0.699	0.041
	1980	0.209	0.656	0.049
Scotland	1871	0.752	0.432	0.060
	1911	0.565	0.428	0.031
	1931	0.404	0.441	0.024
	1961	0.341	0.656	0.031
	1980	0.221	0.615	0.044

	Date	Ig	Im	Ih
Ireland	1871	0.708	0.405	0.014
	1911	0.708	0.339	0.010
	1936	0.570	0.369	0.013
	1961	0.548	0.513	0.011
	1980	0.425	0.557	0.024
Netherlands	1869	0.845	0.438	0.024
	1909	0.652	0.469	0.012
	1930	0.446	0.499	0.008
	1960	0.394	0.630	0.009
	1980	0.203	0.632	0.012
Belgium	1866	0.830	0.403	0.041
	1910	0.444	0.517	0.032
	1930	0.282	0.602	0.018
	1961	0.289	0.705	0.015
	1980	0.204	0.689	0.014
France	1831	0.537	0.514	0.044
	1871	0.494	0.529	0.044
	1911	0.315	0.591	0.043
	1931	0.273	0.613	0.037
	1961	0.323	0.646	0.037
	1980	0.235	0.626	0.048
Portugal	1864	0.682	0.424	0.079
	1890	0.689	0.456	0.075
	1911	0.636	0.471	0.083
	1930	0.544	0.474	0.088
	1960	0.414	0.556	0.057
	1980	0.341	0.615	0.042
Germany	1867	0.760	0.454	0.079
	1875	0.791	0.495	0.073
	1890	0.706	0.497	0.070
	1910	0.542	0.524	0.059
	1933	0.264	0.534	0.033

	Date	Ig	Im	Ih
West Germany	1960	0.301	0.625	0.032
West Germany	1980	0.170	0.603	0.025
East Germany	1960	0.267	0.713	0.071
East Germany	1980	0.215	0.659	0.061
Austria	1890	0.683	0.489	0.113
	1910	0.588	0.517	0.085
	1931	0.186	0.452	0.073
	1960	0.330	0.588	0.060
	1980	0.197	0.575	0.058
Finland	1880	0.698	0.499	0.054
	1910	0.647	0.459	0.043
	1930	0.455	0.404	0.027
	1960	0.343	0.602	0.022
	1980	0.222	0.545	0.039
Denmark	1852	0.671	0.436	0.066
	1880	0.686	0.456	0.064
	1911	0.522	0.486	0.062
	1930	0.327	0.505	0.039
	1960	0.279	0.660	0.045
	1980	*0.234*	0.552	*0.058*
Sweden	1880	0.700	0.409	0.054
	1900	0.652	0.411	0.058
	1930	0.303	0.422	0.043
	1960	0.241	0.626	0.052
	1980	*0.222*	0.461	*0.085*
Norway	1875	0.752	0.406	0.049
	1900	0.701	0.420	0.040
	1930	0.382	0.408	0.020
	1960	0.322	0.660	0.024
	1980	0.215	0.586	0.040

	Date	Ig	Im	Ih
Italy	1864	0.677	0.560	0.044
	1911	0.616	0.534	0.037
	1931	0.471	0.513	0.027
	1961	0.338	0.578	0.011
	1970	0.307	0.616	0.010
Greece	1900	0.688	0.632	0.015
	1928	0.535	0.566	0.009
	1951	0.399	0.502	0.005
	1961	0.327	0.576	0.006
	1970	0.276	0.656	0.006
Spain	1900	0.653	0.559	0.041
	1930	0.540	0.504	0.038
	1960	0.403	0.553	0.012
	1980	0.351	0.605	0.012
Switzerland	1860	0.724	0.388	0.032
	1910	0.513	0.463	0.021
	1930	0.352	0.437	0.012
	1960	0.350	0.570	0.019
	1970	0.268	0.618	0.017
Poland	1897	0.720	0.631	0.050
	1931	0.501	0.544	0.038
	1960	0.335	0.696	0.035
	1970	0.279	0.635	0.024
	1980	0.285	0.674	0.029
Czechoslovakia	1930	0.327	0.558	0.030
	1961	0.254	0.722	0.032
	1980	0.271	0.716	0.035
Bulgaria	1905	0.694	0.737	0.008
	1934	0.379	0.750	0.030
	1956	0.236	0.776	0.057
	1970	0.189	0.778	0.069

	Date	Ig	Im	Ih
Romania	1899	0.645	0.727	0.216
	1930	0.489	0.667	0.111
	1956	0.346	0.694	n.a.
	1970	0.199	0.764	n.a.
(Serbia)	1900	0.649	0.808	0.031
Yugoslavia	1931	0.509	0.682	0.061
	1960	0.322	0.684	0.066
	1970	0.248	0.697	0.052
Russia	1897	0.755	0.696	0.048
	1926	0.665	0.628	0.028
	1959	0.356	0.581	n.a.
	1970	0.233	0.656	n.a.
Australia	1861	0.691	0.696	0.037
	1881	0.736	0.520	0.036
	1911	0.557	0.475	0.030
	1933	0.321	0.522	0.017
New Zealand	1874	0.804	0.677	0.028
	1901	0.566	0.439	0.021
	1911	0.502	0.501	0.023
	1936	0.329	0.508	0.016

Sources: A. J. Coale and S. C. Watkins (eds), *The Decline of Fertility in Europe* (Princeton, Princeton University Press, 1986), chapter 2, table 2.5 and appendix A; and for Australasia: E. F. Jones, 'Fertility Decline in Australia and New Zealand 1861–1936', *Population Index* 37 (1971), pp. 301–38.

Note: Where figures for 1980 were not available for some of the three indices, data for 1970 have been used instead. These figures are shown in italics on the '1980' line (this relates to both Ig and Ih for Denmark and Sweden). For some other countries no data were available for 1980, in which case values for 1970 only have been given.

Notes

An earlier version of this chapter appeared as Working Paper no. 62 (1996) of the Demography Program of the Research School of the Social Sciences, Australian National University. That version incorporates lengthier consideration of various more technical demographic issues, which have been omitted here to save space. I wish to thank the demographers and historians at ANU for their generous hospitality during a period spent as Visiting Fellow during 1996 and in particular I wish to thank Gordon Carmichael and Peter McDonald for their most helpful comments on this paper.

1 M. Mason, *The Making of Victorian Sexuality* (Oxford, Oxford University Press, 1994), in particular pp. 42–4.

2 J.-L. Flandrin, *Families in Former Times: Kinship, Household and Sexuality* (Cambridge, Cambridge University Press, 1979); M. Ingram, *Church Courts, Sex and Marriage in England 1570–1640* (Cambridge, Cambridge University Press, 1987).

3 A. J. Coale, 'Factors Associated with the Development of Low Fertility: An Historic Survey', in *International Population Conference*, Liege, vol. 1 (Liege: IUSSP, 1965), pp. 53–72; A. J. Coale, 'Age Patterns of Marriage', *Population Studies*, 25 (1971), pp. 193–214. See Appendix source note.

4 C. Wilson, J. Oeppen and M. Pardoe, 'What Is Natural Fertility? The Modelling of a Concept', *Population Index* 54 (1988), pp. 4–20.

5 Wilson, Oeppen and Pardoe, 'What Is Natural Fertility?'.

6 Note that entry into marriage was only associated with commencement of reproductive activities, and was not the necessary trigger for it. In many European plebeian cultures throughout the early modern and modern periods, sexual intercourse frequently anticipated the ceremony of marriage and, when accompanied by a verbal promise of marriage exchanged between the two partners, was popularly considered to constitute the principal act creating a marriage, just as the church did not deem a marriage to have occurred without consummation. See, for instance, J. Goody, *The Development of the Family and Marriage in Europe* (Cambridge, Cambridge University Press, 1983).

7 J. Hajnal, 'Age at Marriage and Proportions Marrying', *Population Studies*, 7 (1953/4), pp. 111–36.

8 M. Schofield, *The Sexual Behaviour of Young People* (Harmondsworth, Penguin, 1965); M. Schofield, *The Sexual Behaviour of Young Adults* (London, Allen Lane, 1968).

9 The field has been succinctly summarised in G. A. Carmichael, 'Consensual Partnering in the More Developed Countries', *Journal of the Australian Population Association*, 12 (1995), pp. 51–86; see especially figure 1 and figure 2. See also G. Carmichael, 'From Floating Brothels to Suburban Semi-respectability: Two Centuries of Nonmarital Pregnancy in Australia', *Journal of Family History*, 21 (1996), pp. 281–315.

10 S. Szreter, *Fertility, Class and Gender in Britain, 1860–1940* (Cambridge, Cambridge University Press, 1996), chapters 7–8.

11 Szreter, *Fertility, Class and Gender*, pp. 382–98. This difference was upheld

after allowing for the greater tendency to prenuptial pregnancy among the younger-marriers and the slightly lower fecundity of the late-marriers.

12 A. Hardy and S. Szreter, 'Urban Fertility and Morality Patterns', in M. Daunton (ed.), *Cambridge Urban History of Britain, Vol. III 1840–1950* (Cambridge, Cambridge University Press, 1999).

13 The four exceptions to this statement – Finland and the three Mediterranean countries of Italy, Spain and Greece – will be discussed below.

14 On the characteristics of the north-west European late marriage pattern, see J. Hajnal, 'European Marriage Patterns in Perspective', in D. V. Glass and D. Eversley (eds), *Population in History: Essays in Historical Demography* (London, Edward Arnold, 1965), pp. 101–43; J. Hajnal, 'Two Kinds of Preindustrial Household Formation', *Population and Development Review*, 8 (1982), pp. 449–94; E. A. Wrigley and R. S. Schofield, *The Population History of England 1541–1871: A Reconstruction* (London, Edward Arnold, 1981). Of course the logic of this social development would not necessarily apply at all in societies outside Europe not characterised by the late marriage institution.

15 E. van de Walle, *The Female Population of France in the Nineteenth Century: A Reconstruction of 82 Départements* (Princeton, Princeton University Press, 1974), chapter 7, section IV; D. Weir, 'New Estimates of Nuptiality and Marital Fertility in France, 1740–1911', *Population Studies*, 48 (1994), pp. 307–31.

16 J.-L. Flandrin, 'Contraception, Marriage and Sexual Relations in the Christian West', in R. Forster and O. Ranum (eds), *The Biology of Man in History* (selections from *Annales* trans. E. Forster and P. Ranum) (Baltimore, Johns Hopkins University Press, 1975), pp. 23–47; J.-L. Flandrin, *Families in Former Times: Kinship, Household and Sexuality*, trans. R. Southern (Cambridge, Cambridge University Press, 1979); A. Corbin, *Women for Hire: Prostitution and Sexuality in France after 1850*, trans. A. Sheridan (Cambridge, MA, Harvard University Press, 1990); T. Zeldin, *France, 1848–1945. Vol. I: Ambition, Love and Politics* (Oxford, Oxford University Press, 1973).

17 D. Kemmer, 'The Marital Fertility of Edinburgh Professionals in the Later Nineteenth Century', unpublished Ph.D. thesis, University of Edinburgh, 1989.

18 P. Laslett, *Family Life and Illicit Love in Earlier Generations* (Cambridge, Cambridge University Press, 1977); P. Laslett and C. Oosterveen, 'Long-term Trends in Bastardy in England', *Population Studies*, 27 (1973), pp. 255–86.

19 L. Hall, *Hidden Anxieties: Male Sexuality 1900–50* (Cambridge, Polity Press, 1991); R. Porter and L. Hall, *The Facts of Life: The Creation of Sexual Knowledge in Britain, 1650–1950* (New Haven, Yale University Press, 1995), chapters 10–11; Szreter, *Fertility, Class and Gender*, pp. 396, 402, 407 for references to further evidence, including oral history.

20 K. J. Mumford, '"Lost Manhood" Found: Male Sexual Impotence and Victorian Culture in the United States', in J. C. Fout and M. S. Tantillo (eds), *American Sexual Politics: Sex, Gender and Race since the Civil War* (Chicago, University of Chicago Press, 1993), pp. 75–99.

21 R. P. Davenport-Hines, *Sex, Death and Punishment: Attitudes to Sex and*

Sexuality in Britain since the Renaissance (London, Collins, 1990), chapters 2, 5–7.

22 S. K. Kent, *Sex and Suffrage in Britain, 1860–1914* (Princeton, Princeton University Press, 1987); C. Dyhouse, *Feminism and the Family in England 1880–1939* (Oxford, Oxford University Press, 1989); B. Caine, *Victorian Feminists* (Oxford, Oxford University Press, 1992); venereal disease and the Contagious Diseases Acts had, of course, provided an important focus for feminist mobilisation since the 1860s: J. Walkowitz, *Prostitution and Victorian Society: Women, Class and the State* (Cambridge, Cambridge University Press, 1980).

23 L. Bland, *Banishing the Beast: English Feminism and Sexual Morality 1885–1914* (Harmondsworth, Penguin, 1995).

24 C. Quétel, *History of Syphilis* (Oxford, Polity, 1990), chapters 6, 8–9.

25 Szreter, *Fertility, Class and Gender*, chapter 8. For a brief period, a revisionist view of 'Victorian' sexuality, as hedonistic in private, has held sway, following the publication in 1984 of Peter Gay's two-volume *The Bourgeois Experience* (New York, Oxford University Press), documenting the very uninhibited relationships of two nineteenth-century American women and the apparent implications of a turn-of-the-century survey of the sexual attitudes of a further forty or so American women. However, the latter source – the Mosher survey – has now been shown by Steven Seidman to have been over-enthusiastically misinterpreted by the iconoclastic proponents of a hidden Victorian pro-sensualism: S. Seidman, 'The Power of Desire and the Danger of Pleasure: Victorian Sexuality Reconsidered', *Journal of Social History*, 23 (1990), pp. 46–67. A number of more substantially documented works using a large variety of relevant British source materials have recently appeared in the 1990s, by Michael Mason, Lesley Hall and Lucy Bland (see previous footnotes for references), along with John Maynard's *Victorian Discourses on Sexuality and Religion* (Cambridge, Cambridge University Press, 1993). These all point towards the 'anti-sensualist' (Michael Mason's term) substance of a socially dominant 'Victorian' sexual ideology from the 1850s onwards. This now seems indisputable, regardless of the inevitable existence of individual mavericks and of certain currents of discourse flowing against the tide.

26 A. J. P. Taylor, *English History 1914–45* (Oxford, Oxford University Press, 1965), p. 166.

27 J. Walkowitz, *Prostitution and Victorian Society*; F. Finnegan, *Poverty and Prostitution* (1979).

28 K. Israel, 'French Vices and British Liberties: Gender, Class and Narrative Competition in a Late Victorian Sex Scandal', *Social History*, 22 (1997), pp. 1–26.

29 E. F. Jones, 'Fertility Decline in Australia and New Zealand 1861–1936', *Population Index*, 37 (1971), pp. 301–38.

30 On the nineteenth-century history of Australian marriage and sexuality see P. F. McDonald, *Marriage in Australia: Age at First Marriage and Proportions Marrying 1860–1971* (Canberra, Australian National University, Department of Demography, 1975); G. Carmichael, 'From Floating Brothels'. An important point, of course, is that, from the 1840s and 1850s onwards, the Australian population was recruited from a very

substantial inflow of non-convicts; furthermore the buoyancy of the resource-rich continent's young economy meant that the city of Melbourne famously enjoyed the highest per capita income in the world briefly in the 1880s. The classic study is Graeme Davison's *The Rise and Fall of Marvelous Melbourne* (Melbourne, Melbourne University Press, 1978).

31 P. J. P. Goldberg, *Women, Work and Life Cycle in a Mediaeval Economy: Women in York and Yorkshire c. 1300–1520* (Oxford, Oxford University Press, 1992); D. Herlihy and C. Kalpisch-Zuber, *Tuscans and their Families: A Study of the Florentine Catasto of 1427* (New Haven, Yale University Press, 1985).

32 For documentation of this in Italy see D. J. Kertzer and D. P. Hogan, *Family, Political Economy and Demographic Change: The Transformation of Life in Casalecchio, Italy 1861–1921* (Madison, Wisconsin University Press, 1989).

33 On padrone sexual exploitation, see J. and P. Schneider, 'Going Forward in Reverse Gear: Culture, Economy and Political Economy in the Demographic Transitions of a Rural Sicilian town', in J. R. Gillis, L. A. Tilly and D. Levine (eds), *The European Experience of Declining Fertility: A Quiet Revolution 1850–1970* (Oxford, Blackwell, 1992), pp. 146–74.

34 D. J. van de Kaa, 'The Second Demographic Transition Revisited: Theories and Expectations', in G. C. N. Beets, J. C. van den Brekel, R. L. Cliquet, G. Dooge and J. de Jong Gierveld (eds), *Population and Family in the Low Countries 1993: Late Fertility and Other Current Issues* (Lisse, Swets & Zeitlinger, 1994), pp. 81–126, tables 2 and 4.

35 See Carmichael, 'Consensual Partnering', figure 2. This shows Greece (3%), in particular, and also Italy (7%) with the lowest percentages of all births occurring outside marriage (among developed 'Western' nations in 1990), where comparable figures for Sweden and Denmark were just under 50%. Spain, however, although still relatively low, at about 10%, was showing a distinct upward trajectory by 1985. The only other extremely low non-marital fertility countries were Switzerland (7%) and Germany (10%), both of which also exhibited little increase over the whole period from 1965.

36 On the Swedish 'post-nuclear family' as a supposed harbinger of universal change, see D. Popenoe, *Disturbing the Nest: Family Change and Decline in Modern Societies* (New York, Aldine de Gruyter, 1988), p. 74.

37 On apprenticeship and service see A. Kussmaul, *Servants in Husbandry in Early Modern England* (Cambridge, Cambridge University Press, 1981); and on friends see N. Tadmor, '"Family" and "Friend" in *Pamela*: A Case Study in the History of the Family in Eighteenth-century England', *Social History*, 14 (1989), pp. 290–306.

38 It is relevant to note, in this connection, that immigrant ethnic communities from these southern European countries have continued to exhibit these patterns in Australia: P. McDonald, 'Migrant Family Structure', in K. Funder (ed.), *Images of Australian Families* (Melbourne, Melbourne University Press, 1991).

39 On the important precedence of Danish policies for the Swedish model of the welfare state, see, for instance, D. Levine, *Poverty and Society: The Growth of the American Welfare State in International Comparison* (New

Brunswick, Rutgers University Press, 1988).

40 The OECD Economic Outlook's Historical Statistics showed that in 1984, whereas Sweden, Finland, Denmark and Norway led the OECD table with over two-thirds (and in Sweden's case over three-quarters) of women aged fifteen to sixty-four classified as in the labour force, in Austria and Germany only one-half of such women were so classified; only the three Mediterranean countries, the Netherlands and Ireland returned lower figures of female participation in 1984 (while Belgium and Switzerland recorded comparable levels to Germany and Austria). Source: *Women and Work* (Canberra, Australian Dept of Employment and Industrial Relations, Women's Bureau, July 1987).

41 M. Drake, *Population and Society in Norway 1735–1865* (Cambridge, Cambridge University Press, 1969).

42 Of course it then becomes an interesting question to ask why the other major maritime nations of Europe, those of Britain, apparently did not share these characteristics as strongly.

43 Obviously the Jewish losses in the Second World War were of a different scale altogether than those of any other people. But, in terms of the nations tabulated in the Appendix, it may well be that the German populace suffered a greater proportionate loss of its male population than that of any of the countries which the Nazis invaded, including even the Russians, whose absolute losses were greater but whose proportionate losses were probably significantly less.

44 There is now a large literature on this. For a recent guide see P. Summerfield, 'Gender and War in the Twentieth Century', *The International History Review*, 19 (1997), pp. 1–15.

45 D. J. van de Kaa, 'The Second Demographic Transition Revisited', tables 2 and 4.

46 *Ibid.*, table 2.

47 On the concept of communication communities, as the appropriate units of demographic and social change, see Szreter, *Fertility, Class and Gender*, pp. 350–66, 443–65, 481–558.

48 Van de Kaa, 'The Second Demographic Transition Revisited', table 2.

49 Of course official abortion data remain very variable in quality, and many European countries do not appear to publish such statistics. Comparative information, such as it is, for 1965–92 can be found in A. Monnier and C. de Guibert-Lantoine, 'The Demographic Situation of Europe and the Developed Countries Overseas: An Annual Report', *Population: An English Selection*, 6 (1994), pp. 203–22, table 6A, p. 220.

50 See note 40.

51 Information on divorce ratios calculated in this way from Monnier and de Guibert-Lantoine, 'The Demographic Situation', table 5, p. 218.

52 On the importance of societies' codes of honour see P. Bourdieu, *Outline of a Theory of Practice* (Cambridge, Cambridge University Press, 1977).

53 It may well be the case that those individuals within each European society who are upwardly socially mobile from the proletarian majority into the ranks of the professional and managerial social elite do tend quite disproportionately to leave behind their parental language and code of

childrearing and parenting, adopting instead a more international, 'middle-class' set of attitudes and behaviours most strongly influenced by the values of individual self-assertion and rational consumerism, whose successful manifestation will have been essential for their upward social mobility in the first place. However, this process of class-crossing abandonment of inherited, historic familial values has remained a small minority phenomenon. Regardless of their respective ideologies of liberal meritocracy, highly restricted patterns of upward social mobility have continued to prevail in all European countries since the Second World War, including even such supposedly non-elitist states as Sweden as well as the notoriously class-ridden societies of Britain and France. In most countries, therefore, the majority have continued to adhere to the social codes of the identities in which they were reared. On relatively modest and static rates of social mobility since the Second World War in England and Wales, France, West Germany, Hungary, Ireland, Scotland, Northern Ireland, Poland and Sweden (all the countries studied) see R. Erickson and J. H. Goldthorpe, *The Constant Flux: A Study of Class Mobility in Industrial Societies* (Oxford, Oxford University Press, 1992), esp. chapters 3, 7, 11.

54 J. Lewis and K. Kiernan, 'The Boundaries between Marriage, Non-marriage, and Parenthood: Changes in Behaviour and Policy in Postwar Britain', *Journal of Family History*, 21 (1996), pp. 372–87.

55 On 'the mixed economy of caring' and the history of social policy and the family in England before and since the Elizabethan Poor Laws see, for instance, R. M. Smith, 'Welfare and the Management of Demographic Uncertainty', in M. Keynes (ed.), *The Political Economy of Health and Welfare* (Basingstoke, Macmillan, 1988), pp. 108–35; J. Lewis, 'Presidential Address: Family Provision and Welfare in the Mixed Economy of Care in the Late Nineteenth and Twentieth Centuries', *Social History of Medicine*, 8 (1995), pp. 1–16. On the influence upon the demography of sexuality of the distinctive religious, legal and ecclesiastical institutions of different European states see A. Dittgen, 'The Form of Marriage in Europe: Civil Ceremony, Religious Ceremony. Survey and Trends', *Population: An English Selection*, 7 (1995), pp. 95–124.

9

Cultures of abortion in The Hague in the early twentieth century

Willem de Blécourt

Some advice

The abortion of foetuses, ah, that's only a small matter nowadays. It just depends on how it's done. Most women go to the 'Sanitas' shops. That's all nonsense. All those pills, those mimosa tinctures, that's nothing. The women, in their distress, pay sums of twelve fifty for it. But it doesn't help at all. Tell that black lady of yours, whom you made pregnant: 'one should treat oneself'. The only effective treatment is to spray soap into the womb. To this end she has to buy an ordinary douche. She should unscrew the cannula and buy a catheter to screw on the syringe. The rubber ball should be filled with soap, then the catheter should be placed into the womb. When this is done, then one should squeeze the ball gently. Very carefully. Too strong a squeeze makes the woman pass out. Sometimes the catheter is put into the womb just to keep it open. But the first method is preferable. That's the safest way for women. I also know the practices of the so-called 'experts' quite well. These people are unscrupulous. They demand ample payment. These people also use soap most of the time, but the curse for the woman's health is that they always mix it with a few drops of vitriol. This produces excellent results, the foetus comes off right away, but most of the time the woman gets ill and keeps ailing. It's easy to get rid of the foetus when one knows how to do it right.

Thus the frank advice of a fortune-teller in The Hague in 1925 to a male visitor.[1]

The approach

The abortion issue, so Carroll Smith-Rosenberg argued, 'functions as a sexual language through which divergent gender, economic, regional, and religious groups discuss issues of social change and social conflict far broader than the fate of fetuses or even the sexual rights of adult women'.[2] She may be perfectly right, but in concentrating on groups (a programme for the future rather than the result of past research) she tends, in a sense, to throw away the baby with the bathwater. Examining cultures of abortion certainly requires attention to different sexual languages. It would be rash, however, to disregard the language, experience and actions of those primarily involved: the aborting women, their male partners and the abortionists. As Barbara Brookes stated: 'The problem confronting historians ... is how to uncover the private decision-making that collectively determined the wider history of reproduction. We need to understand why and how individuals limited births and what role spouses, lovers and female friends played in this process.'[3]

The focus on speaking and acting individuals, on abortion practices, has hardly been applied in historical abortion studies. The abortion history of the United States has been called 'a curiously faceless one'.[4] 'Very little research has been done into the practices of illegal male and female abortionists', wrote the anthropologist Lodewijk Brunt about the Dutch state of the art.[5] The few publications in which these topics are addressed for other countries are largely descriptive. Yet as a historical anthropologist I am still, and maybe foolhardily, looking for patterns, for the more abstract and more ordered dimension behind the descriptive one. My starting point, however, is abortion and the choices made by aborting women. That is to say that most of my sources were written down only at the moment when women had already decided to resort to abortion. The choices I will discuss are those between the different possibilities of obtaining the means of abortion, such as presented in the opening quotation. For the women abortion seems to have been the only reasonable option; the choice of having the child seems not to have been realistic. As the gynaecologist Hector Treub disclosed about his sixteen years' practice, of all the women who asked him for abortion, every single one whom he (on legal grounds) had refused to help had found some other means.[6] Similar reports were given in the early 1930s.[7]

Using the concept of 'cultures' involves at least three fields of attention. I have come to consider 'culture' as processes of attaching form and meaning to fragments of everyday life, to experiences people had and situations they found themselves in. The plural 'cultures' points to the differences in these processes, arising from differences in (cultural) characteristics such as gender, class, age and occupation. Above all it points to conflicts about the production of forms and meanings. Looking for the rationales of people's choices on the abortion market amounts to concentrating on specific, situated materialisations of wishes to end a pregnancy – or, as would be more consistent with early twentieth-century discourse, to restore menstruation. The search for means to obtain an abortion can be seen as processes of communication. As only fragments of these processes have survived, the precise considerations of single individuals can be inferred only on the basis of a general, though tentative, outline, combined with selected case material.

Meaning, of course, can be only analytically separated from form; different wordings can refer to differences in meaning, even if the more obscure kind of language (as in the restoration metaphor, or in the designation of abortionists) was primarily used for moral and legal reasons. Current images of abortion and stereotypes of abortionists merely point to the meaning that was attached to the abortion issue by those who utilised these images. Whether they contained verifiable 'truth' or not is of less importance than their function in the political debates. Questions about the different meanings of abortion lead also to consideration of the wider discourses of which the abortion issue was part. Ultimately this would direct the discussion to social change. On a practical level, however, these encompassing discourses are about birth control, about 'women's responses to their physical functions' and 'male and female attitudes towards sexuality'.[8] They deal with norms concerning the place and function of women in society, although this could be a conclusion rather than a presumption.

This chapter attempts to reconstruct the abortion market of The Hague, the governmental seat of the Netherlands, during the early twentieth century. This city is not typical of any 'urban' culture of abortion, but neither is Amsterdam or Rotterdam. The Hague was selected merely because more records as well as records of a greater variety have survived than in the other main Dutch cities. To assess the main source, the verdicts of the court of The Hague, it is necessary to discuss their production, scope and possible bias. A recurrent theme will be the gender division in abortion decisions. Abortion may have been 'part of a female subculture', as Patricia Knight surmised, but advice and help was *not* 'invariably provided by female relations, friends or "midwives"',[9] neither in the Netherlands nor for that matter in England or Germany. The situation was more complex in that the female 'subculture' seems to have been dominant in specific urban settings, even when men were participating. After all, the abortionist's clients were all women.

The legal arena

In the early twentieth-century Netherlands a heightened attention to the abortion issue resulted in a reform of the criminal law regulating abortion. The debates were surely fuelled by a perceived increase in abortion cases, but whether this corresponded with any actual increase remains to be seen. In 1908 the leading gynaecologists Hector Treub and Catharine van Tussenbroek concluded that the crime of abortion was widespread and its frequency was rising alarmingly.[10] Their findings were based on figures showing the proportion of criminal abortions within the total number of abortion cases treated in several women's clinics. Four years later, however, this percentage had fallen again.[11] The medical opinions on these percentages were too divergent, the jurist Valkhoff deduced, they were probably too much influenced by the different gynaecologists' worldviews.[12] Another author pointed to the hitherto unknown existence and proliferation of professional abortionists.[13] Estimates were notoriously vague, but everyone agreed on the expansion of abortion practices. Foreign criminal statistics and impressions from gynaecologists from France, Germany and the United States were presented to underline the seriousness of the Dutch situation.[14]

The firmest figures on criminal abortion are those of the prosecution of abortionists. From 1912 onwards the new Dutch Morality Act, which added a paragraph 251bis to the Criminal Law, facilitated the conviction of abortionists. Before that it had hardly made any sense to prosecute them, as evidence was needed that the foetus had been alive. The new paragraph provided for a procedure in which it had to be legally established only that an abortionist had conveyed the impression that he or she would help a woman who thought she was pregnant. The legal formula ran as follows: 'to treat a woman on purpose by arousing her hopes of disrupting pregnancy' (the legal subtleties probably disappear in translation). In the Netherlands the conditions for prosecuting abortionists thus did not depend on the pregnancy of the woman, nor did the abortionist have to have been operating on her body. To secure a conviction the statement of the aborting woman had to be confirmed by the abortionist, or (in a small minority of cases) by other witnesses. It needed two independent witnesses to establish a 'fact' legally. In spite of an older, but still operating paragraph 295, which prescribed a maximum of three years' imprisonment for the aborting women, they were never brought to trial. The reason behind paragraph 251bis was to protect the woman and to punish the abortionist, and it would have been counter-productive to prosecute the aborting woman, as she was the crown witness.[15] Furthermore, the police as well as the judiciary considered the violation of paragraph 295 the lesser social evil.[16] Prosecution of aborting women was not obligatory, as it was in Germany.

Dutch legal considerations thus differed from those in Germany, where the aborting woman was liable to prosecution; Dutch legal practice also differed from the British approach, where prosecution depended on her death.[17] But although Dutch conviction rates rose sharply after 1911 (and even surpassed the British), they can hardly serve as an indication for abortion rates. Evidence of only one case sufficed to convict an abortionist. The number of abortionists may have been precisely known to the vice squads of the three main cities, Amsterdam, Rotterdam and The Hague, but the scope of their practices varied too much to be of statistical relevance.[18] In the one case in which a cash book, running from 1943 to 1948, has survived, the abortionist performed nearly one abortion a week.[19] But this concerns a professional male abortionist, and he cannot be taken as representative of, for instance, occasional women abortionists.

Women wanting an abortion often had some trouble finding an abortionist. The vice squads of the city police (in the case of The Hague) had the advantage over these women in that they had more information about abortionists and abortion practices than about any other institution. The sources of their knowledge can be divided into two categories. The police monitored professional abortionists by keeping track of their newspaper advertisements and by spying on their houses and shops. Also a stream of incidental information reached the police by way of signed and anonymous letters, telephone calls and oral denouncements. Looking into the letters and journals, one finds family members denouncing their female relatives, a woman who came to complain about her (subsequently estranged) husband of having forced an abortion on her. The language of abortion is aptly illustrated in the case where someone told the police about a conversation he had heard in the street, when a druggist said goodbye to a couple with the woman having difficulties walking: 'I hope all goes well.' The woman had allegedly remarked to her companion: 'I have such a pain; it took long, didn't it, but now I'm glad to have lost the burden.' Even if this did not refer to an abortion, by being understood as abortion speech it does reveal the secrecy surrounding it and the indirect ways it was discussed.[20] Another entry in the files (only a few have survived) concerns a street vendor who told the police that he had occasionally heard moans at a certain address.[21] Even from the few accounts that have survived, the abortion issue appears to be set in an atmosphere of suspicion and distrust. Yet without asking around no woman would find the opportunity of getting what she wanted.

While every report was carefully checked, possible witnesses interrogated and suspect houses placed under surveillance, the police also met with blunt denials ('my wife wasn't even pregnant'), mere gossip and inconclusive evidence. To keep silent about abortion was as important as to talk about it. Doctors who were confronted either with patients seeking an abortion or with those who suffered from the after-effects of the operation were reluctant to break the trust that was put in them; confidentiality was part of their professional conduct and they were willing to violate it only with the woman's permission. Lay abortionists had their own reasons for secrecy, and some of them threatened women with paragraph 295,[22] or even put a bag over their faces, so as to avoid recognition. The aborting women, in their turn, will have had their own ideas about shame and exposure. Those who co-operated with the law were only those who, in some way or other, had resolved to break their silence.

Over the years the most persevering abortionist will certainly have left traces in the court records, the more notorious even several. Apart from recidivism, this points to the finiteness of the reservoir of abortionists. Those who were missed by the prosecuting system would have been the occasional abortionists: those who had tried it once to help an acquaintance in need. Trial figures thus grant only a distorted view of the supply side of the abortion market. This is why it seems more relevant to consider the types of services on offer, rather than their precise number.

Figures are nevertheless not totally useless. Whatever the biases in the prosecution policy and practice, they do not seem to have significantly influenced the male–female ratio. Thus some patterns of distribution, or at least hypotheses about them, may still be revealed. Between 1910 and 1930 the court of The Hague dealt with ninety-five abortionists from that town, sixty-eight of them women and twenty-seven men. (The court also convicted people from the town of Delft and Leiden and the countryside in between.) The fact that women abortionists prevailed in the city becomes even more pronounced when Rotterdam is taken into account, with 111 female and only fourteen male abortionists during the same period.[23] In rural areas, on the other hand, those prosecuted were almost exclusively male. This renders highly improbable the notion of a bias towards prosecuting women.[24] Indeed, if women abortionists had been practising in the rural areas of the Netherlands, they certainly would have been found out, as the norms about the division of labour between men and women were more strictly applied there. Within the towns, especially the urban agglomeration of the provinces of north and south Holland, women abortionists had more opportunities to practise their trade (and to attract clients from the countryside). A high prosecution rate, after all, can also be interpreted as a failure to control abortionists.

Public abortionists

Notwithstanding its secret nature, the abortion market needed a public face. Advertisement by word of mouth was insufficient, for the women seeking an abortion as well as for its suppliers. Open offers of abortion, however, were not just indelicate, they were also legally prohibited. Formulas thus needed to be both recognisable and inoffensive. An 'ex-nurse', for instance, who advertised herself as providing 'all medicines for ladies' and who could be consulted until 10 p.m., 'also on Sundays', was very likely to carry abortifacients as well.[25] From the advertisements alone it could not be inferred that abortions were procured. There merely existed a high probability that this would be the case. Judges, for example, deemed it unlikely that a woman operating a shop in hygienic articles by the name of 'Mata Hari', would restrict herself only to the one abortion for which she was convicted.[26] The statement of a twenty-nine-year-old office clerk may further clarify the way abortion advertisements were worded:

In November 1924 I put an ad in the *Haagsche Courant*. In it I posed as a doctor and at the top I put: 'blood circulation'. The advertisement read: 'Young doctor, gives advice; no drops etc., success ensured.' I inserted this ad several times and I received several letters. I then wrote to the women who had written to me to visit me at an address where acquaintances of mine lived with whom I had agreed to receive visitors there. That is where I treated women, to interrupt their pregnancies.

After talking about a specific case, he admitted: 'The reason for my action was that I needed to earn a living, because I had been fired from the municipal office.' He was sentenced to two months' jail.[27]

One of the obvious places to enquire for abortion services seems to have been a shop for 'hygienic' and 'rubber' articles, like the Sanitas company, which in 1919 had four branches in The Hague. Other shops had similar names like Sanitum and Securitas, to convey notions of safety and cleanliness. This was perfectly legal in itself, as such supplies were in demand also by medical institutions and personnel. Yet the fortune-teller's statement quoted at the start of this chapter was not only confirmed by one of her colleagues: proprietors of 'hygienic' shops were also repeatedly convicted of having procured abortion. Thus a man recommended his girlfriend to seek advice at one of those addresses from the newspaper. The one she chose said: 'Dr. Richters' drops and pills will definitely work. Absolutely harmless.'[28] Because of their visibility, the people running these hygienic shops were among the first to fall victim to the new law. 'Dr. M. Stopes' hygienic Articles and Patent Medicines. Consultations for ladies 1–3 p.m. and 7–9 p.m.', ran the advertisement of one merchant, who became one of the vice squad's regular targets. Thus Marie Stopes's name also drew customers outside Britain, whether she liked it or not. A couple who published a similar advertisement ('Dr. M. Stopes' Speciality, Hygienic Articles, Medicines, Ladies Syringes') explicitly told the police that they had not sunk to 'vile practices', although they did sell medicine for regulating menstruation, a common euphemism for abortion. As far as can be determined from the court verdicts, 'hygienic' shops also attracted women from outside The Hague.[29] Advertisements advising which tram to take to the shop, or telling the reader that the shop is located near a railway station, can be interpreted in a similar way.[30]

There was money to be made in the abortion business. But while abortionists' financial motives are revealed from time to time, the perseverance of some shopkeepers cannot be seen solely in commercial terms. A case in point is a former electrician who in the 1910s advertised under the name of 'Annema'. He seems to have employed commercial, that is high profit producing, methods only later in his career. He started by selling bottles of pills for 5 guilders, and only when these did not help did he offer a treatment for 100 guilders. These potions never produced the desired effect, as can be seen from the statements of the women seeking abortion, as well as from a report of the local health committee of The Hague. This body had some of the 'specialités' analysed and found that they merely served to line the purses of their vendors.[31] Annema's earlier abortion prices had been around 20 guilders (although still a substantial sum of money for an average household, this was more or less the usual price for a non-commercial abortion). Bankruptcy as well as repeated prison sentences did not deter him from his trade. As he usually manipulated women's vaginas with his fingers and boasted of his expertise, procuring abortions probably also satisfied some of his other needs.[32] After his divorce in 1921 he changed his trade name to Van Dam, while his former wife kept the name Annema. She was equally persistent as an abortionist and prosecuted for it at least five times during the 1910s and 1920s. In contrast to her husband, she seems to have shown some concern for the women she aborted. 'Will you write to me?', she asked a woman upon leaving in 1916. And 'do you have the nerve for it?' in 1925.[33] Admittedly these are only fragments to which it is easy to attach too much importance, but it is the difference between the man's practice and the woman's that has been transmitted, rather than the similarity between the partners.

Medical abortionists

'In every middle-sized town of our fatherland', wrote Treub, 'there are one or more physicians and midwives who are known to induce abortion on no other grounds than a woman's wish.'[34] Doctors regarded it their inalienable right to perform abortions, whether on pure medical or social indications.[35] Although in theory they were liable to prosecution, in practice they were usually left alone. In Rotterdam no doctor, and in The Hague only three of them, had to face the court on this account. At first instance it would seem that doctors were usually acquitted (three out of four cases; one of the doctors was prosecuted twice), but two of those acquittals were quashed on appeal.[36]

The Dutch association of (qualified) midwives abhorred abortion. It considered that a midwife's task was to deliver children into the world; to prevent their birth was diametrically opposed to her mission. As in Britain, midwives were 'anxious to distance themselves from the issue of abortion'.[37] The image of the abortionist midwife was apparently strong enough to produce this reaction.[38] A 1911 inquiry of the Dutch Medical Association into midwifery revealed that qualified midwives hardly ever terminated pregnancies. Three years earlier, when Treub and Van Tussenbroek had reported a pathologist's findings that a good number of the abortionists he had come across were former, renegade midwives, the editor of the *Tijdschrift voor Praktische Verloskunde* (*Journal of Practical Midwifery*) expressed his relief by underlining the 'former'. They were no disgrace to the present profession.[39] Yet the Neo-Malthusian League (NMB) favoured midwives as trainees to become birth control consultants. And the general public also linked birth and abortion. 'Midwife' (in Dutch: *verloskundige* rather than *vroedvrouw*) became a label used by abortionists in advertisements to convey the impression of expertise and asepsis. 'Expert' (Dutch: *deskundige*), the title introduced by the NMB for its trainees, became synonymous with 'abortionist'.[40] '*Real* midwives', it was remarked, 'don't advertise their services in the newspapers, and a midwife who lives in Amsterdam wouldn't really expect to perform deliveries out in Rotterdam'.[41]

The abortion court cases of The Hague feature only one midwife. Born in 1858 near the German border, she was found roaming the countryside at the age of forty, performing abortions by applying a bougie. At that time she lived in Amsterdam.[42] In 1912 she advertised in the newspapers as Mrs Bergman (a pseudonym), giving consultations at an address in The Hague. She also distributed leaflets, headed 'Neo-Malthusianism' and dealing with the limitation of offspring. The depositions by witnesses allow some insight into the secret nature of her performance. A woman had visited her, and the pregnancy she feared was confirmed by an investigation. 'If you don't want another child, you can get rid of it here', Bergman told her. The woman decided in favour of an abortion (without telling her husband). 'You don't have to be nervous, I have already helped so many people and I have never failed. It always went well.' After the midwife had completed the operation by sprinkling some blue powder into a tube which she had placed into the woman's vagina, she said: 'If you are stopped by someone from the police in the street, you should tell him that your cap has been adjusted.' Another client was told that there would be no pain. 'If you are going to consult a doctor, he won't see that I've helped you.' Bergman appeared to be well informed about the new law but did not manage to escape its clutches, being convicted in 1912 for two years, in 1916 for one year and in 1925 for six months. While her terms in prison went down (which was rather exceptional, as recidivism usually resulted in more severe sentences), her price went up. In 1912 she charged only 40 guilders, later 100. The extra care for the patient seems to have disappeared in the meantime. In 1925 a witness declared that she had suffered much pain (Bergman had administered curettage), fallen seriously ill soon afterwards and had been admitted to hospital because of it.

The rest of the (para)medical personnel in The Hague prosecuted for abortion consisted of one nurse (the title was not legally protected at the time). She had provided an office clerk with a reddish rubber hose and a four-day stay at her apartment, for which she charged 80 to 100 guilders – the employer paid for it. The nurse was suspected of this one treatment only, and she came off with a suspended sentence.[43] It is impossible to draw general conclusions from these two single cases (although in other Dutch cities a few more abortion-practising midwives and nurses could be found). But the last case can nevertheless be considered as a specific type of supply available on the abortion market, with or without nurses.[44] The midwife merely seems to have ranked as one of the professional 'experts'.

Fortune-tellers

When the label 'expert' had become too transparent for public use, others had to be found. According to a midwife in 1919, it was now the fortune-tellers who 'under the veil of fortune-telling, advise their clients thus' (meaning abortion).[45] She was not the only contemporary to associate fortune-telling with abortion, and indeed enough examples for a convincing argument can be cited of fortune-tellers who performed or at least suggested abortion. But if the two groups are compared as a whole for one city it turns out that, of the roughly one hundred abortionists and one hundred fortune-tellers in The Hague in the first three decades of the twentieth century, there is a potential overlap of only ten. Nevertheless it is worth considering the abortion-providing fortune-tellers here because their practices were especially noticeable. Like the 'experts' and the hygienic shopkeepers, fortune-tellers were closely watched by the vice squads. And without a trade union fortune-tellers could not, of course, present the counter-image official midwives did. A last reason to consider fortune-tellers is that reports of conversations between them and a policeman also afford another rare glimpse into everyday abortion language.

On one occasion the policeman with a remit to check fortune-tellers was brought into what he considered a rather filthy bed-sit. He sat down at a table and the woman asked him to draw seven cards (the number for an unmarried person). She told him that he had worries, that he was a businessman, that he would be lucky in his business but also get himself into much trouble. He took women into his life and they would play an important part in it. They either wanted or were forced to marry him. She also saw a death very clearly. He would have to face doctors and policemen. Then the fortune-teller asked specific questions: 'Did the woman he had made pregnant want to marry him? Did she want to get rid of it? Had she already done something about it?'[46] This same fortune-teller later advised a mother and a daughter who came to visit her about the pregnancy of the latter (which was visible in the cards as well) that she should bathe in luke-warm water in which soda and mustard were dissolved. As this did not help, the girl had to return time and time again; altogether she paid 90 guilders and still her baby was born.[47] The fortune-teller, who had been living above the family before and was thus familiar with their situation, apparently just wanted to exploit them. She was known as an 'expert' in the neighbourhood.

Between fortune-tellers and women seeking abortion, the language could be rather direct. As one woman declared: 'My menstruation was late and I suspected myself to be pregnant, so I had this fortune-teller laying out the cards for me and she confirmed it.'[48] It was not always necessary to consult the cards. Men seem to have been somewhat more cautious, but fortune-tellers were skilled enough to draw things out. A colleague and acquaintance of the first fortune-teller also brought her conversation with the (disguised) member of the vice squad to the subject of girls. From the man's face she deduced that he was weighed down by worries. He agreed whole-heartedly. Next she asked him whether he had perhaps 'shot' too far. He nodded confirmingly. Again studying the cards, she concluded that there was 'young' life in his family; he would not have been unaware of it. Thereupon he told her that he was at his wits' end and was looking for a way out. She consulted the cards anew, saying he would have to let it 'melt'. He answered: 'If that would be possible.' 'That is very well possible', she replied.[49]

The gender divide

'When husbands or lovers took the initiative to terminate a pregnancy they usually picked a male abortionist', Cornelie Usborne concluded from her German files.[50] This was very much the case in The Hague as well, with only one slight modification as the verdicts do not disclose much about who took the initiative (it presumably came from the women). The one incident of a lover insisting on his girlfriend having an abortion (typically?) involves Germans.[51] There is no further sign of lovers enforcing abortions. Women's own agency is more apparent; in a few cases it is disclosed that women themselves demanded abortion repeatedly and were even crying when asking for the abortionist's help.[52]

The more visible class of abortionists was of course consulted by both men and women, but male abortionists also acquired many customers through male networks. There is not only the almost classic image of the employer who went in search of a doctor after he had made his maidservant pregnant (he first suggested that the maid should consult her mother),[53] but also the husband visiting a druggist to buy medicines.[54] On the whole, however, it was mainly lovers who felt responsible and found other men to perform the operation. They made the appointment, paid 50 or 100 or even 200 guilders for it and had to wait outside when the abortionist demanded this in order to avoid extra witnesses.[55] Occasionally a lover treated his girlfriend himself, as in the case when a young woman repeatedly complained that her lover had not found an abortionist and finally got from him a potion consisting of water and essence of vinegar.[56]

Access to a woman abortionist, on the other hand, was often gained through other women. A particular woman living at the Hoefkade, for instance, was known to be experienced as well as cheap. She used Lysol or Sunlight soap and asked only 10 guilders,[57] which was the usual price. When women wanted an abortionist, they first asked around through their networks for advice. As they said in court: 'I heard that she was an abortionist'; 'A woman friend of mine arranged an abortionist and told me to visit a certain address'; 'She came to my house through the agency of another woman'.[58] Another was given by an unknown woman a note which contained a telephone number. A mother arranged a 'lady' for her daughter. Women collaborated to help friends, the one providing room and instruments, the other performing the act.[59] One female abortionist confessed to having learned from a woman who had been living with her how to interrupt the pregnancies of 'women who wanted it'. She operated on women at their home or else outside in the dunes and actively solicited customers, for example noticing that pregnant women visited a fortune-teller, and waiting for them outside on the street and proposing to help to get rid of the foetus.[60]

Some women abortionists hired touts who would earn a proportion of their fee for every woman sent. Or they made a similar deal with a fortune-teller. 'The women who visited me carried a note with a sign and a number from which I could understand that they came for an abortion and how much they would pay', one of them explained to the judges.[61] 'She told me she was short of money', related another woman about the one who organised her practice. 'She asked me if we could take up our former business of pricking again. She would provide the room and make sure that only the patients would notice anything about it' [previously they had both served a few months in prison for the same crime]. 'She already had some customers for me.' In this instance performing abortions was deemed less serious than organising them; in prison terms the difference was six months against eighteen months, also because the organiser had formerly been involved in sexual abuse and had been receiving stolen goods.[62] Women's choice of abortionists could also have been restricted by the wish to avoid involvement with practitioners suspected of petty crime. In The Hague these suspicions would have arisen simply because of the ill-fame of certain neighbourhoods.

Marriage

The bulk of the court material, however, consists of cases about which it is merely noted that so-and-so performed an abortion on certain (usually married) women in such-and-such a manner. Even the amount of money paid is not always specified. It is difficult to avoid the impression that the cases that carry more information are exceptional and that the best-known abortionists who were regularly prosecuted stand out amongst the many practitioners who operated on a less commercial basis. In other words, by focusing on hygienic shops, experts and even fortune-tellers it appears that the ordinary is slipping through, is escaping attention. Historians must not only break through the veil of obscurantist and euphemistic abortion language, they must also take into account what is left unspoken because it was so obvious that it did not need to be entrusted to records. Of course, this is an invitation for speculation.

The fortune-teller I quoted at the beginning of this chapter appears to have been well informed about the abortion market, although it is not certain how many women would have followed her advice about self-help as these did not end up in the criminal records. The method she proposed may have been the most safe and effective (as long as one operated with clean instruments and made sure that no air entered the bloodstream), but soap was not the most popular abortifacient used in The Hague (unlike Rotterdam from whence she came). It was catheters (small rubber hoses) which were most frequently applied in The Hague.

Yet it would be unwise to write off the hygienic shopkeepers and experts as uncharacteristic. Precisely because they showed the public face of abortion, they imply the hidden, female abortion culture by contrast. If they caught the police's attention, they also caught that of customers who were not informed about the inner abortion market: women from out of town and men. One of the main features of the public abortion supply is its commercialism. Choosing a male abortionist through male contacts, or even a well-known female expert, meant that the customer had to dig deep into his or her purse. Lovers seem to have paid most. An unwritten rule on the abortion market appears to have been that the responsibility of boyfriends and lovers for pre- or extramarital pregnancies entailed a large sum of money, in contrast to the small sum women usually paid. It was expected on both sides as proper restitution of the woman's honour, at least as long as marriage was not considered.

Husbands, on the other hand, were almost entirely absent from the abortion market. Within marriage the decision to abort was the woman's province. Her plight was reflected in the price; no one thought of extorting money from her. Early twentieth-century (Dutch urban) abortion, it turns out, has to be understood within the prevailing norms of marriage.[63] Outside marriage abortion was shameful; inside marriage it was almost normal. And if marriage was the stable and all-encompassing point of reference in women's lives, abortion (and by implication sexuality) was not only a means to discuss social and economic change; for women it was also a way to react to it.

Notes

1 Municipal Archive (henceforth GA) Den Haag, archief gemeentepolitie, 2558, nr 27.

2 Carroll Smith-Rosenberg, 'The Abortion Movement and the AMA, 1850–1880', in *Disorderly Conduct: Visions of Gender in Victorian America* (New York, A. A. Knopf, 1985), pp. 217–44.

3 Barbara Brookes, 'Women and Reproduction, 1860–1939', in Jane Lewis (ed.), *Labour and Love: Women's Experience of Home and Family, 1850–1940* (Oxford, Blackwell, 1986), pp. 148–71, p. 156.

4 Suzanne Poirier, 'Women's Reproductive Health', in Rima D. Apple (ed.), *Women, Health, and Medicine in America: A Historical Handbook* (New Brunswick, Rutges University Press, 1992), pp. 217–45, p. 237.

5 Lodewijk Brunt, 'Engeltjesmaaksters', *Vrij Nederland* (22 December 1979), p. 27.

6 Hector Treub, 'Abortus provocatus en strafwet', *Tijdschrift voor Strafrecht*, 9 (1896), pp. 1–24, esp. pp. 16, 23.

7 J. Valkhoff, 'De omvang van de kriminele vruchtafdrijving in Nederland', *Mensch en Maatschappij*, 8 (1932), pp. 38–57, esp. p. 47.

8 Quotations are taken from Angus McLaren, *Birth Control in Nineteenth-century England* (New York, Croom Helm, 1978), p. 231.

9 Patricia Knight, 'Women and Abortion in Victorian and Edwardian England', *History Workshop*, 4 (1977), pp. 57–68, p. 67.

10 Hector Treub and Catharine van Tussenbroek, 'Over den crimineelen abortus in Nederland', *Nederlandsch Tijdschrift voor Geneeskunde*, 52, IB (1908), pp. 1149–61.

11 Hector Treub, 'Eenige medisch-statistische cijfers over abortus criminalis', *Weekblad van het Recht*, 9311 (1912).

12 Valkhoff, 'De omvang', p. 41.

13 P. A. de Wilde, 'Toeneming der bevolking en stijging van den levensduur', *Mensch en Maatschappij*, 2 (1926), pp. 79–83, esp. p. 81.

14 P. van Heynsbergen and G. C. van Balen Blanken, *Abortus criminalis* (Amsterdam, Holland, 1925), pp. 56–62.

15 *Ibid.*, pp. 48–50.

16 J. Valkhoff, 'De vervolging en de bestraffing van den crimineelen abortus in Nederland', *Tijdschrift voor Strafrecht*, 41 (1931), pp. 136–58, esp. p. 139.

17 Barbara Brookes, *Abortion in England 1900–1967* (London/New York/Sydney, Croom Helm, 1988), p. 29.

18 Valkhoff, 'De omvang', p. 44.

19 Cornelis Nicolaas Peijster, *De onbekende misdaad* (The Hague, Nijhoff, 1957), p. 42.

20 GA Den Haag, archief gemeentepolitie, 2532, dd. 18 IV 1923.

21 GA Den Haag, archief gemeentepolitie, 2531, nr 18, dd. 25 I 1925.

22 Valkhoff, 'De vervolging'; Archive of the province of south Holland (RAZH), district court, arr. Den Haag 462, nr 712.

23 Figures are based on the indexes of the court records. RAZH, arr. Den Haag, nrs 49–67; arr. Rotterdam, nrs 732–9.

24 For a further discussion of the distribution and the different percentages of male and female abortionists, see Willem de Blécourt, *Het Amazonenleger: Irreguliere genezeressen in Nederland, ca. 1850–1930* (Amsterdam, Amsterdam University Press, 1999), chapter 8.

25 *Nosokómos*, 9 (1909), p. 493, from the *Haagsche Courant* (this advertisement did not turn up in my own sample).

26 RAZH, arr. Den Haag 619, nr 751.

27 RAZH, arr Den Haag 595, nr 230.

28 RAZH, arr. Den Haag 620, nr 1090; 619, nr 753.

29 RAZH, arr. Den Haag 492, nr 712; 507, nr 47.

30 See e.g. *Haagsche Courant*, 2 July 1919, 2 September 1925.

31 'Gevaarlijke en bedriegelijke handel met geneesmiddelen', *Tijdschrift voor Sociale Hygiëne*, 24 (1922), pp. 329–34.

32 RAZH, arr. Den Haag 467, nr 40; 507, nr 47; 589, nr 274; 613, nr 853.

33 RAZH, arr. Den Haag 504, nr 861; 598, nr 976.

34 Treub, 'Abortus provocatus en strafwet', p. 23.

35 Cf. Lodewijk Brunt, 'Het schandelijk misdrijf: Artsen in de strijd tegen abortus omstreeks 1900', *Amsterdams Sociologisch Tijdschrift*, 6 (1979), pp. 210–26.

36 *Weekblad van het Recht*, 11103 (9 November 1923).

37 Nicky Leap and Billy Hunter, *The Midwife's Tale. An Oral History from Handywoman to Professional Midwife* (London, Scarlet Press, 1993), p. 90.

38 Cf. Jean Donnison, *Midwives and Medical Men. A History of Interprofessional Rivalries and Women's Right* (London, Heinemann Educational, 1977), pp. 128, 130, 147 on the role of the abortion image in the discussion preceding the British Midwife Act. See also Leslie J. Reagan, *When Abortion was a Crime: Women, Medicine, and Law in the United States, 1867–1973* (Berkeley/Los Angeles/London, University of California Press, 1997), pp. 90–1.

39 *Tijdschrift voor Praktische Verloskunde*, 12 (1908), p. 29.

40 *Maandblad tegen de Kwakzalverij*, 20, 3 and 20, 4 (March and April 1900).

41 *Tijdschrift voor Praktische Verloskunde*, 23 (1919), p. 144.

42 *Weekblad van het Recht*, 7038, 7064, 7113.

43 RAZH, arr. Den Haag 506, nr 1153.

44 Cf. RAZH, arr. Den Haag 481, nr 600; 549, nr 2141.

45 *Tijdschrift voor Praktische Verloskunde*, 22 (1919), p. 329.

46 GA Den Haag, archief gemeentepolitie, 2558, nr 40.

47 RAZH, arr. Den Haag 599, nr 1244.

48 RAZH, arr. Den Haag 613, nr 808.

49 GA Den Haag, archief gemeentepolitie, 2558, nr 14. See also Piet Bakker, *Misdadige praktijken: Een onderzoek in de duistere wereld der aborteuses* (Rotterdam, n. p., 1931), p. 5.

50 Cornelie Usborne, 'Wise Women, Wise Men and Abortion in the Weimar Republic: Gender, Class and Medicine', in Lynn Abrahams and Elizabeth

Harvey (eds), *Gender Relations in German History: Power, Agency and Experience from the Sixteenth to the Twentieth Century* (London, London University Press, 1996), pp. 143–76, p. 152.

51 RAZH, arr. Den Haag 612, nr 613.

52 RAZH, arr. Den Haag 490, nr 345; 496, nr 982; 564, nr 270.

53 RAZH, arr. Den Haag 556, nr 532.

54 RAZH, arr. Den Haag 595, nr 72.

55 E.g.: RAZH, arr. Den Haag 486, nr 1108; 555, nr 490; 556, nr 535; 614, nr 1075.

56 RAZH, arr. Den Haag 619, nr 688; cf. 614, nr 1241.

57 RAZH, arr. Den Haag 606, nr 880; 616, nr 1880.

58 RAZH, arr. Den Haag 490, nr 361; 597, nr 688; 619, nr 754.

59 RAZH, arr. Den Haag 618, nr 512; 619, nr 751; 509, nr 400; 572, nr 1409.

60 RAZH, arr. Den Haag 481, nr 555.

61 RAZH, arr. Den Haag 506, nr 1131; cf. 561, nr 1424; 574, nr 189.

62 RAZH, arr. Den Haag 613, nrs 895, 896; cf. 592, nrs 909, 910.

63 Cf. Reagan, *When Abortion was a Crime*, pp. 32–3.

10

'Didn't stop to think, I just didn't want another one': the culture of abortion in interwar South Wales

Kate Fisher

Historical treatments of abortion are frequently clearly affected by the current, highly politicised, abortion climate, dominated by the awareness of the dangers and horrors of 'back street' abortions and the moral rhetoric about the right to life of the unborn foetus. Illegal abortion is generally perceived by historians as an unpalatable, dangerous, ethically disturbing family-planning option. That it was resorted to by many women is thus seen as testament to the desperation of many women and to the lack of alternative reproductive choices. Angus McLaren is typical in asking: 'why would women be so determined to avoid childbearing as to risk the dangers of abortion?'[1]

In my research, described below, respondents' representations of abortion were strikingly different from the late twentieth-century, Western culture of abortion and revealed that it is not useful or valid to assume that abortion was an illegal, dangerous and morally questionable method of fertility control employed by women only reluctantly. First, although most interviewees gave the impression that they were aware that going to an abortionist was illegal, there was less perception that self-induced abortions were criminal.[2] Second, respondents were often ignorant of, or at least indifferent to, the arguments which stress the rights of the unborn foetus and the sanctity of foetal life. Third, it was the perception of the health risks associated with terminating a pregnancy that dominated the testimony on abortion and predominantly determined women's preparedness to attempt to abort. In working-class circles there seems to have been very little condemnation of abortion, rather an acceptance of its practical importance. As Leslie Reagan agrees, 'the widespread acceptance of abortion, expressed in word and deed during the era of its illegality, suggests the persistence of a popular ethic that differed

213

from that of the law and the official views of medicine and religion'.[3]

This chapter considers the practice of and attitudes towards abortion as part of a wider oral history of contraceptive use, using a sample of men and women married during the interwar years. I interviewed a total of fifty-nine people, forty-one women and eighteen men. Three of these also took part in a group interview which included twelve other women. Most were widows or widowers, but there were five interviews with couples.[4] Three women refused to be taped. In addition, preliminary interviews (untaped owing to equipment failure and one woman's desire to be interviewed over the telephone) were also conducted with a further nine people. Interviews lasted up to four hours, covered various questions about marriage, family, courtship and sexual attitudes, and concentrated, in particular, on birth control practices. Dates of birth ranged from 1899–1925.[5]

I avoided self-selected samples and obtained interviewees largely through visits to old people's homes, day centres and social clubs.[6] Obviously, there remains a question as to whether those who agreed to be interviewed had atypical sexual experiences. Interestingly very few declined to be interviewed, and moreover I did not find that those who eagerly agreed to be interviewed and those who needed gentle encouragement differed noticeably in their experiences. All interviewees were guaranteed anonymity, and interviews took place in private, generally in the respondent's own home. Oral history is an important research tool for studying the subject of abortion, about which qualitative material is scarce. Oral history enables one to look carefully and in depth at how individual women felt about abortion and how they made decisions when faced with an unwanted pregnancy. It enables one to analyse the different experiences of a number of women and to examine what distinguished the women who were prepared to go to an abortionist, the women who were prepared to try and induce an abortion themselves and those who would do neither. Attitudes are revealed by the way stories are told as much as by what is said. For example, oral historians must pay attention to what is said unprompted, what juxtapositions and contrasts are drawn and what words are chosen.[7]

South Wales is a particularly interesting area in which to study attitudes towards abortion: during the interwar years abortion was widely perceived to be on the increase and South Wales was thought paradigmatic of this trend. This was linked by the medical authorities with the rising maternal mortality rate. The 1930 Report of the

Chief Medical Officer of the Ministry of Health expressed alarm at the maternal death rate in South Wales particularly, and the Ministry of Health report of 1932, 'High Maternal Mortality in Certain Areas', singled out Wales; it was the only area which warranted a separate chapter.[8] Abortion was thought to be both 'a public health problem of great gravity' and 'terribly rife in South Wales'.[9]

Respondents were seldom concerned by either the legal or the 'moral' issues surrounding abortion. Many were aware that abortion was illegal, though some gave the impression that they felt self-induced abortions were within the law. Abortifacients were commonly and easily available from 'reputable' outlets. Many ordinary chemists sold slippery elm bark, for example, which was one of the most common methods, and for which, according to the Birkett report on abortion, in bark form, there was no other 'legitimate' use.[10] Fear of being caught, or sent to jail, was not mentioned as a reason why abortion was not attempted or decided against. At all stages almost all the women interviewed seem to have made a decision about whether or not to attempt an abortion without considering the rightness or wrongness of destroying an unborn foetus. Many respondents gave no indication that they were aware of the existence of arguments condemning abortion on the grounds that a foetus has a right to life; no one seemed to feel the need to defend their or anyone else's actions against such 'moral' objections. When I specifically presented the 'pro-life' argument to them, some admitted that they now realise that many people think that abortion is a form of killing and a few agreed with this position. However, they affirmed that this was not an opinion they held at the time.[11]

Only two women unequivocally suggested that they felt that abortion was 'morally' wrong.[12] Aileen:

> The only thing I'm dead nuts against is abortion … 'cos I know quite a lot of my friends had abortions and it, that's really, I mean, that's taking a life, isn't it?[13]

Concerns about health dominated the discussion of abortion. Abortions were widely felt to be dangerous, and stories emphasised the gruesome. Doris:

> They knew ways and means of getting rid of them which I would never do.
> *Why was that?*

> Oh God, too dangerous. A friend of mine, across the road there,
> she did all sorts of things ... to get rid of it ... it was a wonder she
> didn't kill herself. I remember once she was walking around, blood
> pouring from her. How the heck she survived, I don't know.[14]

The perceived degree of danger was also the main criterion used to
distinguish between the different methods for terminating a pregnancy.
My respondents appear to have viewed going to an abortionist, as
opposed to any self-induced method with drugs or instruments, as
the most risky means of inducing a miscarriage. This was probably
at least in part due to the greater public awareness of tragedies
resulting from a visit to an abortionist, as such incidents were more
likely to result in a prosecution and wide newspaper coverage.[15]
Going to an abortionist was reported to have been very common,
and many gave details of relatives who had visited an abortionist.
However, no one admitted to having taken such a risk personally.
Edith was persuaded by her husband to go, but in the end was so
frightened that she might die that she could not go through with it.
She was very forthcoming with her narrative, which was long, detailed
and beautifully structured (refined through repeated tellings?).

So why didn't your husband want too many children?
Well, he had two sisters himself and they were very much against
having children, 'cos I know, when I was going to have my
daughter, they persuaded him, for me to have an abortion, which,
those days, wasn't a legal thing, it was done illegal by an old
woman. It was done illegal. And, they were very much, 'Oh, Bobby
you don't want more children, you don't want more children', they
were very much, his sisters were very much against, 'cos they
knew I was from a big family, and they were rather reluctant
about what was going to happen, whether I would have a big
family, because, I mean, some people can't have children, and some
have lots of children, especially as, years ago when we didn't know
any different, like, but of course it's different today. But they didn't
want any children, except they kept saying, 'Oh, Bobby, don't
want to have more children like', and when I was, they knew I was
having my daughter, they persuaded him and he did ask me to get
rid of her. Well, funny enough, he made this appointment, through
his sister, and it was a lady out in Canton that I was to go this
day, to this house, to get rid of her. Well, I know my sister she
was terribly upset when I told her that I was going. I went, and I
got as far as the lady's door, and d'you think I could knock that

door? I couldn't knock the door. I just couldn't go through with it myself, you know. So I stayed out till gone ten at night, and this was, I went and sat in the park and everything, did everything but rather go back home. But eventually I went back home and I said, 'I haven't gone', but I was supposed to have gone and had this old woman perform this abortion, which of course is, was a very wrong thing to do those days, I mean, you know, because I mean they used to, the girls used to, sometimes used to peg out didn't they? You know, they would, er, it wasn't done like in a hospital, it was just in a, in a woman's room, somewhere, I don't know where, I don't know what it was but, I just couldn't go, couldn't go. Any rate, I came back home and I said I couldn't go. I know he said, 'Well we'll try', he'd ring her up and it wasn't ringing her up, he'd go and see her and see again, but I, I definitely refused to go any more. I wasn't going to get, er, it wasn't so much the child I was thinking about, it was thinking about my own health, I thought I was going to die if she cut me open, I thought she'd be cutting me open, like, you know, to get this baby out, and I was so afraid of it myself that really I was afraid to go, although I went, I still couldn't make it, no.[16]

Dilys revealed, very tentatively, the attempts she made to 'shift' her foetus and interspersed this admission with denials. Health considerations, particularly the fear of failing to abort and having a handicapped child as a result, determined which methods she was prepared to try and which she never took. Her testimony reveals the way in which women discussed the different pills and potions rumoured to be efficacious, distinguishing between the ones she was prepared to take and the ones she was not.

Oh, they used to have a bottle of gin, that's why they called gin, 'old woman's ruin'. Because that was supposed to bring everything on, you know, but it didn't.
So what did you, you just drank the bottle?
We just drank it hot, you know, gin and, er, now they're giving you whisky now for heart trouble, and aspirin. I never took gin or anything like that, couple of doses of salts, nothing shifted, leave it alone.
So you tried?
Yes, well, you know, only on salts or anything like that, no gin, no nothing like that. Well, it could, it could bring on, if you took quinine, things like that now, it could bring on blindness in the child, and German measles does that now too.

> *So what was quinine?*
> Quinine, oh, horrible, bitter, I did take that.
> *You took that when you were pregnant?*
> Didn't do no good, not a bit of good.
> *So how much did you take and where did you get it?*
> Um, well, you could buy a bottle of quinine then, and put some in water or something like that, but it is very very bitter. Soldiers used to have that abroad, um, because of malaria. Very strong, but I wouldn't do anything like that, in case it harmed the child.[17]

Similarly, a midwife who gave evidence presented by the Midwives Institute to the Birkett Committee felt that 'the reason women so frequently asked if the baby was "all right" at birth was because they had so often taken abortifacient drugs'.[18]

Leslie illustrates well the dominance of health considerations over 'moral' ones. When discussing the pills that women frequently took to 'restore menses' by 'removing obstructions', he asserted that he 'never believed in them' because 'they might do more harm than good, might cause cancer'. When we discussed people who 'had abortions' he revealed the centrality of health issues and the marginality of 'moral' ones.

> *How did you feel about people who [had abortions]?*
> Well it's only looking after their interests.
> *What reasons are there for them, why they shouldn't, maybe shouldn't try?*
> Well, to me, it's detrimental to your health, innit?

Later in the interview I specifically asked him about the 'moral' issues associated with abortion, which had been totally absent from his testimony.

> *A lot of people now think that people who have abortions are killing children inside them.*
> Well they are, they definitely are, aren't they? They're stopping life, aren't they?
> *Did you use to think that years ago?*
> No. Never thought about it.[19]

The only indication that women were aware that abortion was felt to be illicit (either legally or morally) is revealed in the way in which abortion is discussed during the interview. Frequently abortion is discussed late on in the interview (once a closer relationship between the interviewer and interviewee has been established?) and often after a direct question on my part, rather than being mentioned unprompted during the general discussions of sex and birth control. Most of the abortion stories were told in the third person, and a few of those who admitted having attempted, or having thought about attempting, an abortion explicitly denied doing so at first.

Muriel is a good example. She began by talking about what her sister did, while claiming that she herself never took anything. Then a few seconds later she admitted to having tried Widow Welch's Pills. A few sentences further, however, she reasserted that 'she never bothered'.

Well, my sister did for one. She took different things, er, what they call it bitter, bitter something she used to take. In fact, she told me to take it, but I never.

And why didn't you?

No, I never done. I never. All I took was some Widow Welch's pills.

What are those?

'Cos they say they help to bring you on, you know. Anyhow, it didn't do nothing. I don't think I took enough really. But my sister took nearly everything, you know. She went to the herbalist and all got, got things, herbs. Lots of women used to go to women for them to try to, um, get rid of, you know, babies, but I never bothered.

Was it just you couldn't be bothered?

Well, I never both, I never, I wouldn't do it because I thought it was dangerous, you know.[20] Oh, I knew a few that went and had, you know, had the babies taken away, like. But, it was dangerous, see. I know a young girl died through it. Yeah, she used to, she lived in Oakdale and, this was after, ooh a long time after, I was married, and we lived in Springfield and, er, she was living with this, she was minding his children she was, and she got pregnant by him, and he had somebody to do something, you know, and, anyhow she died.

And it wasn't because you felt that it was wrong to go to one of these women?[21]

No.

It was just because it was dangerous?

It was dangerous, yeah. That's the only thing I took was Widow Welch's Pills.[22]

The overwhelming majority of women I spoke to who attempted to abort a child failed. Most stories involved botched attempts. Betty, for example, almost admitted having successfully aborted. She also began by telling me about the attempts her neighbour made to 'try and get rid of it' (though this was unprompted), but when recalling what this friend took she, perhaps unwittingly, revealed subjective knowledge of the method which prompted her to reveal her own experience. However, she was careful to point out that the period she brought on did not contain a 'clot', signifying that she had not been pregnant after all.

> She was taking tablets, and other stuff, you know ... well her mother in law ... she said, I don't think she ever take it mind, what was it now? Oh heavens, I forget the name of this stuff now, but, ooh, it was nasty to take. It was something you had to do yourself, it was a herb and, you know, put the boiling water on it, like, and drink that, you had to drink a cupful of that, you know, a couple of times, and um, whether she took that, I don't know. But during the war, now, um, I had two evacuees ... and I had lost my periods then the one month like, and I thought, Oh heavens, Oh, I hope I haven't now ... So, whatever, I went then for two or three months, think it was, I hadn't seen anything, so, I said, 'Well I'm taking that stuff', and I done it, and I took it ... I did come, that's right, but there was nothing, it was only just a natural period, you know, it was all clear. Well, if they'd been anything wrong you'd have a clot, wouldn't you? But there wasn't, it was all clear.[23]

Thus there is some indication, perhaps, that interviewees were wary of discussing abortion with a stranger and that they were careful not to incriminate themselves to an outsider. It is difficult to tease out what might lie behind the hesitation on the part of some of the interviewees to reveal their knowledge and experience of abortion. I do not wish to suggest strongly the existence of ulterior motives in the tendency to provide anecdotes that involve a third person or in the presentation of failed rather than successful terminations. Most women freely provided frank and detailed responses to my questions about abortion. What I do want to argue, however, is that, even if we conclude that some of my respondents were reluctant to reveal familiarity or involvement with abortion, this was not because they were wary of being seen to have transgressed codes of 'morality'.

This finding is particularly interesting with respect to the perception of community regulation of behaviour and the effect such values have on the attitudes of respondents. The influence of restrictive 'chapel culture' particularly influential in South Wales cries out for examination. The chapels were undeniably 'dominant social institutions', though their influence was on the wane.[24] There is evidence that communities in Wales were adept at regulating social behaviour and that traditions of public shaming were evident, even during the 1984 miners' strike against 'blacklegs'.[25] Rosemary Crook's oral history presents a picture of the Rhondda as one dominated by 'standards ... based on the values of the Chapel'. She depicts the society as an intimate one of 'involvement and interdependence between women', and feels that this 'very intimacy was a major factor in regulating women's behaviour'. Each woman was socially reliant on her inclusion in such support networks. Crook emphasises a moral consensus in which 'chastity ... was ferociously enforced by mothers' and 'contraception and abortion were apparently almost unknown' and regarded as practised only by 'the worst' women 'in the face of God'.[26] Russell Davies interprets the force of religion as a factor in many nineteenth- and early twentieth-century suicides in Wales.[27] Margaret Douglas interprets the closure of a birth control clinic in Abertillery in 1926 with nonconformist opposition, and those involved in the birth control clinic campaign in Wales frequently argued that nonconformist influence was a factor behind disappointing attendance figures.[28]

It is certainly true that my interviewees sometimes referred to the morality expected by the outside community. They mentioned notions of respectability and the need to be 'good' or 'tidy'. Such concerns, however, did not dominate discussions of abortion or contraception or appear to influence attitudes towards birth control or various methods (including abortion).[29] It is striking, perhaps, how seldom religion was mentioned in my interviews, and how infrequently quasi-religious language was used in the context of the discussion of personal birth control use.[30] Interestingly, Moya Woodside and Eliot Slater also found that religious beliefs 'had remarkably little influence on the men and women of our sample' with regard to family size and contraception.[31]

It is likely that one reason why many women did not consider themselves to be 'destroying life' was that they took abortifacients before they were certain they were pregnant, as soon as a period was late or even when a period was due in order to ensure that it came. It is not surprising that in such instances abortion was easily divorced from 'moral' considerations; taking pills was a regular practice, seen as a way of restoring a late period, rather than removing an unwanted foetus, and associated more with menstruation than with pregnancy. One woman wrote to me:

> Now you could go to the pharmacy in Newport and ask for pills to bring on your period a few days before you were due. They were called 'Penny Royal Bitter Apple and Steel'. I only have one daughter who was sixty years on the 28th of October, yesterday. There were no condoms or any other prevention as I know of. However, another tip, *before* a period put your feet in a bowl of mustard water. Every month before a period. I have to say it always worked for my six sisters.[32]

Documentary sources also provide evidence of women who would take abortifacient pills regularly. For example, Moya Woodside's survey of women abortionists in Holloway prison found one who claimed: 'Sixty percent of married women use the Higginson's syringe regular every month just to be sure they bring the period on.'[33]

In making a decision to take abortifacient pills women did not necessarily face up to the possibility that they might be pregnant, and still less to its further implications. They simply knew that if they wanted no more children they had to make sure that they menstruated. This is not to say that they were totally unaware of what they were doing – most of my evidence for abortifacient pill-taking comes as a result of questions that mention the word 'abortion', or questions that ask about methods used to 'get rid of a child when unwillingly pregnant', and the language used by the respondents is not overly euphemistic (foetuses are frequently referred to as babies, for example), but the thought process behind the practice sometimes avoided facing up to the implications that a child might have been conceived.[34]

Iris was quite aware that Beechams' pills caused miscarriages, but nevertheless reports that her mother took them in order 'never to be pregnant again'.

> Beechams', they used to swear if you took Beechams', before your monthly period that it would help you, you know, that might've worked.

So, do you take that, you don't take that when you think you might be pregnant?[35]

No, you took that just before you were, your monthly period, like. *Just in case.*

Yeah, that's right. I think it used to be three, three Beechams'. Funnily enough there used to be gypsies come round then, you know, I don't know if you'd be interested in this bit. Gypsies used to come round, they used to tell us daft things, and we used to be petrified of gypsies, and this gypsy told my mother, she said, 'cos my mother, like I told you, had a lot of miscarriages, and she said, 'Every time your period's due take three Beechams' and you'll never be pregnant again.' And she told my mother that, and my mother took them for years, and on the box it used to be, um, 'worth a guinea a box',[36] used to be on the lid of it, like.[37]

The distinction drawn between abortions and bringing on periods (a practice completed before one was certain that one was pregnant) was clearly revealed by Dolly:

So what did people do when they were pregnant and they didn't want to be pregnant?

I never heard nothing like that! Didn't know, we'd get on with it. We still had old-fashioned pinnies and ... [continues talking about pinnies]

Oh, so there weren't any abortions in those days?

No, never heard none of that.

Did you ever hear of things to bring on a period?

Well, I never had anything like that. Some perhaps would, you know, if they hadn't come, they'd take a pill. No, I never went in for anything like that.[38] Let me think, after I had Karen, I think I was on the way to another, and I did go to Blaina, then to Robertson – he told me, the clothesman, he go up to my brother and give him this letter, and they had to pay a pound for a tablet – it was like a brown pea. And I took that and that fetched mine on. Yes, I think I would have had another one after Karen. I do.[39]

All these examples show very clearly how many women did not perceive a significant difference between abortifacients and forms of birth control that aimed to prevent conception. Contraceptives and abortifacients were often obtained from the same source, for example, chemists and mail order companies, and some methods, such as quinine, could be used either before or after conception. In fact the blurring of contraception and abortion was a widespread popular misconception. Marie Stopes had to remind even those working for her of the 'moral' difference between abortion and her 'constructive birth control':

> I must be quite clear about abortion. You do understand don't you, that birth control work must be so carefully distinguished from abortion. We always ask a specific promise from everyone associated with us on our medical and nursing staff, that they will not have any contact with abortion work in any shape or form, our enemies are always on the look-out to associate the control of conception with the destruction of the embryo.[40]

Elizabeth conflated caps and abortifacients and was convinced that Stopes's clinic in Cardiff (Splott) provided abortions:

> Marie Stopes, she was in London, I think, yeah, a lot of people used to write to her and she used to send them pills and things like that … I'm sure there was a Marie Stopes in Splott some-where, there was, she had an old shop made into a clinic, ay. A friend of mine went there, I don't know, she never had any children, so she must have come on.[41]

The tendency to perceive abortifacients as a way of anticipating a period or ensuring regular menstruation was capitalised on, and/or fostered by, advertisements for abortifacients, which, in order to circumvent the law, presented their wares as remedies for such things as 'suppressed menstruation' or 'female irregularities', and prom-ised to 'remove obstructions even in the most obstinate of cases'.

However, early abortion, in which the implications of carrying a child could be easily ignored, was not the only circumstance in which abortion was attempted without much deliberation about the 'moral' acceptability of the practice. Some women also took aborti-facients when it was clear that they were actually pregnant and they did not ignore the realities of what they were doing. Whereas women who took pills early often described such practices evasively as 'bringing on a period' rather than as aborting a pregnancy, later attempts were often explicitly presented.

> And then of course there was a lot of people, lot of people I knew, friends, they used to take stuff to get rid of the babies because they didn't want them, because they already had three or four.
> *Yes, so what sort of stuff did they take?*

They used to take, um, oh, what'd they used to take now? Oh, my one friend what did she used to take now? Gin with, um, something else, they used to put it in the oven, and, um, when it used to go down to about that much they used to drink it. Well, of course that used to, it was like a sedative to get you to go to the toilet, and used to use it that way. Can't remember what, other, and then there was another one, O God, what was it? I did forget, memory and what not, um, as they say, slippery elm and the leech. *So how would you use the leech?*
The leech, you'd put that, inside you and then it would attack the womb, and open the womb up, and of course you'd lose the baby then.
Yes.
I know one of my aunties done it.[42]

Even though in these instances the 'foetus' is recognised as being a potential child, any 'moral' questions about the legitimacy of trying to 'get rid of it' are absent.

Birth control clinic data also show the popular acceptance of abortion. The Walworth Clinic found that women 'habitually brought on miscarriages' and in Salford attempted abortion was felt by the birth control pioneers interviewed for a 1969 BBC documentary to have been 'almost a convention'.[43] Nor did patients necessarily prefer contraceptive methods or find them 'morally' more satisfactory. One woman at Stopes's Cardiff clinic thought the cervical cap she was given was 'disgusting': she had 'got rid of things regularly for years', which was 'much easier'.[44]

The question as to whether there was a stage in pregnancy when abortion became unacceptable is difficult to ascertain; the interview data are not clear. Other documentary sources certainly suggest that such a cut-off point existed and was important, and traditionally 'quickening' appears to have been a widely accepted signal to working-class women. Betty is the only one of my interviewees who made a distinction between early and late abortion. Above, she reported her experience taking abortifacient pills. This is how she felt about abortion:

I wouldn't have an abortion.
Why's that?
Well it's like this, if you don't want children, don't play with the fire and then you don't get burnt.
So what do you think's wrong with abortions?

Well, it's taking a life, innit?
So there's something different between taking a pill and having an abortion?
Well, if you take a pill, you could take a pill and that pill could work straight away and you could, well they'd only just be a little seed there, wouldn't there? Well, if you have abortions, I mean that baby's formed.[45]

Most respondents did not make any mention of any cut-off points, quickening or otherwise. The timing of abortion was also not alluded to. Many could not remember how many periods they'd missed before attempting an abortion, and gave vague answers to questions I asked about when abortions would be attempted. On the other hand, all the examples of abortions presented took place before the pregnancy was well developed and it seems likely that a distinction would have been drawn between early and late abortions in practice. However, this question is very interesting, linguistically. Aborted foetuses were not always referred to in emotionally neutral terms; in fact, 'getting rid of a baby' was one of the most common descriptions of abortive acts. This perception of a foetus as a 'baby' does not seem to have deterred women from attempting abortion, nor excited any censure from friends or neighbours. Kathleen was shown the dead foetus her friend had aborted. It was treated as a 'little thing' that had been alive and was (decently?) buried. Yet Kathleen did not seem to disapprove of her friend, though she found the sight a little gory, and the story suggests that there was no shame in showing a dead foetus to friends, even when it was the product of an extramarital liaison.

My friend was in the army, I don't know if I should tell you this,[46] and, um, her husband was in the army and she got pregnant with somebody and she got rid of it. But um ...
How did she do that?
Oh, somebody got rid of it for her, like, you know, and they brought it up to show us, it was in a little bottle like that, this little thing in a little bottle, I always remember that, and they buried it, at that time. It was only little, it was only, she must have been about six weeks, you know. But, er, always remember that, and, er, but she had it, 'cos her husband was in the army, and a funny thing she went away with this bloke after, she, yeah, she left her husband. But I always remember that, that little thing stick in your mind don't it [can't hear, a few words mumbled].

What did it look like?
We was only young see, weren't we. It was like a little baby, only, I should imagine when, you know, when they get pregnant first, it's nothing much, isn't it, you know. I remembers it in the bottle and they but it, they, they buried it and all.
So describe it in the bottle?
Something like a bit of something, like a bit, it was supposed to have been a baby anyways, I don't know what the hell it was, but anyway, *ych a fi.*[47] That's the only thing I can remember about anybody having any abortions or anything.[48]

In my discussions of abortion it has proved far from straight-forward to analyse what effect I, as the interviewer, had on the presentation of my respondents' comments, and equally unclear what views I was perceived to hold. I tended not to discuss my own views on various aspects of abortion politics with my interviewees; I did not disagree with the few that expressed moral disapproval of the practice, nor, obviously, did I condemn those who accepted the practical inevitability of abortion. More interesting, however, are the retrospective representations of attitudes towards abortion. First, the fact that the majority of abortions attempted by respondents failed did not lead many to regret having tried to 'get rid' of a child subsequently born and loved or to re-evaluate their opinions on abortion.[49] Second, respondents were also peculiarly unconcerned about 'modern' debates about abortion – this is particularly surprising as almost all expressed opinions, repeatedly, on modern sexual behaviour and modern contraceptive methods, especially the pill. They did not talk much about any changes in the 'culture of abortion' – neither the fact that it is now legal nor the fact that it is condemned by many, though some did assess the contrast in attitudes towards abortion when I explicitly presented it to them. It is quite possible that the stresses placed on the dangers of abortion reflect the influence of modern rhetoric on the horrors of backstreet abortions, yet such a contrast was not explicitly drawn. Changes in abortion law did not seem to tap into the particular historical concerns of my respondents, and do not appear to be one of the changes that they see as especially significant or as particularly noteworthy. In contrast the increased availability of contraception (especially condoms and the pill) was seen as responsible for certain perceived changes in the sexual behaviour of young people (especially the unmarried) which respondents were particularly concerned to point out and contrast with their own experiences. In fact their lack of awareness of modern debates and issues about abortion was sometimes astounding. Elizabeth argued:

> I don't know why they don't make a law that, yes, you can go in a hospital and have an abortion if you're satisfied to do it, you know. They shouldn't rule your life like that.[50]

In conclusion, abortion was a not insignificant method of fertility limitation for some families. While no respondent presented it as the main or only method used, it was an accepted part of many working-class people's lives. Oral testimony brings this into sharp relief, providing striking examples of the contexts in which everyday abortion decisions were made.

The attitudes towards abortion expressed by my interviewees reveal most clearly the importance of recognising that there is nothing obvious or natural about our perceptions of the issues raised by the practice of abortion, and that there is nothing inevitable about the premises we use to frame debates about abortion. The working-class women interviewed were little worried by the 'moral' problems associated with abortion, and rarely concerned that abortion might be considered a form of killing. Nor was abortion invariably resorted to only as a last resort, or only when the negative consequences of having another pregnancy or child were particularly high and when motivation reached extreme or desperate levels.[51] Nor was abortion always resorted to reluctantly, in the absence of contraceptive alternatives. Little moral agonising seems to have taken place, and decisions could be reached somewhat casually, as is well illustrated by Iris's memory of her conversation with a friend when they were both pregnant.

> I can tell you a funny bit. Um, my neighbour next but one, she had three children I think, and she went in for a fourth, and she'd read somewhere that there were these tablets, two and six each, which was a fortune then, half a crown like, so she said, 'Do you want one, Iris?' I said, 'No,' I said, 'I don't think I'll bother,' 'cos we were pregnant at the same time. 'Oh, I'm going to have one.' They were great, big, dark green jellies, like a jelly sweet like, oval sweet. So, anyway, she took it. [Laughing.] Done nothing for her. She was still pregnant. We used to laugh and do things like that. Then she'd take blue, she took a square of blue in a glass. Stupid things she used to do, you know, because she didn't want any

more children like. But, er, it's funny looking back at it, but she could have killed herself couldn't she? [laughs] [52]

Iris's account focuses wholly on the pregnant woman: there is no concern expressed for the foetus. It is clear that women did not have to be 'desperate' before contemplating an abortion; pregnant women could take abortion-inducing steps in a very light-hearted manner, even as something of a joke between friends. [53] Moreover, as Iris's account of such an incident strikingly illustrates, often it was the (imagined) health risk for the woman, rather than the perceived taking of a life, that was the source of negative attitudes to abortive practices. We should do well to recognise that, for many or most ordinary women in the 1930s, as revealed in their own testimonies, the 'abortion debate' as we see it was not a factor in practical decision-making.

Notes

1 Angus McLaren, 'Illegal Operations: Women, Doctors and Abortion, 1886–1939', *Journal of Social History*, 26, 4 (1993), p. 799.
2 It is difficult to provide numerical data to support such conclusions since they are the result of my interpretations of testimony that is sometimes impressionistic and ambiguous.
3 Leslie Regan, *When Abortion Was a Crime: Women, Medicine, and Law in the United States, 1867–1973* (Berkeley and London, University of California Press, 1997), p. 21. See also Angus McLaren, 'Women's Work and Regulation of Family Size', *History Workshop Journal*, 4 (1977), p. 75.
4 All had been married.
5 The research was funded with the assistance of a Wellcome Trust Studentship, for which I am very grateful.
6 Initial attempts to solicit interviewees through newspaper appeals were rejected at the pilot stage as unsatisfactory and, moreover, produced a disappointingly low response.
7 Names have been changed.
8 Ministry of Health, *Interim Report of the Departmental Committee on Maternal Morbidity* (London, HMSO, 1930); Isabella D. Cameron and Dilwys M. Jones, *Reports on Public Health and Medical Subjects, No. 68, High Maternal Mortality in Certain Areas* (London, HMSO, 1932). See also Ministry of Health, *Report on Maternal Mortality in Wales* (London, HMSO, 1937), cmd. 5423, pp. 1936–7, xi.
9 BMA Report, *Medical Aspects of Abortion*, (1936), p. 6; *Birth Control News*, 8, 6 (October 1929), p. 91.
10 Ministry of Health, Home Office, *Report of the Inter-Departmental Committee on Abortion* (London, HMSO, 1939), p. 62.
11 It is difficult to ask such questions in the interview without appearing to

attack or challenge their actions or ethics. I do not push them as far as I might when presenting them with the 'pro-life argument' as I do not want to put them on the defensive or imply that they should have thought or acted differently.

12 By 'moral' I wish to refer only and specifically to the arguments that proclaim a foetus's 'right to life' and condemn abortion as a form of murder.

13 Aileen, bc3sw#14. One Catholic man also opposed abortion because of his 'religious teachings' – even though he freely admits that he 'broke all faith' and 'was wrong' in deciding to use french letters.

14 Doris, bc3sw#6.

15 Without accurate information on the number of attempted abortions or the number of injuries or deaths resulting from abortion attempts it is very difficult to estimate how dangerous abortions were. Barbara Brookes argues that 'women knew from experience that, despite the protestations of the medical profession, abortion was relatively safe', especially within a context in which maternal mortality was not insignificant. It is likely that the dangers of abortion are exaggerated by respondents just as much as by contemporary commentators. Barbara Brookes, *Abortion in England, 1900–1967* (London, Routledge, 1988), p. 42.

16 Edith, bc2#23.

17 Dilys, bc2#13.

18 Malcolm Potts, Peter Diggory and John Peel, *Abortion* (Cambridge, Cambridge University Press, 1977), p. 258.

19 Leslie, bc3sw#1.

20 Note again the dominance of health concerns influencing abortion decisions and the way in which perceptions of the health risks determine which methods are tried and which rejected.

21 This is rather a leading question.

22 Muriel, bc2#3.

23 Betty, bc3sw#19.

24 David Gilbert, *Class, Community and Collective Action: Social Change in Two British Coalfields, 1850–1926* (Oxford, Clarendon Press, 1992); Chris Williams, *Democratic Rhondda Politics and Society, 1885–1951* (Cardiff, University of Wales Press, 1996); D. W. Howell and C. Baber, 'Wales', in F. M. L. Thompson (ed.), *The Cambridge Social History of Britain 1750–1950*, vol. 1 (Cambridge, Cambridge University Press, 1990), pp. 329–36.

25 Rosemary A. N. Jones, 'Women, Community and Collective Action: The "Ceffyl Pren" Tradition', in Angela John (ed.), *Our Mothers' Land: Chapters in Welsh Women's History, 1830–1939* (Cardiff, University of Wales Press, 1991), pp. 17–41; Jaclyn Gier, 'Miners' Wives: Gender, Culture and Society in the South Wales Coalfields, 1919–1939' (unpublished Ph.D. thesis, Northwestern University, 1993).

26 Rosemary Crook, '"Tidy Women": Women in the Rhondda between the Wars', *Oral History*, 10 (1982), pp. 40–6.

27 Russell Davies, '"Do Not Go Gentle into that Good Night": Women and Suicide in Carmarthanshire, c. 1860–1920', in John (ed.), *Our Mothers' Land*, pp. 102–3.

28 Margaret Douglas, 'Women, God and Birth Control: The First Hospital

Birth Control Clinic, Abertillery 1925', *Llafur*, 6, 4 (1995), pp. 110–22.

29 Rosser and Harris found, however, that active Welsh nonconformists tended to have the smallest families. Colin Rosser and Christopher Harris, *The Family and Social Change: A Study of Kinship in a South Wales Town*, (London and New York, Routledge & Kegan Paul, 1965), p. 180.

30 My interviews did not, however, particularly focus on religion. While some questions on religious affiliation and activity were asked, I felt that the complexities of religious belief and the intersection of religious morality and personal life would require a subtle, sophisticated and time-consuming set of questions that was beyond the logistical scope of this research. On the complexities of oral interviews about belief see Sarah Williams, 'Popular Religion and Oral History', unpublished paper presented at a symposium on Working-class Religion and Oral History, Birmingham, 2–3 April 1996.

31 Eliot Slater and Moya Woodside, *Patterns of Marriage: A Study of Marriage Relationships in the Urban Working Classes* (London, Cassell, 1951), pp. 188–9.

32 This letter is one of only three I received in response to a newspaper appeal requesting memories of birth control. She was not well enough to be interviewed.

33 Moya Woodside, 'Attitudes of Women Abortionists', *Family Planning*, 12, 2 (July 1963), p. 33.

34 Madeline Kerr commented on the similar attitude of a Roman Catholic woman she spoke to in a 1958 study of Liverpool who 'considers birth control a sin. "It is definitely a sin". Yet under certain circumstances she appears to consider abortion permissible. She said, "I mean to say I don't say I've never taken anything. We all do at times don't we? You just say to yourself it's late."' Madeline Kerr, *The People of Ship Street* (London, Routledge & Kegan Paul, 1958), p. 83.

35 I led Iris slightly here. However, she does independently provide evidence that Beechams' pills were taken regularly, before pregancy was suspected.

36 Maureen Sutton argues that the slogan 'worth a guinea a box' was a veiled reference to the rumour that back-street abortionists charged a guinea; Maureen Sutton, *We Didn't Know Aught: A Study of Sexuality, Superstition and Death in Women's Lives in Lincolnshire during the 1930s, '40s and '50s* (Stamford, Paul Watkins, 1992), p. 95.

37 Iris, bc2#8.

38 Note, again, the denial: a third-person account which then shifts into a first-person story.

39 Dolly, bc3sw#17.

40 Marie Stopes to Jean Peterson, 5 July, no year, 1937?, Marie C. Stopes papers in the Contemporary Medical Archives Centre at the Wellcome Institute for the History of Medicine, CMAC/PP/MCS/C.24.

41 Elizabeth, bc3sw#12.

42 Use of the leech was not mentioned by any other respondent, nor is it a method that appears in any other sources for the period. The factual accuracy of Rosie's memory here, however, is not crucial to my argument. The point is that she deliberately presents abortion in the past as having been accepted and widely resorted to, however gruesome the method.

'Collective memory' appears to place importance on highlighting the horrors and dangers of the practice rather than any 'moral' implications of their actions. Rosie, bc1#2.

43 See Brookes, *Abortion in England*, p. 6.

44 Gordon to Stopes, 21 July 1939, Marie C. Stopes papers in the Department of Manuscripts at the British Library, Add Ms. 58625.

45 Betty, bc3sw#19.

46 It is my belief that she puts this proviso in because she feels she should not be telling tales about her friend's extramarital affairs, rather than because abortion was 'morally wrong', though it might also indicate awareness that abortion was illegal.

47 A Welsh phrase expressing squeamish disgust, equivalent to the English 'Ugh'.

48 Kathleen, bc2#16.

49 American research into a number of women who had illegal abortions in the 1950s and 1960s revealed similar attitudes (although the researchers did not acknowledge this): 'I felt nothing. I didn't feel anxious. I think I was stupid. No, I was not stupid ... I just went to take care of business ... I just got on the train. Not only did I not think about the moral or ethical implications, I didn't think about the physical possibilities.' Ellen Messer and Kathryn E. May, *Back Rooms: Voices from the Illegal Abortion Era* (New York, St. Martin's Press, 1988), p. 21.

50 Elizabeth, bc3sw#12.

51 A survey of abortion cases in a Camberwell hospital similarly judged that in 13 per cent of cases reasons for resorting to abortion were 'trivial'. T. N. Parish, 'A Thousand Cases of Abortion', *Journal of Obstetrics and Gynaecology*, 39 (1935), p. 1110.

52 Iris, bc2#8.

53 Mary Zimmerman also argues that abortion was not always characterised by conflict or trauma. Mary Zimmerman, 'Experiencing Abortion as a Crisis: The Impact of Social Context', in Barbara J. Risman and Pepper Schwartz (eds), *Gender in Intimate Relationships: A Micro Structural Approach* (Belmont, CA, Wandsworth Publishing, 1989), p. 134; see also Rowena Woolf, 'Changes', in Family Planning Association, *Abortion in Britain* (London, Pitman Medical Publishing, 1966), p. 70, who argues that 'guilt that women are supposed to feel after an abortion is exaggerated; what guilt there is, is imposed on them by conventional attitudes, and the conditions of the abortion'.

11

French Catholics between abstinence and 'appeasement of lust', 1930–50

Anne-Marie Sohn

Translated by Lisa Greenwald

Although the official discourse on sexuality is known, this is not often the case in respect of the intimacy of couples. Yet certain documents – judicial dossiers, memoirs, private journals – permit us to lift the veil on private life.[1] The correspondence addressed to the Abbé Viollet is part of these unhoped-for treasures.[2] It contains only 255 letters but the cohesion of the collection, which reveals the personality both of the addressee and his correspondents, makes them precious. The Abbé gave his own point of view when the letters were published in his newspaper, but unfortunately his individual replies to correspondents have not survived.

Born in 1875, priest at Plaisance (Paris, fourteenth arrondisement) from 1902, Jean Viollet founded a number of social organisations, for example Les Oeuvres du Moulin Vert. In 1918 he founded the Association du Mariage Chrétien (AMC) with his friends the vicar Emmanuel Chaptal and Jean Verdier, future archbishop of Paris. It aimed at reawakening the Catholic family, raising the birth rate and developing conjugal spirituality. The AMC propagated its ideas through conferences and brochures, and by its newspapers which reached thirty thousand subscribers. Abbé Viollet was therefore a beacon of the new conjugal and natalist moralism at the point when the papal encyclical *Casti Connubii* of 31 December 1930 'appeared in the French church as an inspiration of the work that Viollet undertook from 1918'.[3] The surviving letters, principally written in the 1930s, were provoked by the open debates in the AMC newspapers which published 'matters of conscience' submitted by readers.[4] They are a revelation of the new Catholic policy and of the stiffening of conjugal moralism which found its apogee with the encyclical.

Of these correspondents we know at once much and very little. Their sex (equally divided between men and women) and their civil status (90 per cent were married) are known, as are their provincial origins.[5] However, only 40 per cent gave the number of their children and their profession. From the letter writers' professions, but also from the writing – elegant, stylised, flowing – we may conclude that they belonged to the bourgeoisie.[6] The fact that so many priests wrote to him (as many as 10 per cent of the authors) reveals the influence exercised by Abbé Viollet on his peers. They were practising, even militant, Catholics.[7] All were assiduously loyal and well informed. They read the encyclical and the Bible, they cited Thomas Aquinas and St Augustine. All were scrupulous penitents. Many were not content to have a confessor: they yearned to confide to a 'director' and not finding one, addressed themselves to the emblematic priest of couples, Abbé Viollet. They solicited advice, revealed their 'matters of conscience', and found themselves recounting their life stories. They sometimes confessed unwittingly. As one parent concluded his missive: 'Pardon me, Monsieur Abbé, for these confidences, I must say this confession, for it is one.'[8]

As has always been the case, the epistolary genre, between confession and matters of conscience, allows for enormous candour on sexuality. Catholics dared to approach all its facets, as individuals conscious of current secular trends, but also as believers during these years marked by Rome's hardened position on the limitation of births – of which the encyclical *Casti Connubii* is a witness.

To surmount silence and ignorance

Following the example of Abbé Viollet, who opened the press of the AMC to troubled spouses, these correspondents spoke naturally about life and wanted to break the 'conspiracy of silence'.[9] By such candour, these authors of a new generation broke with the preceding one. As a correspondent remarked, 'Our mothers evidently didn't have such subjects of conversation and were completely shocked to hear them.'[10] But a worker from the north judged such evolution insufficient: 'We only speak with prudence and in general terms of such things, perhaps too veiled to really address the question directly.'[11] The majority of the authors always tried to be precise without being vulgar, and they tried to describe their various loves with an alacrity rarely found in the archives. They had, nevertheless, a vocabulary which was their own. They spoke of 'appeasing lust', and they preferred 'enjoyment' (the Biblical word) to the usual term 'pleasure'.

It is no surprise that almost one author in ten denounced the ignorance of too many young people, both Catholics and non-Catholics. Such ignorance could be astounding, as in the case of a twenty-five-year-old woman from Nantes: 'Maybe it is wrong and I will say something stupid and ridiculous, but it makes me crazy with fear to ask myself if one kiss could be enough to get pregnant ... If you would tell me that I have nothing to fear and that *other things* are needed, you will deliver me from such torment.'[12] Innocence, far from protecting, engendered terrors and anxiety. Certain authors blamed narrow religious instruction, like one newly wed: 'In the convents young women are brought up far more to become nuns than to become wives and mothers.'[13] The winds changed, however, and the gulf between the generations widened. 'When I got married', confirmed a Normandy woman who married in 1920, 'I was ignorant of all marital duties like all other young women, for, at this epoch, we wrongly left young women in the dark about all these things.'[14]

A dozen letters go further in defending the principle of sex education. The priests and the teachers were the toughest defenders of this new pedagogy, which they emphasised was then revolutionary if not considered immoral.[15] A curate of the Saône-et-Loire rejoiced at its introduction: 'We have for too long treated the question by vague and grand euphemisms.'[16] This concern with openness was exceptional for the epoch, even if words were freer after the First World War. But the partisans of open dialogue did not defend an unbridled sexuality. Far from it. They were convinced that prohibitions had to be respected.

Ordinary prohibitions

Acts popularly considered against nature – bestiality, paedophilia, incest – were ignored by the correspondents. Homosexual penchants show through five letters, but only two of the authors were able to name their impulses, such as the student 'attracted to children' who confessed: 'I fear to fall into mortal sin ... It is against nature.'[17] The others had a fuzzy perception of normality: 'What do you think of demonstrations of affection between friends: kisses, caresses and other things? Could there be a danger?' enquired one woman.[18] Masturbation, in contrast, was largely tolerated by the general public but provoked strong concerns among Catholics who had internalised bourgeois medical discourse.[19] A young woman who discovered the 'solitary vice' in reading a book by Abbé Viollet described the habitual masturbation syndrome: 'I will even tell you that I am weary of life. And one other thing: From morning to night, my eyes burn brightly in deep darkly rimmed sockets; my pallid face frightens me and questions me on the nature of my wrong. Do things like this exist in others, or am I a monster, or one possessed?'[20] Numerous correspondents also enquired about means of preventing children from succumbing to these 'bad habits.'[21] Furthermore, and because of their background, the cases of priests succumbing to the sins of the flesh were exceptionally high.[22] The debauchery of a chaplain of a boarding school, reported by a priest whose young sister 'had been entirely shattered in her soul, perhaps for ever', is classic.[23] Denounced by the anticlericals, but rarely proved, there were cases of both married and unmarried women being seduced by clerics: 'Twice (please pardon this confidence) she appealed to priests, alas, she found other things entirely than spiritual help!'[24]

Legitimate couples were most concerned about prohibitions from the moment of their engagement. The writers searched first to distance themselves from sexual provocations, however indirect these were. They applied to adults a strategy of negation that ordinary French men and women used only for children and adolescents. An officer from Angers marvellously summarised this line of conduct: 'Put on guard very early against the danger of life, I fled dangerous occasions as I was advised to do by the church.'[25] From such arguments came the condemnation of balls, of bad reading material and films which led to further interrogations: 'One can generally agree that it is permitted to admire paintings and sculptures which are found as works of art in museums – the Vatican and others – but which in other locations might be considered wounding for the eyes.'[26] Feminine coquetry, especially, interpreted as flirting, was condemned. 'May the fashion of going around with uncovered legs be accepted by a Christian?' Such were the problems of young Catholics when the middle classes framed the questions, but in terms of suitability and not of morality.[27] As for make-up, it was a sign of loose living. Such standards bring us to the matter of conscience of a young husband, 'attracted by made-up women' who wanted his wife to take up the habit of putting on make-up. Alas, 'my wife bridled at it, not in absolute refusal but because she found it deeply repugnant.

I realised that at the base of my wife's attitude was the greatest conformity to Christian morality.' To assure himself, however, he asked 'what the church doctrine was on the subject of the employment of make-up: (a) for married women; and (b) for young women, and single women in general', distinguishing between 'loud' and 'discreet make-up'.[28] A few letters such as one from Algeria confirm the co-existence of two conflicting normative systems among the religious: 'On the one hand, my wife is a perfect spouse in the sense of Fray Luis de Léon. On the other hand, I feel that I am married to my grandmother who could be a Quaker or a Seventh Day Adventist ... All the fantasies that are permitted to young modern women – short hair, pyjamas, bathing suits – are considered by her an abomination of desolation. Horror, sin!'[29]

The 'liberties' between engaged couples divided the correspondents, especially between the generations.[30] A mother grieved because her 'daughters raised in such a Christian fashion ... have displayed the latest modern effronteries' instead of maintaining a respectful reserve. 'It has become habitual, even indispensable, to allow special interviews to affianced couples (naturally at the home of the young woman but with her parents out of the room)', sighed the mother, shamefully admitting a concession to the ideas of the day. But she rebelled against dangerous familiarity. 'It is in these instants of freedom that the young woman is used to sitting down completely naturally on the same sofa as her fiancé, and both of them embrace as if the marriage had already occurred.'[31]

This pervading climate eroded the barriers long held against desire. It also affected the conjugal bed and led to painful doubts. Certain particularly prudish believers remained prisoners of a pessimistic conception of sexuality, sullied by the stain of original sin. Since St Augustine authorised coitus only for procreation, argued a prudish spouse, 'these things are therefore not without sin'.[32] 'She considered intimate relations vulgar, perhaps so as not to call them forbidden', sighed a frustrated husband.[33] Although most of the correspondents had a freer conception of sexuality, they asked just as many questions concerning their obedience to rules decreed by the church. They recognised that the secondary aims of marriage authorised the satisfaction of the senses, but only in order to guard against lechery. The faithful were thus persuaded, as many correspondents reported that 'all is permitted' in the framework of marriage. They believed this because confessors had preferred, until the 1920s, to practise the art of understatement by not asking precise questions. They were dismayed at the about-face of clerics who henceforth vigorously condemned 'lustful pleasures', as did Abbé Viollet. 'What are lascivious acts? I swear I have not understood', asked a reader who did not know of any prohibition other than masturbation.[34] Thus, a worker in Wattrelos asked for a guide 'on the manner and the only way to perform the sexual act', with a list 'of permitted caressing gestures allowed before the conjugal act'.[35]

In practice the correspondents stumbled on the same taboos as their more secularised contemporaries, who distinguished between ordinary caresses and 'things particularly incorrect'.[36] In the face of theologians divided on the subject, young women worried about 'French kissing'. This was considered before 1914 as a *risqué* favour, able on its own to constitute an indecent assault, but it became widespread after the war.[37] Catholics also seemed to enjoy genital caresses which consenting lovers considered banal preliminaries, but they saw them as a particular problem in the degree to which they could arouse female pleasure independent of coitus. A French woman from Algeria clearly articulated this problem, which was broached in a dozen letters: 'If sexual pleasure is not obtained during the conjugal act, must touching received either after or before the act which provokes sexual excitement be considered reprehensible?'[38] It comes as no surprise that oral stimulation was rarely mentioned. Firmly condemned by the church, reserved in the nineteenth century to prostitutes or to brazen mistresses, it made a timid breakthrough during the interwar period but provoked the embarrassment of honest women.[39] The correspondents of Abbé Viollet knew therefore that they violated a social and religious taboo. Thus only two were willing to do so. 'Permit us to submit to you a delicate question that we don't dare to bring up in confession', ventured one of them. 'In the accomplishment of the [sexual] act, my wife doesn't experience any sensation. It takes a prolonged excitement with the tongue on the small part of the vagina.'[40] Likewise, only one person attempted anal intercourse, abhorred by women, rejected by popular opinion and exceptional even today: 'During my conjugal life, I sometimes searched for particular sensations (of a homosexual nature). It all ended evidently in the right direction ... I rarely did these things; they strongly displeased my wife who accepted them only out of obedience.'[41] Finally, a single missive described erotic scenarios which I have never encountered in other sources.[42]

Does a husband have the right to demand that his wife undress with him so as to dance naked together? ... Does he have the right thus nude to look at himself in a large mirror while striking different poses with his wife? ... May he demand that his wife put on men's underwear or other male clothing at the same time that he puts on women's clothing, and thus rigged out the two of them could go mad in the bedroom?'[43]

The spouse of a 'bestial' man, as the expression went, suffered less in her faith than in her modesty, a modesty common to all women, who were embarrassed by nudity and voyeurism until the middle of the twentieth century.

Yet the correspondents did not pose any 'cases of conscience' on sexual positions, perhaps because the missionary position – the only one allowed for practising believers – was the most widespread.[44] They also seemed to ignore the ban on sexual relations during pregnancy and breast-feeding, although it was supported by the church and the medical establishment. Nothing was said of abstention during menstruation since this was the popular custom for women generally, and for men frequently, but for reasons of hygiene more than of morality.

Evidently, AMC supporters were shocked by the same sexual differences as were their contemporaries, although the unmarried were more easily shocked. They carried out, however, a double reading of taboos, both social and Christian. Yet this difference did not prevent them from recounting their sensual fulfilment.

Pleasure and sexual discord

The authors, like their interlocutor Abbé Viollet, displayed a lofty ideal of Christian marriage, founded on love. This deep and durable love – 'we love each other not as much but more than we did twenty years ago', as one mother wrote – was both physical and affective.[45] Consequently the authors rehabilitated and even exalted pleasure. Seventeen among them broached a subject that normally belonged to the secrets of conjugal life.[46] 'Is this enjoyment one of those that is permitted by the Good Father?' asked one spouse who 'desired' and 'gave myself up to the plenitude of sexual pleasure'.[47] A husband even defended something rather new – women's right to pleasure – and he enquired about authorised pleasures 'not wanting to displease

God but also not wanting to deprive my wife of joys to which to my mind she has a right'.[48] Three neglected wives finally dared to confess the unquenched desire which tortured them since, as a general rule, women kept quiet so as not to seem like nymphomaniacs. 'How many times did I try to master my desires?' exclaimed a woman from Alsace.[49]

The confidants poured out their feelings concerning their marital failures. Women and men expressed their disappointment with the same wealth of precision as that of modest couples torn apart before the judge, family or friends.[50] Discord rested on the distortion of desire and of pleasure. Women's refusal, whether it was unexpressed or aggressive, was the major complaint. Some allowed only what all women called 'conjugal duty'. The expression always signalled resignation rather than happiness. But from passivity one passed rapidly to disgust. 'The reality of marriage has always been distasteful for me', proclaimed a woman from Rennes.[51] Frigidity was thus not far away. It appeared from the moment of the engagement for one young woman who permitted her future husband 'caresses in the most intimate places of my person', but who remained impassive. 'I let him do it, experienced absolutely nothing, no sensation.' The situation did not improve: 'Never have I experienced pleasure in the conjugal embrace!'[52] Frigidity could even lead to serious pathological troubles. 'I have *never once* not suffered before or after conjugal relations ... I sometimes had veritable nervous attacks, only with crying and screaming without being able to stop myself', complained a Breton woman who even consulted a doctor.[53] As for men, they often denounced the 'cold' woman. 'I always reproached my wife for being too indifferent to her husband, for being too cold and like marble', complained an overseer.[54] The open debate on the subject in the newspaper of the AMC in 1934 might lead to the conclusion that such problems weighed on Catholic women especially. Yet the mildly religious or non-religious said the same thing in the same way.

The causes of sexual incompatibility were also identical in the devout and secular. Marriage without love led to a fiasco. Five writers blamed such repulsion from the shock on their wedding night and imputed it to the ignorance of their partner, which was widespread among young Catholics who were advocates of virginity.[55] As one young woman, whose husband finally explained the act to her, wrote, 'this act is too humiliating, I could never resolve myself to accomplish it.'[56] 'Marc' wrote a remarkable criticism of his marital failures stemming from his inexperience and the erroneous advice of his spiritual director. Consulted on the eve of the wedding, the director affirmed that 'all is permitted at the moment of procreative act', but that outside of coitus, he had to consider his wife 'as a sister and treat her as such'.

> The consequences of this narrowness of vision caused my wife, a delicate and sensitive spouse, much pain. I showed her a great coldness outside of the act itself. 'You never seem to love me except when you do that', she told me a few days after our marriage. Another consequence was that the procreative act was my only release. I accomplished it with passion (the everything permitted), without measure, without consideration for the delicate feelings of my young wife who had been a virgin only a few days before.

And he concluded, 'my manner of acting has killed physical love inside her and it is only in crying that she sometimes accepts the resumption of contact'.[57] Lacking explanations, the speakers came to blame 'temperaments'. Men were represented as 'impassioned', and 'extremely sexual'. This vocabulary was common among all the French men, who attributed their masculine desire to an irrepressible compulsion. Women, in contrast, passed for less sensual. 'Woman in general is psychologically colder, and the Christian woman more so than others', affirmed a scholar.[58] Finally we may conjecture that the fear of pregnancy could bring women to cut out all sexual relations.[59]

Devout men experienced conjugal frustration as much as secular men. They were sometimes able to resign themselves, like this Lyon man: 'She has refused so often that I have come to stop asking.'[60] Many egotistically took their pleasure without concern for th.eir partner. Some of them practised emotional blackmail. 'My husband told me that if I *wouldn't do it*, he'd immediately find a mistress because his health wouldn't allow him to abstain', mentioned a spouse affected with vaginismus.[61] Women repelled by coitus freed themselves by using avoidance tactics, denounced by unhappy husbands and perfectly summed up by an anonymous author: 'Each time when she receives me it is never until after repeated supplications and after a respectable number of refusals.' From there came a long list of pretexts and ruses.

> She is disposed when she knows that I don't want it, that I cannot miss work ... Or, in order to free herself, she promises later, 'lunch

or evening', etc. The great excuse is that 'I'm tired'. At the end of our arguments, she never hesitates to reject me by provocation, retorting, 'you only have to go relieve yourself elsewhere', or even 'go relieve yourself with your sister', or 'relieve yourself alone'.[62]

All these couples, victims of sexual discord, were worn down by a disunion without escape. The correspondents of Abbé Viollet, too religious to accept the alternative of infidelity or the rupture of divorce, had as their only hope the annulment of an unhappy marriage. This was highly improbable, at least for couples with children.[63]

'To have a child each year' or 'To live like brother and sister'

The principal subject of enquiry in the Abbé's collection – how to live between sin and chastity and still limit one's family – appeared in 40 per cent of the letters. With the exception of loyal ascetics, none of the writers contested the necessity of limiting natural fecundity, particularly as neither the Pope nor the encyclical *Casti Connubii* condemned it on principle. If the enquirers proclaimed their desire to stop giving birth, they rarely mentioned the ideal number of children – when their secularised contemporaries during the 1930s had as their idea a single child or two. At first these religious couples conformed to religious prescription and accepted the children that God gave them, but when the births became both too numerous and too close together they were incited to revolt.[64] 'Are we obligated to have a child each year?' asked one woman who had produced 'what is conventionally called a beautiful Christian family. In ten years' time, we will have had eight children.'[65] From this point the refusal to procreate was as powerful as that shown by non-Catholics. It sometimes took an obsessive turn, so much so that the concerns of the child, the first goal of Christian marriage, figure less in the correspondence. Worse, the birth of children was presented not as a joy but as a 'duty'.

The arguments advanced for justifying the limitation of births were, for the most part, common to all groups in French society. Neo-Malthusian arguments found followers among Catholics of both sexes anxious to ensure a future for their children. 'One can help along one child but not six at the same time', otherwise, they are all destined to 'loss', wrote a French man from Algeria.[66] Professional and economic difficulties played a growing role in the crisis. 'I know well that one must have confidence in God, but at the same time, when one looks clearly at the situation, must not one be prudent and think of the future and of the daily bread to feed the children that we already have?', considered a saleswoman.[67] Some went so far as to see the large family as a privilege that the church reserved for rich people. Moreover, in this very Malthusian France of the 1930s, practising Catholics felt themselves distanced from ordinary people. Such sentiment bred bitter remarks: 'I wanted children', one father wrote. 'I must support them and drag the flock out for the smallest outing under the ironic eyes of the passers-by; for, if I'm not wrong, the compliments that I receive are touched with commiseration, or even malice.'[68] 'One easily has a mocking smile for those who are simple enough to let themselves get "knocked up" so many times', grieved a mother.[69]

These letters reveal, above all, a correlation between birth control and a new conception of women's condition. Women and most men were refusing to confuse their destiny with constant reproduction which reduced them to the level of animals. 'Woman is not a female rabbit', declared a mother to a social worker. 'Woman is not just a machine to procreate without limit', echoed a father of a large family.[70] It is, in fact, on these women that the sufferings of childbirth and educational tasks fell. 'Children tire you out', it was said between neighbours.[71] 'We walk like automatons, accomplishing the work that is imposed', wrote an overtaxed mother.[72] But it was without a doubt the 'country woman unrecognised by all at the heart of her isolated farm', a mother of ten children in fourteen years, and pregnant with an eleventh, who best described her maternal cross. 'I must furnish all the labour for the farm and the house, milking the cows, the care of the animals. I cannot even find a girl from the town who will consent to walk in the mud of the lanes, for there are too many children to care for, too much laundry to wash.' She enjoyed not one moment of repose. Worse, 'right after giving birth, the mother gets up immediately because there is no one to take care of the little ones.' These charges weighed even more heavily upon her because she found no support for her suffering from her 'indifferent' husband who 'believed himself the uncontested authority' and refused to assume paternal responsibilities.[73] These exhausted women were embittered and their family suffered. 'Exhausted by their closely spaced births, exasperated by the cries and the agitation of their children, these mothers began to hate them. The husband is not satisfied with his life with an always grumbling and withered spouse who evades sexual relations as much as possible.'[74] Some saw their spouse imposing on them an insupportable burden. 'At the bottom of the hearts of these mothers who are too tired, you will find bitter thoughts and perhaps unjust ones such as this: Men are egoists.'[75] A sixty-year-old widow posed the problem in general terms: 'According to the articles of the Holy Father, a woman must make sacrifices for the pleasure of her husband.'[76] The male correspondents of Abbé Viollet, however, were for the most part sensitive and concerned about the health and happiness of their spouse.

Health, in fact, was one haunting preoccupation which recurs in about thirty of the letters. It infused them with a tragic aspect, especially since thirteen of the women had been warned that a new pregnancy could mean death. This gave rise, among Catholics particularly, to serious matters of conscience since the increasingly severe medical prohibitions contradicted the injunction to 'be fruitful and multiply'. 'My doctor (who is a dedicated Catholic) *insists* that we do not have a large family and confirms that closely spaced pregnancies will be dangerous for my health', a tuberculosis patient, who had just submitted to a pneumothorax procedure, clearly stated.[77] Nine letters concern tuberculosis sufferers with this particular problem. For men tuberculosis was seen in terms of the offspring's health. A father of eleven children, hospitalised for the disease, wrote that 'different doctors consulted have been unanimous in affirming that I should *not have children* as there will be a strong risk of contamination'.[78] For women it was their survival that was in question, and the practitioners thought almost unanimously that pregnancy could reactivate the sickness.[79] Treated at Sainte-Feyre and already the mother of one child, a patient refused a possibly fatal gamble: 'To have another child would be the equivalent of suicide', she said.[80] The dangers inherent in pregnancy pushed even some writers to ask whether marriage with a tuberculosis patient was compatible with Catholic morality. Confronted with a necessary limitation of births, believers thus suffered worries unknown to their secular contemporaries who, without second thought, followed medical advice.

For a long time clerical silence permitted Catholics to get around the 'crime of Onan'. If the correspondents of Abbé Viollet were unanimous in impugning abortion, twenty-one of them admitted that they 'took care'.[81] The doctrinal stiffening in regard to sexual matters, symbolised by *Casti Connubii*, turned the innocent into the guilty. Pope Pius XI exalted the 'chaste conjugal union', and he affirmed that 'all usage of marriage ... in the exercise of which the act is deprived of the natural power to procreate life by the artifice of men, offends the law of God and natural law'.[82] What is more, not content to combat masturbation, he condemned the silent or overly complaisant confessors, shaking the serenity of the confessional.

The shake-up led to the 'horrible dilemma' of believers: 'First, to have an unending number of children; second, to live like brother and sister; third, to be in a state of mortal sin.'[83] Abstinence remained, in effect, the only means authorised by the church to limit pregnancies. Occasional abstinence was accepted by the writers after a sickness or during periods of nursing. In contrast, it was rejected as a contraceptive solution because it destroyed the life of the couple. Twenty-seven correspondents considered this part of their suffering. Abstinence, they suggested, killed conjugal love. 'If the husband is neither brutal nor egotistic, he will not oblige his wife to do what is considered such a great sin. But what a chilling between the couple! ... What *anxiety* to see what makes him *destroy with deliberate intention* this precious and unstable edifice of harmony, of reciprocal love.'[84] What is more, this method was unusable when one of the spouses, the husband most frequently, refused. Moreover, abstinence was hard to bear. 'Do you frankly admit that a couple of our age where mutual love reigns must and should live without sexual relations?' enquired a farmer.[85] Many letters described the psychological troubles provoked by abstinence: 'It is such a privation from all points of view that my husband and I have come to be in a nervous state and a worrying depression.'[86] Solutions proposed by the clerics in order to escape the temptation – separate beds or bedrooms – left correspondents sceptical. The 'imperfect acts' that the church authorised – caresses and even penetration – far from appeasing the senses, generated new torments. The church's theory was remarkably well defined by 'Marc'. '[My spiritual director] explained to me that the uncompleted act was not illicit on two conditions, that the husband and wife do nothing against nature, and that they accept in advance the normal function of the act if the sperm rises up.' Marc experimented successfully with this last idea and he found such relations 'very soft, very restful, very calming: I could "enter" (it is true, with precaution, and in choosing the right moment, and in strongly maintaining control) in order to "leave" without "seeing" the sperm rise up.'[87] Most people did not have as much control over their bodies, however, and accidental 'pollutions' were sources of remorse, especially since contradictions from confessors generated confusion. The understanding ones made a distinction between material sin and intentional sin: 'He told me that caresses were permitted and that even if a pollution was produced it wasn't the worst thing', mentioned a penitent.[88] Others admitted liberties but plunged into hypocrisy: according to one writer, as soon as there is an ejaculation, 'you declare these freedoms *shameful* and you ban them'.[89]

Finally, about fifteen correspondents went beyond anxiety in order to make a more theoretical analysis. Six of them denounced the paradox of an institution – the church – which forced spouses to 'live like brother and sister' according to the consecrated expression. A dozen attacked the foundations of this prohibition. Chastity was first presented as heroic and inaccessible to a simple lay person. 'One has to be a saint to observe the law rigorously, for the temptation is always there', remarked a correspondent for whom monastic chastity was much easier.[90] 'Catholic morality, such as the encyclical formulated, demanded neither more nor less than pure and simple heroism', wrote another author, who ironically remarked, 'I am persuaded that the Catholic couple is only a fraud in the sense that nine times out of ten "Christian spouses" must *very quickly* no longer become spouses, if they want to remain Catholic.'[91] In brief, as a militant of the AMC said, 'conjugal love was never before envisaged to be platonic', and he denounced the campaign in the press led by Abbé Viollet in favour of chastity. One officer even pointed out a contradiction in the teaching of the church. 'Do we not go against one of the ends of marriage which is to consecrate by union the love between the spouses?'[92] It was thus the best-trained Catholics who formulated the most pertinent critiques against the new course of the church. Sexuality thus became a fundamental crux between clerics and followers.

Sexuality and dechristianisation

Faced with the demands of the Vatican, believers obeyed, tried to circumvent them or rebelled. Twenty-four authors conformed to Papal teaching with conviction or resignation. Six letters argued for natural fecundity. A woman from Lille was surprised by these 'singular doctrines when frequent motherhood is the cause of all ills'.[93] Certain letters aligned themselves along the positions of Abbé Viollet, criticising the 'couples who search for pleasure in wanting to avoid "the act"', and condemned even incomplete acts.[94] Four couples made abstinence their ideal, including this couple from the Vosges: 'Between the births of our children, we have always practised a complete abstinence, offering this mortification – certainly difficult at times – for our two bodies which are full of youth and life', wrote a husband.[95] Four correspondents made the vow of chastity to thank God for a kindness or to atone for a sin, but they sometimes lived this trial as a 'conjugal hell'.[96] Finally, four women were ready to give their life to conform to the divine law, like this correspondent: 'I believe more strongly in accepting the *eventuality of death* than in engaging in fraudulent relations'.[97] Their consent was serene. It was desperate, however, in one farmer of Sainte-Pazanne: 'Thus, the law of God absolutely must be obeyed and since abstinence is impossible, children, no matter how many, must be accepted. On earth there should only be martyrs of marriage … Now I have offered my life to God … it is a total immolation.'[98]

The majority sought accommodations with the rule. 'In religion, as in everything, there are *attenuating circumstances* which do not make us as guilty as we would believe', suggested a married woman.[99] 'Without encouraging guilty abuse, one could be a little less intransigent', suggested a second.[100] Besides the sarcastic retort, letter writers substituted theology for emotional arguments in the call to the Blessed God and to the compassionate church. 'Is that a mortal sin considering the conditions in which we find ourselves? No, I don't believe it is; God does not ask the impossible', pleaded a young female tuberculosis patient.[101] From 1933 onwards, many believed in finding their 'salvation' in the discoveries of Ogino and Knauss.[102] Judging from its poor success rate among ordinary couples, Ogino's method was imperfect. Relying on periodic abstinence, it nevertheless allowed a harmonious sexual life. It therefore had everything to attract believers concerned with reconciling religion and private life.[103] The church could not condemn partial abstinence. One part of the clergy remained reticent, however, fearing that this would mean the 'death knell for motherhood', or even, as Abbé Bragade put it, that the method 'went directly against the principal goal of marriage'.[104]

Certain correspondents finally responded by rebelling against pontifical injunctions which threatened to distance them from the church. Twenty-four writers allowed themselves to reveal their uncertainties, their sense of deception and their anger. The encyclical which shook the former peace was received as 'a theological staggering blow', a 'hard hit'.[105] One letter even mocked the text, implicitly challenging pontifical infallibility:

> I was too interested (much more *truly* than the pope!) in aspects of marriage to wish to receive this document 'ex-cathedra'(!) − this naive encyclical *Casti Connubii*, of which the title alone could be considered a joke if it was permitted to believe Pius XI had a dry sense of humour. Before accepting as exhaustive and unchallengeable this naive document which crushes Christian spouses, I wish that gentlemen and doctors and theologians would look at it twice.[106]

The 'Catholic father of a large family' was exasperated by 'the preponderant, if not exclusive importance today', that Catholics gave 'to the question of abstinence' to the point where 'the main effort of thinking and of Catholic action is polarised between sin and the flesh'.[107] Two letters saw in the encyclical a new proof of the congenital incapacity of the church to adapt itself to the modern world. The demand for doctrinal modernisation was at the heart of these critiques: 'Isn't it better to definitively abandon positions that no longer mean anything?', suggested a follower.[108] Certain believers no longer hoped for even the smallest change, and described the church as a cold monster which required its adherents to sacrifice their lives rather than concede on certain principles. 'We are on the earth to suffer. Consequently, why fear the children who are born? If their number drives their mother to the tomb, what does it matter when suffering elevates one?', inveighed an officer.[109] He went further, however, accusing the church of betraying the Bible. 'Pius XI decreed a universal law which does not rest on any Christian morality … For the first time, I envy the Protestants.'[110]

In effect, from the moment that believers dared to doubt the church, they moved from challenging the institution to questioning their own faith. This is well illustrated in an anonymous letter: 'I feel that what the church asks is unrealisable … This prohibition comes from a human and not a divine church … It is neither happiness nor the wisdom of God. I feel that I weaken, I even worry about the strength of my faith … The Blessed Father no longer appears to me as I feel he is, in other words perfectly just and good.'[111] The tone is identical in this Parisian's letter: 'The intransigence of the church on the question of marriage has really irritated me. The confidence that I could have in the teachings of the church has been shaken and my faith unfortunately somewhat altered.'[112] An industrialist from Charolles bore at the same time the hell of abstinence and 'that other hell, that of the absence of God'.[113] Women especially depicted an implacable and especially sexist God. 'The heart of God is hard on women', wrote one anonymous correspondent.[114] An elderly woman continued to hope but was gnawed by doubt. 'Women's role is hard … God is too good (since we call him the *Blessed Father*) to order a different lot for man and woman.'[115] The rupture hinted at abandonment of prayer – 'we don't even have the strength to raise our hearts towards God', complained an exhausted mother, who became radiant with her distance from the confessional.[116] 'I naturally stopped confessing in the last months', noted one of Abbé Viollet's correspondents, who continued, 'Am I still Christian enough to practise? For to be Christian, God must be worshipped in church, but for the last four months, I have been caught in this dilemma: either the encyclical has exaggerated or God has. If Jesus Christ really imposes this on me, where is his wisdom and his goodness?'[117] 'In order to confess, one must be conscious of having committed a fault, but I am not', an officer stationed in Morocco told his confessor. Less arrogant in their rebellion, women felt the same as this sales-woman: 'It bothers me to confess on the subject of conjugal relations.'[118]

The most scrupulous Catholics looked very much like their more secular compatriots. Like them they wanted to bind spiritual love and physical love together but in the framework of an indissoluble Christian marriage. Similarly to their contemporaries, although unwilling to reject the idea of a large family, they desired to control their fertility. The church, in banning *de facto* the realisation of their aspirations, brought them to these painful matters of conscience which aggravated the frustrations of ordinary conjugal life and estranged the most conscientious from their faith. This qualitative study on sexuality and conjugality joins thus with the conclusions of religious history. Historians explain male dechristian-isation in the nineteenth century by the refusal to accept clerical interference in private life. From the correspondence received by Abbé Viollet, one sees that the phenomenon became stronger in the 1930s, and it henceforth affected women especially. A final confirmation is given by quantitative research which shows, in the 1950s, a correlation between the decline of women's observance after marriage and the establishment of a limited family.[119]

Notes

1 On the evidence that can be retrieved from the judicial archives, see my thesis, *Chrysalides: Femmes dans la vie privée (XIX–XXèmes siècles)* (Paris, Publications de la Sorbonne, 1996); *Du premier baiser à l'alcove: La Sexualité au quotidien (1850–1950)* (Paris, Aubier, 1996) and 'Les Attentats à la pudeur sur les fillettes en France (1870–1939)', *Mentalités*, special issue entitled 'Violences sexuelles' (Paris, Imago, 1989).

2 The archives are held by the Commission Episcopale de la Famille de l'Archevéché de Paris. They contain the newspapers and some, but not all, of the published letters, together with other letters that were not published.

3 M. Sevegrand, *Les Enfants du Bon Dieu: Les catholiques français et la procréation au XXème siècle* (Paris, Albin Michel, 1995), p. 49. This book contains the best analysis of the problems and devotes a few pages to the Abbé Viollet, as does M. Bernos, C. de la Roncière, J. Guyon and P. Lécrivain, *Le Fruit défendu: Les chrétiens et la sexualité de l'antiquité à nos jours* (Paris, Centurion, 1985).

4 Of 194 dated letters, 182 were written between 1929 and 1939. These correspondents had the courage of their opinions, since 156 signed their missives.

5 We know the communes in which 173 of the authors lived. Eighty-four lived in small towns and rural communes, forty in mid-size cities, and twenty-five in the department of the Seine. If the twenty ecclesiastics who wrote letters are left out, out of 179 lay persons of known civil state, there were only seventeen unmarried individuals.

6 They included industrialists, officers and white-collar workers such as shopkeepers and employees. The working classes were, not unsurprisingly, under-represented. I counted only three workers, three farmers and one maid.

7 A third were members of the AMC or readers of its bulletins, and seventeen were engaged in Catholic activism but many, without a doubt, neglected to mention their activities.

8 Saumur (Maine-et-Loire), 12 October 1930.

9 The expression was employed by a young woman. Tarascon (Bouches-du-Rhône), 30 March 1938.

10 Lyon (Rhône), 6 December 1930.

11 Wattrelos (Nord), 29 May 1935.

12 Nantes (Loire-Inférieure), undated.

13 Place of origin unknown, undated.

14 Athis-de-l'Orne (Orne), 8 February 1938.

15 Only teachers of the communist-led trade union CGTU wanted to include the exempted education. See Anne-Marie Sohn, 'Féminisme et Syndicalisme:

Les Institutrices de la Fédération Unitaire de l'Enseignement (1919–1935)', Thèse de 3ème cycle, Université de Paris X, 1973.

16 Cuiseaux (Saône-et-Loire), 1 July.

17 Albi (Tarn), 13 July 1938. This compares with twelve cases of female homosexuality found in the judicial archives.

18 Tarascon (Bouches-du-Rhône), 30 January 1938. Two young women and a young man were ignorant and two young men perceived the danger.

19 Thirteen letters. On tolerance among the working class see A.-M. Sohn, *Du premier baiser à l'alcôve.*

20 Nancy (Meurthe-et-Moselle), 21 April 1936.

21 The AMC and Abbé Viollet put this subject on the agenda from 1929 onwards.

22 There were eight cases, in two of which priests were defrocked, married, but continued to believe. This problem appeared very rarely in the judicial sources except in cases of attacks on morals.

23 Saint-Michel-de-Maurienne (Savoie), 27 June 1939.

24 Le Puy (Haute-Loire), 18 April 1936. Case reported by a director of a boarding school and concerning a third.

25 Angers (Maine-et Loire), undated.

26 Lacroix-Barrez (Aveyron), 29 May 1936. See on this point G. Houbre, who addresses these worries for the nineteenth century. *La Discipline de l'Amour – l'Education Sentimentale des filles et des garçons à l'âge du Romantisme* (Paris, Plon, 1997).'

27 Tarascon (Bouches-du-Rhône), 30 January 1938. Although make-up was limited before 1914 to artists and to tarts, after the war it was permitted to married women and advised against for well-behaved young ladies.

28 Paris, 5 December 1935.

29 Oran (Algérie), 26 September 1939.

30 Two cases only.

31 Place of origin unknown, 11 January 1931.

32 Bourg-en-Bresse (Ain), 29 September, year unknown.

33 Dinard (Ille-et-Vilaine), 2 June 1939.

34 Saint-Hilaire-Saint-Florent (Maine-et-Loire), 21 October 1930. In the language of clerics, masturbation, or the crime of Onan, was directed against the ejaculation outside of the 'vase dû' ('in the right place').

35 Wattrelos (Nord), 29 May 1935.

36 According to the words of a domestic from Strasbourg. Proceedings of the examining magistrate of Strasbourg, 10 April 1925, Archives Départementales, Bas-Rhin, AL 112.

37 According to a ruling of the Cour de Cassation dated 5 November 1881.

38 Tiaret (département of Oran), 18 September 1935.

39 Women never asked for cunnilingus and, if they passively accepted it, they were disgusted by fellatio. As with anal intercourse, the church condemned them to between three and fifteen years of penitence. See J.-L. Flandrin, *L'Eglise et le contrôle des naissances* (Paris, Flammarion, 1970).

40 Rennes, 4 June 1938.

41 According to the survey of A. Spira, N. Bajos et le groupe ACSF, *Les Comportements sexuels en France* (Paris, La Documentation Française, 1993),

3 per cent of the French practised anal sex often and 10-12 per cent sometimes. 'Marc', undated. Place of origin unknown. He never confessed it.

42 All in all, out of 7,250 juridical dossiers concerning private life, only three contain similar facts.

43 Craon (Mayenne), undated. The husband also practised oral sex.

44 There was one case of coitus with the woman on top. Catholic militants thought that this position impeded fertility because it was unnatural.

45 Baugé (Maine-et-Loire), 22 December 1931.

46 Out of the 7,250 dossiers, I found only forty-two mentions of pleasure as opposed to seventeen in 220 letters written to Abbé Viollet. See Sohn, *Chrysalides.*

47 Angoulême (Charente), 14 December 1939.

48 Place of origin unknown, 26 November 1939.

49 Saverne (Bas-Rhin), 19 October 1938.

50 I found only sixty-four dossiers on this subject in the judicial archives as opposed to thirty-nine letters in the collection of Viollet, which are exceptionally rich on this subject. See Sohn, *Chrysalides.*

51 Place of origin unknown, undated.

52 Place of origin unknown, 16 November 1934.

53 Rennes (Ille-et-Vilaine), undated. There were three cases of vaginismus, more or less emphasised.

54 Alès (Gard), 22 July 1940.

55 I found in the judicial archives only five accounts of a ruined wedding night against five in the Abbé's collection.

56 Lyon (Rhône), 26 January 1937.

57 'Marc', undated. Place of origin unknown.

58 Poitiers (Vienne), 6 June 1934

59 Six cases.

60 Lyon, 26 January 1937.

61 Rennes, undated.

62 Place of origin unknown, undated.

63. Fifteen authors mention adultery: men in order to evoke the temptation more than the fall, women in order to flaunt their bitterness as neglected spouse (the fall being a feminine temptation). Otherwise, it should be noted that, even for the slightly practising or non-religious French, divorce remained a social trial that many did not yet dare to face. There were during the 1930s at most fifteen thousand divorces per year.

64. Half had between four and twelve children.

65 Place of origin unknown, 11 January 1931.

66 See Sohn, *Chrysalides.*

67 Saint-Geoirs (Isère), 14 February 1932.

68. Oran, 24 September 1929. This makes clear, moreover, that the high birth rate in Catholic regions was beginning to fall.

69 Alès (Gard), 27 February 1940.

70 Rieupéroux (Isère), 16 December 1936; 'Problème de la vie conjugale dans le mariage chrétien vu par un catholique père de famille nombreuse', memoire of fifty-nine pages, undated. Place of origin unknown.

71 Place of origin unknown, undated.

72. Place of origin unknown, undated.
73. Sainte-Pazanne (Loire-Inférieure), 12 April 1939.
74. Oran, 24 September 1929.
75. Place of origin unknown, undated.
76. Montmorency (Seine-et-Oise), 10 March 1931.
77 Châteauguyon (Ille-et-Vilaine), 12 April 1938.
78 Savoie, 12 February, 1930.
79 Very reluctant to countenance therapeutic abortion even when the Académie de Médecine recognised it in principle, doctors were willing, nevertheless, to save tubercular patients by pregnancy termination.
80 Sainte-Feyre (Creuse), 6 January 1939.
81 They used methods common to all couples. The condom, the sponge or the cotton tampon were not favoured. Nor were they convinced of the virtues of hydrotherapy, although three women went as far as to ask whether post-coital washing, or even douching, was allowed. Evidently it was *coitus interruptus* or, in the language of sinners, 'cheating', which was the most used and was tolerated by some confessors. Four letters posed the problem of therapeutic abortion and five mentioned attempting abortion
82 Sevegrand, *Les Enfants*, p. 61.
83 Paris, 30 October 1930.
84 Lyon, 6 December 1930.
85 Monceaux (Oise), 20 November 1934.
86 Angoulême (Charente-Inféfieure), 14 December 1939.
87 Place of origin unknown, undated.
88 Narbonne (Aude), 14 February 1930.
89 Charolles (Saône-et-Loire), 25 October 1930.
90 Monceaux (Oise), 20 November 1934.
91 Paris et Amiens (Somme), letters of 8 February 1932 and 18 January 1931.
92 Villefranche-de-Rouergue (Aveyron), 28 August 1933.
93 Lille (Nord), 15 September 1937.
94 Macon (Saône-et-Loire), 21 September 1935.
95 Letter from the front, 13 October 1939.
96 Charolles, 24 June 1930. This previously cited middle-aged industrialist and his wife wanted to obtain the 'redemption' of a posterity limited to three children, to support the religious vocation of a son and make an act of grace for the 'conservation' of the spouse.
97 Argentan (Orne), 19 August 1934.
98 Sainte-Pazanne (Loire-Inférieure), 2 April 1939.
99 Montmorency (Seine-et-Oise), 10 March 1931.
100 Lyon, 6 December 1930.
101 Sainte-Feyre, 6 November 1939.
102 Saint-Cloud (Seine), 4 July 1935. On the Ogino method see Sevegrand, *Les Enfants*.
103 Twenty-six letters are devoted to the Ogino method.
104 Note of Abbé Bragade to a priest, January 1936, and note of Bragade on a letter of a priest from Lille, 27 April 1936.

105 Paris, 18 January 1931 and Sanatorium of Leysin (Switzerland), 10 February 1932.
106 Vanves, 19 April 1931.
107 Typed notebook, undated. Place of origin unknown.
108 Place of origin unknown, 8 February 1932.
109 Craon (Mayenne), undated.
110 Angers (Maine-et-Loire), undated.
111 Marseille, 21 May 1932.
112 Paris, undated.
113 Charolles (Saône-et-Loire), 24 June 1930.
114 Place of origin unknown, undated.
115 Montmorency (Seine-et-Oise), 10 March 1931.
116 Place of origin unknown, undated.
117 Vanves, 19 April 1931.
118 Rabat (Maroc), 20 May 1947 and Saintes (Charente-Inférieure), 24 January 1950.
119 See the example of the parish of Saint-Poplain at Lyon, studied in 1954 by Emile Pin and cited by C. Langlois, 'Toujours plus pratiquantes: Le permanence du dimorphisme sexuel', *Clio: Femmes et Religion*, 2 (1955).

Index